P9-ARC-553

# Columbia University Contributions to Anthropology

## Volume XXX

---

# SOCIAL ORGANIZATION
# OF THE PAPAGO INDIANS

BY

RUTH MURRAY UNDERHILL

# SOCIAL ORGANIZATION

## OF THE PAPAGO INDIANS

BY

RUTH MURRAY UNDERHILL

AMS PRESS
NEW YORK

Reprinted with the permission of
Columbia University Press
From the edition of 1939, New York
First AMS EDITION published 1969
Manufactured in the United States of America

Library of Congress Catalogue Card Number: 74-82347

AMS PRESS, INC.
New York, N. Y. 10003

# FOREWORD

The American Papago are found on three reservations, a large one and two small ones, in the southern part of Arizona, near the Mexican border. To the south are the Mexican Papago who live in the same villages with Mexicans and have largely intermixed with them. To the north are the Gila Pima, another branch of the same people who have had much more contact with White Americans than have the Papago. To the west and south are the small groups of Sand Papago, still largely unknown.

American Papago, Mexican Papago and Pima were once part of a large corn raising culture which included the Opata, Tepecano, Tepehuane, and other Sonoran peoples now extinct. The nature of their culture has been a matter of great interest as a link between Mexico and the cultures of the Southwest. The Papago were chosen for study because, though they were not so advanced as their congeners, their position in the desert has left them far less subject to White influence. Their reservation was set apart only in 1917 and they still retain many customs and ceremonies abandoned both by Pima and by Mexican Papago.

Five sojourns were made with the Papago: in June — October 1931, September — October 1932, February — October 1933, November — January 1934, October — November 1935. Most of the time was spent on the Sells reservation, the largest of the three though a few weeks were spent at San Xavier and some days below the Mexican border.

Even among the American Papago it was found that there were decided differences in dialect, customs and ceremonies and an effort was made to get data from each of the three important groups. One of these was often completely ignorant of traditions known to the others, so that it was no uncommon experience to have an informant in one village deny with amusement the possibility of some practise which those in the next village acknowledged as traditional. Since there are over 5000 Papago it was possible to get many points of view and their presence makes one realize how many shadings are found in a living culture which are lost or even distorted in those where only one or two informants are available.

Interpreters were used through the whole period, since I did not trust my rough conversational knowledge of the language for accurate discriminations. It was found that the interpreter must always be of the same dialect group as the informant and, if possible, of the same village. On the one occasion when an interpreter had to be taken into what was, to him, a foreign village, the general distrust interfered seriously with work.

The informants were chosen because each was expert in some particular line but sometimes a period of probation was necessary on my part before one would consent to instruct me. Consent obtained, the sessions usually ended with the declaration: "I have told you to the best of my knowledge. If some one tells you differently, let me know. I do not wish you to write a mistake." As often as possible various people were consulted, and the variation in their accounts was usually found due to regional differences. Two informants refused to speak at all and their portion of the Wiikita ritual is lacking. The list gives each informant's occupation and the affiliations which might influence him such as sib, village and dialect division. It is realized that to gain a full understanding of regional differences and therefore, perhaps, of the past history of these people, an even more intensive study should be made in each locality.

The present work was made possible by grants from the Columbia University Humanities Council and from special funds. It was suggested by Dr. Franz Boas, to whom, like all his students, I owe the deepest appreciation for inspiration, for keenly constructive criticism and for discipline in thinking. Dr. Ruth Benedict, under whose direction the work was done has been my constant reliance, not only for administrative help but for the use of her own rich material and for constant suggestion and stimulation. To Dr. Gladys Reichard, Professor of Anthropology at Barnard College I owe much kindly help in the field and out of it. Dr. J. Alden Mason, of the University of Pennsylvania Museum and Dr. George Herzog, of Columbia University, have generously made me free of their material on the Papago and Pima. Dr. Byron Cummings, Dr. John Provinse and Miss Clara Lee Fraps of the Department of Anthropology of the University of Arizona have given me every courtesy and assistance.

On the reservation, I have received valuable aid from Father Bonaventura Oblasser of the Franciscan missions, whose knowledge of the Papago, both from church records and from long experience cannot be duplicated. The two superintendents, Mr. Elliot and his successor, Mr. Hall, have been generous with assistance and hospitality. Mrs. Bennet, Miss Shorten, Miss Rouse, Mr. and Mrs. Carruth and Mr. and Mrs. Moyer all have given me hospitality, transportation and other most necessary aid, often at personal sacrifice to themselves. Mr. and Mrs. John Pancho have not only interpreted for me but entertained me at their house.

The number of my very competent informants and interpreters is too great for separate mention. Some gave information which will figure more largely in a subsequent volume on Ceremonies but all contributed toward the present discussion. There follows a list of their names and affiliations which may make clear the number of local differences which must be considered in obtaining a picture of Papago life.

# INFORMANTS[1]

m = moiety   s = sib   v = village   d = dialect

1. Jose Anton, m Coyote   s aapap   v Pisinimo   d Koloti.   Chief of Pisinimo.
2. Bernabe Lopez (Donkey Shoulder), m Coyote   s apki   v San Pedro d Archie   Chief of San Pedro village, orator at drinking ceremony.
3. Jose Enos, m Coyote   s aapap   v Kaka   d Huhura   Sub-chief of Kaka village, in charge of liquor ceremony, hereditary dancer at green corn ceremony.
4. Jose Morano, m Buzzard   s maam   v Covered Wells   d Archie Hereditary Mocking Bird speaker at drinking ceremony and orator for salt expedition, Covered Wells.
5. Jim Thomas (Dionisio), m Coyote   s apki   v Anegam d Archie One of the elders who accompanied Anekam salt expeditions; Keeper of the Anekam calendar stick.
6. Jose Marcellino, m   s   v Akchin   d Archie   One of the elders who accompanied Akchin salt expeditions.
7. Juan Gregorio, m Coyote   s aapap   v Santa Rosa   d Archie Enemy Slayer in mock battle, but therefore possessing war trophy and ritual.
8. Albert Anton, m Coyote   s aapap   v Santa Rosa   d Archie Enemy Slayer in mock battle with war trophy and ritual; village elder versed in ceremonials; wiikita singer.
9. Santiago Maristo, m Coyote   s aapap   v Comalick   d Archie War shaman; father, an Enemy Slayer whose trophy he now tends; one of the four official narrators of the origin myth.
10. Juan Marcos, m   s   v Little Tucson   d Archie   One of the four official narrators of the origin myth.
11. Justin, m Coyote   s aapap   v Quitovaca   d Koloti   Official keeper of regalia for Quitovaca wiikita and deer dance.
12. Juan Lopez, m   s   v Santa Rosa   d Archie   Hereditary clown for wiikita ceremony; one of the hereditary song composers for wiikita ceremony; a composer of modern song cycles.
13. Jose Pancho, m Buzzard   s maam   v Santa Rosa   d Archie A young man with good memory who had learned much from his two grandfathers, shamans, and his father, hereditary clown and song composer.
14. Jose Xavier, m Buzzard   s okori   v Cowlic   d Koloti   Organizer of Cowelick Easter Ceremony.
15. Pete Jim, m Buzzard   s maam   v Santa Rosa   d Archie   Elected speaker for moral talk at drinking ceremony.
16. Patricio Lopez, m Coyote   s apap   v Choulic   d Archie   Shaman and eagle killer.

---

[1] For brevity, informants quoted in the text are referred to by number.

17. Tomaso Flores, m Coyote  s aapap  v San Miguel  d Koloti
Professional herb doctor and singer for curing.
18. Donkey Tail, Professional herb collector and peddler.
19. Jose Castillo, m Coyote  s aapap  v Choulic  d Archie  Professional
singer for curing, especially disease caused by war trophy.
20. Juan Diego, m Buzzard  s okori  v Tecaloti  d Koloti  Professional
singer for curing, especially eye trouble.
21. Jose Santos, m Buzzard  s maam  v San Xavier  d Archie
Keeper of the calendar stick for San Xavier.
22. Jose Ramon (Salt in the Coffee), m Coyote  s aapap  v Big Fields
and San Isidro  d Archie  Professional hunter of deer.
23. Joaquin Lopez, m Buzzard  s maam  v Iron Pump  d Archie
Professional hunter and worker in hides.
24. Harry Leonardo, m  s  v San Xavier  d Archie  Professional deer hunter.
25. Ben Johnson,  Ajo  d Koloti.
26. Maria Chona, m Coyote  s apki  v Santa Rosa  d Archie  Expert
basket maker; had learned much from her father, a chief, her first
husband, a shaman, and her second, a singer, hereditary clown and
keeper of calendar stick.
27. Angelita Lopez, m  s  v Santa Rosa  d Archie  Expert
potter; composer of songs.
28. Angelita Tapia, m Coyote s apki  v San Isidro  d Archie  Expert
potter amd basket maker.
29. Lupe Garcia, m Buzzard  s maam  v Poso Verde  d Koloti
Expert potter; storyteller.
30. Juan Harvey, m Buzzard  s maam  v Choulik  d Archie  Phoenix
Indian School, Cook Bible School, Phoenix  interpreter.
31. John Pancho, m Buzzard  s maam  v Santa Rosa  d Archie
interpreter.
32. Carmen Pancho (wife of above), m  s okori  v Koloti  d Koloti
interpreter.
33. Rafael Gonzalez, affiliation lost  v Tucson  d Archie  Sherman
Institute, Riverside, California  interpreter.
34. Lucy Cachorro, moiety lost  s okori  v San Miguel  d Koloti
interpreter.
35. Ella Lopez, m Coyote  s aapap  v Santa Rosa  d Archie  interpreter.
36. Frank Vasquez, moiety lost  s okori  v Pisinimo  d Koloti  interpreter.
37. Pablo Santos, m Buzzard  s maam  v San Xavier  d Archie
interpreter.
38. Enos Francisco, m Buzzard s maam  v Poso Verde d Koloti interpreter.
39. ha piitchim (Happy Jim), keeper of hunting ritual  v Kaka  d Huhuhra.
40. Louis Petero (komaki, gray), m Coyote apki  v Cirenaca  d Archie.
41. Ismil Luis, m Coyote s apki  v Emita  d Huhuhra (shaman).
42. Harry Pablo, m Coyote  s apki  v Anegam  d Kuhatk.
43. Rosa Thomas,  (consulted for genealogies)  v Sikorhimat  d Archie.

# PHONETIC SYMBOLS

The symbols used here, with a few variations, follow those recorded by Kroeber, U. Cal. Pub. vol 10, no 5, p. 242.

*a, i, o, u,* roughly as in Spanish

*i′,* the back tongue, unrounded vowel found in many Shoshonean languages

*p, t, k* are intermediate stops

Phonetic Transcription of Indian Languages, Smithsonian Miscellaneous Collections, vol LXVI, 1916, no 6.

*t* is a dental stop, *ṭ,* retroflex

*s* is a dental sibilant: *c* represents    retroflex *s.*

*r* is always retroflex.

*w* is a phoneme.  Before *i′, o, u,* it is the usual semi-vowel: before *a* and *i* it becomes bilabial *v.*

Papago words are accented on the first syllable of the stem: prefixes are unaccented. When a word stands alone, its last consonant, if sonant, becomes surd and, if surd, strongly aspirated. This influences surrounding sounds and often causes the whole last syllable to sound whispered. The process does not take place in running speech, and therefore has not been indicated in orthography.

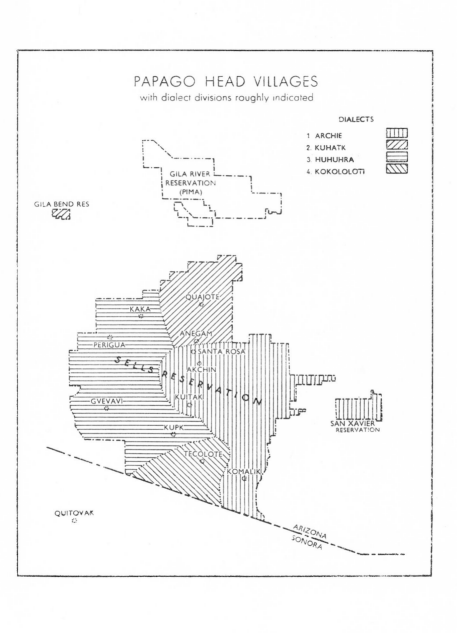

PAPAGO HEAD VILLAGES
with dialect divisions roughly indicated

DIALECTS
1. ARCHIE
2. KUHATK
3. HUHUHRA
4. KOKOLOLOTI

GILA RIVER
RESERVATION
(PIMA)

GILA BEND RES

QUAJOTE

KAKA

ANEGAM

PERIGUA

SANTA ROSA

SELLS RESERVATION

AKCHIN

GVEVAVI

KUITAKI

SAN XAVIER
RESERVATION

KUPK

TECOLOTE

KOMALIK

QUITOVAK

ARIZONA
SONORA

# PAPAGO SOCIAL ORGANIZATION

## APPENDICES

# LOCATION AND HISTORY

## LOCATION

The Papago are to be found on three reservations in the southwest corner of Arizona, adjoining Mexico. Their country was under Mexican rule until the Gadsden Purchase of 1853 and, with that of the Gila Pima, it once bore the Spanish name of Pimeria Alta (Upper Pimeria). All its inhabitants were known as Pimas by the Spanish and by themselves as o'otam. They consider themselves one people, though they distinguish River People now called by the Whites Pimas, and Desert People, called Papago. For convenience we shall allude to the combined people as Pimans. Their language is the same, with minor variations, many of them due to the influence of English on the north and Spanish on the south. Migration and interchange have been so constant that statements as to habitat and history must include both groups.

The Pimans were found by the first Spaniards living where they do now though in a little wider territory. Their stretch of desert, two hundred miles long by two hundred and fifty wide, lay like a roughly shaped diamond, with its long axis along the present international boundary. It was a barren stretch, containing no streams at all, but it was roughly outlined by water courses: at the north the Gila, at the south, the little Altar, which loses itself in the sand before reaching the Gulf of California, at the east, the San Pedro flowing north to the Gila. At the west, the driest part of Pimeria, nearly uninhabited, touched the Gulf of California.

The Pimans are the northernmost of an almost unbroken line of Uto-Aztecan speaking peoples, stretching from the neighborhood of Mexico City along the western edge of the plateau with extensions into the foothills and the plains beneath. All practised agriculture, wherever the country permitted and often irrigation also. On the plateau, at the south, were to be found such people as the Aztecs, with their intensive agriculture and complex organization; beyond, in the mountains, the Cora and Huichol, whose agriculture had, of necessity remained simple but whose ceremonies and handicraft were most elaborate. Further north came the ruder Cahita and Tarahumare and, stretching down past them, through Sonora and Durango, a group of agriculturists and irrigators comprising the Tepehuane, the Nevome or Lower Pima, the Opata, Tepecano and, at the north, extending into desert country, our subject, the Upper Pima.

1

This series of southern Uto-Aztecans has been variously classified into sub-groups[1] but recent studies tend to minimize the distinctions.[2] However, there is agreement to the effect that Piman, as spoken by both the Upper and Lower Pima, finds its closest affiliations with Tepecano and Tepehuane. Whorf would even call the three one language, with separate dialects.[3] These linguistic relatives of the Pimans are now so merged with the Mexican population that it is difficult to reconstruct their culture. Information must come largely from Spanish sources, which mention their irrigation;[4] their houses of wattle and daub or of adobe;[5] their cotton raising and cotton garments.[6] They were apparently, agriculturists and irrigators who shared many customs with the Pima, as first known to history. Similar in culture, though slighty variant in language, were the Opata, wedged between the Upper and Lower Pima so closely that Spanish writers sometimes generalized about the whole area as one.

The country occupied by these congeners of the Pimans ranged from the tree clad mountain slopes of the Tepehuane to the lowlands of the Opata where oak and grass began to give way to desert vegetation. It was cut by small streams, flowing ultimately toward the Gulf of California and in whose valleys clustered the wattle and daub houses, with their irrigated fields. But, toward its northern end, it dipped into the hot, low Colorado Desert and the last of its irrigated valleys, that of the Gila, was separated from the others by an expanse of arid country where agriculture could scarcely survive. This was the country of the Papago. It was a tongue of the western desert thrust into an agricultural area and it forced its inhabitants to a different way of life from that of their congeners to north and south.

North of it was the Gila whose valley was, as far as the accounts can show, a cruder version of the irrigated valleys of Sonora. This was a frontier beyond which irrigation stopped, for to the west, stretched the Colorado Desert: to the north the Colorado Plateau rose in an abrupt wall. At this point, the line of Uto-Aztecans was broken. It was resumed on the Plateau, in the Hopi villages and continued north through the Basin and Range Country, among groups of largely nomadic food gatherers. To the west, beyond the

---

[1] Kroeber, 1934, p. 16.
[2] Whorf, 1935, p. 608.
[3] Whorf, 1935, p. 608.
[4] Beals, 1932, p. 158.
[5] Beals, 1932, p. 176.
[6] Beals, 1932, pp. 170, 172, 173.

Colorado, other food gatherers, the Southern California Shoshoneans, extended it almost to the sea. But, between the Pimans and these congeners of simpler culture, was thrust a wedge of another stock, the Yuman, occupying the Colorado River valley and its adjacent highlands so as effectually to separate the southern agriculturists from the northern and western food gatherers.

Pimans thus found themselves at the meeting point of several areas, both cultural and geographic and, because of their situation in open desert country, they were in easy communication with all. Well worn routes led to the south where they traded with their more prosperous linguistic relatives. To the west, a few days journey over identical desert country brought them to the River Yumans, whose living conditions were so similar that the equipment of the two peoples often coincides, point for point. To the northwest, open Basin and Range country continued into the great stretches occupied by their Shoshonean kin.

Travel was more difficult to the northeast, where the Pueblos stood on the high plateau that marks the change from torrid to temperate country. At least in historic times, the intervening rough country was held by Apache, enemies of the Pimans. Yet, in prehistoric times, it was down over the Mogollon Rim that Pueblo immigrants filtered into the Gila and it is with the Hopi, above the Rim, that the Papago show some of their most obvious likenesses.

It was only at the east that communication stopped. There, in historic times, lived the Apache, whom the Pimans met only in war skirmishes and from whose country they brought not a shred of booty to spread its evil magic. Pimans owe nothing to the Athapascans except the constant stimulus derived from two centuries of warfare and any likenesses between the two peoples must be traced to a common source in the Pueblos.

The country of the Pimans themselves is a southern extension of the Basin and Range area which has been roughly described as a desert parallelogram, outlined by streams. It was the Pima, the River People, who occupied the stream valleys, while the Papago, the Desert People, made the best of the arid interior. Their land was a succession of flat valleys, floored with wind blown pebbles and interrupted by low mountain ridges, water and wind eroded into gullies and pinnacles. The ridges are never continuous and a wandering people could thread its way to and fro over the whole desert without encountering any obstacle but thirst. On the lower slopes grow giant cactus, cholla and prickly pear, widely spaced so that each may have its share of water and with their succulent stems veiled from the blinding light by forests of white thorns. Along the dry

1*

stream beds the bean bearing mesquite and palo verde stretch their roots down to underground water. On the plain grows the creosote bush and sometimes nothing else.

This is one of the hottest and driest areas in the United States, the annual rainfall in the interior being about five inches.[1] Yet those five inches rendered subsistence possible for the Desert People. They are concentrated in the summer months of July and August when the daily cloudburst produces a temporary flood which may cover the flat plain to a depth of six inches for a square mile. In a day or two there sprout the seeds of annuals which may have remained inactive for several seasons, awaiting sufficient moisture. The succulent cacti swell, storing water for the dry months. The deciduous trees put out tiny leaves, exposing to the glare as little green as possible.

For two months while the desert bloomed, the Papago picked and stored every root, stalk, leaf and fruit that it produced. Where the flood water had softened the soil, they planted small gardens which, begun in mid-July, had just time to mature before frost. All the harvest was dehydrated in the blazing desert sun and stored to furnish food in the dry months. Then the rain ceased; the rain reservoirs which had supplied drinking water for the valley dwellers dried up; life was impossible unless the population moved to the foothills where there were springs.

Until very recently, when the United States government has dug wells in the valleys, this was the life of the Papago. It precluded their having permanent houses, either for dwellings or for ceremonies. It prevented a centralized form of organization such as has been suggested for the Pima, both on the Gila and the San Pedro. But it kept the Papago unmolested until long after these others had disappeared or had assimilated White ways.

Yet the Desert People, harassed by Nature as they were, found opportunity to practise all the arts described for the more fortunate Pima,[2] with only minor differences, due to materials. We may picture them, up to a few generations ago, living in round, semi-subterranean houses, often earth covered. They dressed in skirts and breechclouts of buckskin and, less often, cotton and wore sandals when they had any footgear at all. Their pottery was of coarse red clay, shaped by paddle and anvil with, only rarely, a decorated jar for offerings and seed storage. The bulk of their utensils was of basketry: plaited, coiled or netted in the intricate technique known as coil without foundation. These are old arts in

---

[1] Bryan, pp. 29—30.
[2] Russell, pp. 68—181. Castetter and Underhill, pp. 48—63.

the area and at least the house and the red pottery rank with the simplest of the equipment once used there. Far more elaborate developments have taken place in Pimeria and been forgotten and one of the most absorbing questions occupying present day archaeology is the tracing of these developments and the connection with them of the modern Pimans.

## PREHISTORY

The whole of Pima and Papago country is dotted with ruins, ranging from small, almost obliterated villages to elaborate communal buildings of several storeys, like that which still stands at Casa Grande. Villages may be found in the open desert[1] but the communal houses are clustered in the valleys of the large streams, the Gila and Salt, while a few are found on the smaller Santa Cruz. The valleys themselves are a network of ancient irrigation canals. The most recent survey reports a hundred and twenty five miles of such canals in the Salt River valley and half as many in the Gila[2] and the oldest of them so far excavated has been dated at 800 A.D.[3]

Until recently, communal houses and canals were thought to have belonged to one culture; a culture obviously so much more elaborate than that of the present Pimans, that it could have no connection with them. But the investigations of Gladwin[4], Woodward[5], and the University of Arizona, make it obvious that there have been two cultures in the area, the earlier, which built the canals, of long duration and the later which built the great houses, short and transitory. The canal building culture has some points in common with that of the modern Pimans and the question of their relation to it is now under debate.

---

[1] Huntington, 1914, p. 47.

[2] Halseth, 1936, p. 42.

[3] Haury, 1936, p. 49.

[4] Gladwin, 1928, 1933. This paper went to press before the publication of Gila Pueblo's extended work on a Gila River site: Excavations at Snaketown, by Harold S. Gladwin, Emil W. Haury, E. B. Sayles, Nora Gladwin. Medallion Papers, XXV, Gila Pueblo, Ariz. 1937. The result is an unnecessarily extended statement on some points, both of history and prehistory, instead of summary and quotation. Our reading of the Spanish sources gives slightly different results from those of the Snaketown report. Nor do we here attempt a complete analysis of Mr. Gladwin's assumption of a Pima-Hohokam relationship which, while a tenable hypothesis, requires more penetrating and thorough work than it has yet received.

[5] Woodward, Arthur, The Grewe Site, mimeographed by Los Angeles Museum.

The bulk of recent work in the area has been done by Gila Pueblo, under the direction of H. C. Gladwin, who with W. J. Gladwin has published a series of papers on the canal building culture, called by him the Red on Buff, from its distinctive pottery and also the Hohokam from the Piman word meaning Vanished People.[1] After a series of surface sherd surveys, made throughout Piman country, the Gladwins conclude that the Red on Buff culture extended from Casa Grande south to Sonora; west almost to the Colorado and east into the valleys of the Santa Cruz and San Pedro, and almost to the New Mexico line.[2] The Hohokam lived at first in earth lodges, with an entrance vestibule or roof opening[3] and then progressed to one story houses of wattle and daub or reinforced adobe, compactly grouped and surrounded by an adobe wall.[4] Their Red on Buff pottery was made with paddle and anvil, and has been called by Kidder "strikingly different from all other groups of pottery in the Southwest".[5] They made also pottery figurines and effigy heads.[6] They used decorated slate palettes for paint mixing[7] and they did work in carved shell.[8]

Another trait differentiating the Hohokam from the Pueblos is that they cremated their dead, placing the unburned bones at first in small pits, then in pottery jars.[9] The skeletal material from Hohokam sites is therefore so very limited that it is impossible to establish any correlation between it and later physical types.

The Gladwins believe that the Hohokam "entered the South-west as a group and from an exterior source," but, in spite of sherd surveys made in every direction around their habitat, there is no trail to indicate from which direction they came. However, the signs point to their having been already agriculturists, since they chose a desert area necessitating irrigation, rather than the neighboring mountains which would have appealed to a hunting people.[10]

---

[1] The word is a reduplicated plural, used by both Pima and Papago to indicate finished, vanished or gone. It was used by Russell (1926, p. 24) and quoted by Huntington (1914, pp. 23, 24). Russell applied the term, as do the Pimans, to the great house builders, while Gladwin uses it to designate the canal builders. Since it has become popularized in the latter sense, it will be so used here.

[2] Gladwin, 1933, pp. 203—204.

[3] Gladwin, 1933, p. 222.

[4] Gladwin, 1928, p. 23; 1929, no. 3, pp. 26—27.

[5] Kidder, 1924, p. 111.

[6] Gladwin, 1933, p. 235.

[7] Kidder, 1924, p. 112.

[8] Kidder, 1924, p. 105.

[9] Gladwin, 1933, p. 248.

[10] Gladwin, 1933, pp. 252, 226.

The time of their arrival is also uncertain. There is no tree ring data in Piman country and the dates of Hohokam culture must be established by cross finds of pottery, not always available. Gladwin has divided their history into five periods; Pioneer, Colonial, Sedentary, Classic and Recent. These correspond in character to the five Pueblo periods but are slightly ahead of them in time, for pottery finds show the Colonial to be contemporary with Pueblo I and possibly with Basketmaker III.[1] The last phase of the Colonial is dated by Haury from 700—900 A. D.[2] which would push the Pioneer, the indefinite early period, well back toward the beginning of the Christian era. In Pioneer times, agriculture was already well developed and the inference is that the Hohokam may have been tilling the soil before the Basketmakers. Gladwin, in fact, calls them "the earliest farmers in Arizona."[3]

Their progress continued until about 1300 A. D. and, says Haury, "In the richness of their material attributes and the length of time through which the sequence of their culture's growth can be traced, the Hohokam stand alone in the American Southwest.[4] But between 1300 and 1350, they suffered an invasion of peoples from the Little Colorado pueblos and Flagstaff "whose presence is marked by a distinctive polychrome pottery; the use of stone if possible in wall construction and the custom of inhumation."[5] These were the builders of the great houses who, attracted by the fields and the irrigation systems, placed their settlements on the very sites formerly occupied by the Hohokam. Gladwin's theory is that it was a peaceful invasion, "the two peoples continued to live together and their cultures remained separate and distinct"; the Hohokam continued "to live in one storey houses of pole, brush and clay construction, they went on making the Red on Buff pottery . . . they carved images in shell . . . and they continued to cremate their dead placing the unconsumed remains in Red on Buff redware urns." They also brought their irrigation systems to the point of greatest development. Meantime the Pueblo people "continued to build their multi-storeyed houses, used stone when it was available . . or caliche. They made Gila polychrome pottery, buried their dead in the earth, often under the floors of rooms.[6]

The invasion did not even reach to all parts of the country for, out of fifty-nine sites surveyed, Gladwin found three with no traces of polychrome pottery.[7] And it was brief. Cross finds of pottery

[1] Gladwin, 1933, p. 250.
[2] Haury, 1936, p. 49.
[3] Gladwin, 1933, p. 277.
[4] Haury, 1936, p. 48.
[5] Gladwin, 1929, p. 37.
[6] Gladwin, 1933, p. 251.
[7] Gladwin, 1933, p. 252.

indicate that the great houses were abandoned between 1400 and 1450 A. D.[1] Discussion is still rife as to whether the cause of abandonment was waterlogging of the fields[2] or enemy attacks,[3] and as to the final refuge of the builders. The Pima in 1694, three hundred years at the latest after the exodus had taken place, told their first Jesuit missionary that "the ancestors of Montezuma deserted and depopulated it (Casa Grande) and, beset by the neighboring Apaches, left for the east or Casas Grandes (of Chihuahua) and that, from there they turned toward the south and southwest finally founding the great city and court of Mexico."[4] Pima words for Apache and for enemy being the same, this tradition may have referred to any other warlike tribe as well as the Apache. The tale of the Aztecs, so persistently repeated by the Spaniards, has been as persistently rejected by historians, since the Aztecs were in Mexico City before the great houses of the Gila were built at all. But the suggestion of Chihuahua remains a possible one, with some archaeological support.

The point of importance for this study is the relationship of the modern Pimans to both Hohokam and Puebloan cultures, and on this archaeologists are not all in agreement. Gladwin suggests many likenesses between the Hohokam and the modern Pimans who do, in fact, live on the old sites, use the old canals, build wattle and daub houses and make paddle and anvil pottery. The likeness is most obvious with the Papago "whose pottery shows a definite relationship to prehistoric Red on Buff and whose manner of life appears to be the same as that indicated by Red on Buff settlements of the Sedentary (third) period."[5] An interesting possibility would be that the Papago represent a fringe of the Hohokam which according to the sherds "pushed west and south .... where, owing to unfavorable natural conditions, their development was retarded."[6] This branch had no irrigation[7] and their pottery, instead of developing like the rest, remained set in a local variation.[8] Offering no temptation to invaders, they remained untouched throughout their stay and it is possible that, "the ancient life of the Red on Buff people persists here (in Papago country) suspended in sur-

---

[1] Gladwin, 1933, p. 252.
[2] Turney, 1929, pp. 44—45; Halseth.
[3] Russell, p. 26; Bolton, 1936, p. 370.
[4] Bolton, 1936, p. 285.
[5] Gladwin, 1929, No. 4, pp. 70—71.
[6] Gladwin, 1929, No. 4, p. 129.
[7] Gladwin, 1929, No. 4, p. 80.
[8] Gladwin, 1929, No. 4, pp. 129—130.

roundings sufficiently adverse to have discouraged intrusion by an alien people less qualified to deal with desert conditions."[1]

This suggestion, rejected by some archaeologists, has much to recommend it. The chief difficulty is that the Papago bury their dead, instead of cremating as the Hohokam did. It is true that they burn a warrior killed by the enemy but so do they burn everything which has touched an enemy, through fear of evil magic. Such fear would preclude their gathering the bones in a jar as did the Hohokam, for the cremation pyre is left as soon as lighted and no one revisits it. Gladwin mentions jars, hidden in the mountains, which might be burial jars but these are, actually, receptacles of fetishes too dangerous to leave near human dwellings. The Papago form of burial, on the other hand, is a primitive one, widely spread among congeners of the Pimans in rocky country. The corpse is seated upright in a rock cranny as often in the Basin, in northern Mexico and with the ancient Hopi. The custom might thus have been learned from Puebloan invaders but might equally well be indigenous.

The house also presents a certain difficulty. The present Papago house, built of wattle and daub or of what Gladwin calls reinforced adobe (adobe smeared on a framework of crossed poles), is indeed a duplicate of late Hohokam houses. But such a house has only been used within the last fifty years and apparently was adopted from Sonora where the Yaqui have used it for some time. The old Papago house, still used for ceremonials, was a dome shaped structure of brush, the floor excavated to 18 inches or two feet. It presents likenesses to the houses of the Mission Indians and the Paiute and also to the old Hohokam pit houses. This was also the Pima house,[2] and if the Pima and Papago are relics of the Hohokam we should have to suppose that they did not pass beyond the earliest stage in house structure, or that they lapsed back into it. Nor did they continue all the Hohokam arts. They do not work in shell and when they dig up, in their fields, the carved frogs or the slate palettes mentioned above, they regard them with the superstitious awe shown by the Navaho toward Pueblo relics. But there are scraps of tradition to support the theory that they have survivors of the Hohokam among them. Russell was told that the Red moiety, among the Pima, represent the old inhabitants of the land, while the White moiety were the invaders,[3] and the present writer heard that the old inhabitants are the speakers of the Huhuhra dialect, who live at the extreme west of Papagueria, just where

[1] Gladwin, 1929, No. 4, p. 130.  [2] Russell, pp. 154—155.
[3] Russell, p. 26.

they would have been pushed by intruders. It is true that this western country is more primitive and more conservative than the rest and also that it lacks a ceremony, the Wiikita, proved to be definitely Puebloan in origin. However, the locality has no tradition of cremation beyond that of the enemy victim. Unsolved elements enter into the problem here.

Another possibility is that the Pimans represent a recent invasion of nomads who drove out the great house builders. Gladwin's objection to this is that their perfect adaptation to their desert habitat precludes their having arrived there as late as 1400 A. D. and data in the following pages go to support such a statement. Nomads warlike enough to conquer the great houses would hardly settle down so soon to a life of industrious agriculture such as the Pimans practise, and if the houses were voluntarily abandoned it would be because the fields were unusable, so no other agriculturists would move in. Gladwin also argues that they have no songs to commemorate such a conquest which should be recent enough for great vividness. They have, as a matter of fact, an elaborate saga, describing how they themselves destroyed the houses,[1] but the writer is inclined to think it a late creation, for the Pimans have, at various times, told quite different versions. Besides the Aztec story, they have said that the houses were built by their own ancestors,[2] by foreigners from the north[3] and, even, specifically by the Moqui "because they alone know how to do such things".[4]

It seems just possible that *the* Pimas who told such contradictory stories were different groups of Pimas, including some who were actually descendants of the Pueblo invaders or of those who had assumed their culture and some who represented a previous settlement. But, in course of time, the Pimans have evolved a myth which recounts, with topographical detail, how they destroyed the houses, marching through the country from east to west and working magic to crumble the walls of the "sacred houses" or "rain houses" where lived the *sivanyi*, the rain magicians. Granting that such a tale has no ranking as history, it may afford implicit ethnological evidence and, for that reason, we quote a summary of the present Papago version as told by the official narrators.

Elder Brother and Earth Magician, having made human beings, quarrelled and Earth Magician retired with his creations underground. Elder Brother's people, who spoke the same language, remained above. He cared for them until he finally offended them and they killed him. He came to life and went underground to ask

---

[1] Russell, pp. 226—230.
[2] Bandelier, 1892, p. 464.
[3] Bolton, 1936, p. 370.
[4] Coues, II, pp. 386—387.

help of Earth Magician and his men in revenge. These latter were the present People.

They sent gopher above ground as a spy and he reported the people there were playing all sorts of games and "speaking our language". The underground people, in the legend called the Emergents, decided to come up. They emerged at a place called Smooth Ground, an alkali plain at the extreme east of the present Papagueria, near Benson. Here they divided into three armies and marched west. One army went north, through the Gila valley, one south through the Altar and the third in the middle through the present Papagueria. The great houses fell before their magic and the inhabitants fled, some far to the north, and some far to the south. These latter are still to be found in Sonora and are called Jackrabbit Eaters.

The People marched west across a great water (Colorado River ?) which parted to let them through but closed again so that many of them could not get back (floods ?). On the far side of this water they fought with the Fox Enemies, who had underground houses like fox holes; the Bat Enemies, who attacked at night and so swiftly that they seemed flying; the Owl Enemies, who crept up like dead men. The People were beaten, so finally they crossed the water again. But they had delayed too long: it closed while they were crossing and left many on the other side where they are now.

The remainder came back to Pimeria and, under Elder Brother's direction placed prayersticks (there has been no mention of prayer sticks in the former tales) at Archie in the north and at Quitovaca in Sonora. Elder Brother then taught them the Wiikita ceremony. The scalp ceremony he had taught during the march of conquest. From Archie and Quitovaca, the people went out to settle the land.

This tale may have echoes of the walls of Jericho and the Red Sea, attributable to the missionaries. But it also sounds like a Pueblo migration myth. Its march of conquest is completely out of keeping with the peaceful and sedentary nature of the Pimans and, particularly the Papago, who abhor war and lack any pattern for boasting over its exploits. It is true that the myth speaks of the houses as crumbling by magic rather than in battle but even the idea of leaving their homes to appropriate the lands of others is contrary to Piman thought, and one wonders if it has not been borrowed from the annals of a more nomadic race.

But the story of the conquest is not the whole of the tale. The first part, abbreviated in the summary into a paragraph is what, to most Papago, constitutes the origin myth. It relates to the ancient people and ends with the death of Elder Brother, while the second part begins with Elder Brother's resurrection and ends with the march of conquest. In spite of the logical form given the tale by orators whose hereditary function it is to tell it dramatically, many informants are vague about the connection between the two parts. They tell the first part as though it had happened to the present Pimans, describing carefully how Elder Brother taught them many of their arts (though never great house building). Then comes the resurrection, unique in the myths of the area, and Elder Brother reappears as a war leader. But again his people are the present Pimans.

It seems obvious that two myths have been joined to produce the narrative. The first, dealt with in detail under Ceremonies, shows likenesses with the myths of Mexico, of the Yumans and of the southern California Shoshoneans who were in contact with them. It mentions specifically the origin of the drinking ceremony which is Mexican in affiliation. The second, beginning with the emergence from underground, resembles the migration myths of the Pueblos, and mentions distinctly that the Wiikita (prayerstick ceremony) the one completely Puebloan ritual, was instituted after the march of conquest.

The tale indicates intimate connections of the Papago with the Sonoran cultures and so do such ceremonials as the drinking feast, the intervillage games, and the salt pilgrimage so similar to the Huichol pilgrimage for peyote and containing, perhaps, a reminiscence of a time when the Gulf of California was not so distant from the Papago habitat. It also shows Pueblo connections in the point for point correspondence of the Wiikita with Hopi ceremonials and in scattered resemblances, constantly appearing. But other Papago traits have their most direct resemblance with the Shoshoneans of the Basin or of California. Such are the extreme importance attached to the menstruating woman, the cult of the eagle, the local organization of the ceremonial leader and the fetish. Many of these are not unknown to the Uto Aztecans to the north or to the south, but they appear there obscured by other more elaborate developments. Their important place in Papago life needs historical explanation.

Such explanation involves careful study, ethnological and archaeological, of the Piman Sonoran area and the trails leading to it. Kroeber has pointed out the resemblance of pottery made by the Mission groups, Cahuilla, Luiseño and Diegueño and by the Seri of Tiburon Island to that of the Papago.[1] Sauer and Brand found on the fortified hills of southern Papagueria and northern Sonora a pottery unlike Hohokam,[2] and the connection of these

[1] Kroeber, 1925, p. 703.
[2] Sauer, 1931, pp. 116, 117.

finds with the past of Pimeria is not clear. Spanish documents may eventually yield more information as to the agricultural people of northern Sonora, now absorbed in the Mexican population. The Opata, and Tepecano who formed one area with the Upper Pimans, should have shared many Hohokam traits possessed by them, perhaps brought them to a higher point. The Lower Pimas, acknowledged by the Upper Pimas to be their kinsmen, present a further problem for they not only had irrigation and colored cotton clothing,[1] but lived in fortified communal houses.[2]

The present study, concerned with ethnology, can offer only such information as is implicit in the extent of Papago likenesses to one region or to another. There have been compiled in appendix II such data as time would permit showing the affiliations of the Papago with northern Mexico, with the Pueblos, the Shoshoneans and their only neighbors who were not Uto-Aztecan, the Yumans. From elements shared with these diverse cultures, the Papago have built a system suited to their life as small groups of peaceful agriculturists, frugal in equipment, informal in organization, intent on hard work and the compelling of the supernatural.

## The Pimans as First Seen by the Whites

Between 1450, the latest tree ring date for the abandonment of the Gila by the Pueblo invaders, and 1687, when the first White missionary came, there is a gap in Piman history. At a stone ruin, north of Phoenix, there has been found Gila redware which seems to belong to a date after the departure and in the forests near Prescott there is Red on Buff, in company with black on gray belonging to another people.[3] These are the only pottery finds which point even vaguely to the history of the Hohokam after the invaders had left.

Spanish exploration began, according to tradition, only a hundred years after the exodus but the first travellers if, indeed, they crossed the country at all, left no recognizable account of it. Legend credits Fray Marcos de Niza with passing through the valleys of the Santa Cruz and San Pedro in 1539 though Sauer doubts if he got much above the Mexican border.[4] In 1540, the main Coronado party

---

[1] Alegre, 2: pp. 70, 124, 174, 186; Perez, pp. 240—241, 385.
[2] Alegre, 2: pp. 70, 124; Doc. Hist., 4, Series 3, p. 359.
[3] Gladwin, 1933, p. 259.
[4] Sauer, 1932, p. 28.

went the same way and "some poor Indians" who came out to meet the general may have been Sóba Jípuris of the San Pedro.[1] Melchior Diaz, a Coronado scout, went from Sonora to the mouth of the Colorado, probably through Mexican Papagueria[2] but left no description. The first historian and geographer of Pimeria is Father Eusebio Francisco Kino (Kühne) the Austrian Jesuit, who labored for its conversion from 1687 to 1711.

Kino found the River and Desert People well established, in the very localities where they are now. As far as can be told from his casual comments, their culture was just what it was when seen by later American visitors and what it has remained almost to the present. But kinsmen of theirs were spread over a much wider territory than is now occupied and his description of all these inhabitants of Pimeria may help us to some deductions as to the components of its population.

When Kino was assigned to the Upper Pimas, no more was known of them than their location and that but vaguely. Spain had conquered Mexico City in 1523 and since then had been pushing gradually northward through the unconquered territory. These excursions had of necessity been along the coastal plain, the rivers which traversed it to the sea acting as landmarks. Each expedition passed a new river until in 1687, the next to last, the Magdalena had been reached. Beyond it lay unexplored desert. In the valley of the Magdalena, however, mission stations had been established and two silver mines were in operation. There was a Spanish governor, Spanish mayors of the mining towns and Spanish settlers, both mining and ranching. They regarded "this Pimeria" to the north of them as an ultima thule, of low savages and deadly thirst.

It was known, however, that the inhabitants were related to the Lower Pimas, or Nevomes. These agriculturists, long since "reduced", had obtained their nickname from the Spaniards because of their phrase "pi nyi matc", I don't know. From them Kino took interpreters so that he was equipped to meet his new charges.

His aim was not only to evangelize the Upper Pimas but to explore and map the country. In fact, during his twenty-three years of service he made fifty journeys throughout its length and breadth, many of them dipping into what is now the Papago reservation and two cutting through the heart of it. During these two, Kino not only explored but baptised, distributed seeds and appointed native officials. Bolton[3] has carefully traced the course of these

---

[1] Sauer, 1932, p. 36.
[2] Sauer, 1932, pp. 37—38.
[3] Bolton, 1936.

journeys and we shall adopt his painstaking identification of localities. Not only Kino but his military escorts, Bernal and Manje, have left in their diaries brief glimpses of the Pimans describing them in greater detail than did the padre whose mind was on God and how to get to California.

The whole country, from the Altar to the Gila, from the San Pedro west to the "Cocomaricopas" and even, at one point to the gulf, was occupied by people known as Pimas. Manje says of them: "although in different regions and divisions, yet is it one and the same, the language which they speak, with a little difference here and there in some verb or noun".[1]

All these people practised agriculture if there was the slightest opportunity and, wherever there was water, they irrigated. But there was not water everywhere and because of the varying conditions, Kino found the population divided into groups, differently named and with slightly different food, dress and housing.

Kino established himself in Sonora, in the valley of the little San Miguel river and his mission station Dolores soon became famous. Near the south-flowing San Miguel were two other little streams which flowed in the same direction and joined: the San Ignacio and the Altar. In the valleys of all of three were people whom Kino calls simply "Pimas": agriculturists, who had irrigation "wherever there were good arroyos".[2] Caborca, which may be taken as a sample town had "fertile and rich lands all under irrigation with acequias where they harvest plentiful maize, beans and calabashes."[3] It was among these Sonoran towns, that Kino established his missions and the actual "reduction" proceded.

But Kino was always anxious for a northern extension and he soon pushed down the two parallel streams, the Santa Cruz and the San Pedro, which flow northward into the Gila and form the eastern boundary of the desert. Here were "extended plains with pleasing and delightful valleys,"[4] the San Pedro having 2000 people in fifteen villages.[5] The Pimas on these rivers bore the added title of Sóba Jípuris, sometimes spelled Soba y Jipuris. The term is untranslatable but there was a western group called Sobas and Jípuri may be an old descriptive or locative.

The villages of the Sóba Jípuris extended from the Gila as far up the two little streams as irrigation was possible. Tumacácori,

---

[1] Manje, p. 259.
[2] Manje, p. 225.
[3] Manje, pp. 216—222; Bolton, 1936, p. 274.
[4] Bolton, 1936, p. 377.
[5] Bolton, 1936, p. 367.

almost at the Mexican border of Arizona was one of their settlements and Bac, outside Tucson, another. They were prosperous agriculturists raising corn, beans, pumpkins and melons, which may mean a variety of pumpkin since the Pimans had two. In some of their districts "there is not so much agriculture," says Bolton "or so large a population, at the present day".[1] They gave the soldiers of the escort "so much maize flour that they did not have bags in which to put it",[2] and the Father Visitador, Kino's superior, thought the fields of Bac could support 30,000 people,[3] as in fact they do now. Beside their food, the Sóba Jípuris raised cotton which they wove and dyed for clothing and they were "dressed and adorned with colored mantas (cotton blankets) belts and strings of beads around the neck".[4] Their large town Bac, contained 800 people,[5] and Quiburi, the next, 500.[6] Both were "fortified,"[7] though the nature of the fortification is not described. Did it resemble a Hohokam compound? The houses, at least were not of the wattle and daub variety for they are always described as being made of mats,[8] a custom neither Hohokam (so far as known) nor present Piman, but common in Sonora and the south.[9] The Spaniards credited the Sóba Jípuris with a federal organization and speak of "the principal chief of all the rancherias" in a district,[10] even of the "head chief of all the Pimas",[11] but we cannot be sure how truly they interpreted the situation.

The Sóba Jípuris were far more warlike than the Papago of the present paper and even Kino admits that those of Quiburi were "somewhat less docile than the foregoing people of the West."[12] They were on the frontier of Apache country and constantly subject to attack. Kino describes a battle like those recorded later for Pimas and Yumas[13] with five hundred and six hundred men on a side, a formal challenge and a fight by selected champions, ten Sóba Jípuris and ten Apaches. The Sóba Jípuris won and chased the enemy for four leagues killing three hundred with their poisoned arrows.[14] But they did not fight merely for defense. They quarrelled among themselves and a war between two powerful chiefs on the San Pedro had caused sixty miles of the fertile valley to

[1] Bolton, 1936, p. 361.
[2] Bolton, 1936, p. 366.
[3] Manje, p. 277.
[4] Bolton, 1936, p. 367.
[5] Bolton, 1936, p. 268.
[6] Bolton, 1936, p. 360.
[7] Bolton, 1936, pp. 361, 381.

[8] Bolton, 1936, p. 376.
[9] Beals, 1932, p. 178.
[10] Bolton, 1936, p. 365.
[11] Bolton, 1936, p. 361.
[12] Bolton, 1936, p. 269.
[13] Russell, p. 41.
[14] Bolton, 1936, p. 381.

be deserted.[1] One wonders if this warlike people could have had an Apache mixture. They were fighting the Apache in Kino's time but a Spanish record some years previously had called Quiburi, their principal town, a settlement of Pimas and Jocomes (a nomad group) intermingled.[2]

These easterners had the most elaborate culture found among Kino's charges. Their irrigation, so admiringly commented upon, recalls Hohokam practise and might indicate a long period of establishment. But Kino, occupied with teaching them to bake bread and herd cattle, says nothing to indicate whether they also made the shell carvings, slate palettes, three quarter grooved axes and funeral urns which characterized the Hohokam. Excavations along the San Pedro and Santa Cruz may help to elucidate their history.

The Sóba Jípuris were already moving from the Apache border in Kino's time,[3] and later they all scattered among the other Pimas. The writer, when on the Gila, had a certain family unexpectedly pointed out as Sóba Jípuris. Ultimately, all the villages were deserted except Bac, the seat of Kino's one mission, whose Spanish affiliations may have helped to protect it. It was through that channel that Spanish influence, what there was of it, was kept alive in the territory of our study.

The next two groups found by Kino differed from the Sóba Jípuris only as their environment had forced a simplification of their culture. Kino speaks of them all as Pimas and feels no doubt as to their being the same people. Those on the Gila, he regarded as identical with the Sóba Jípuris and sometimes called them by that name.[4] He had time only for three visits to these distant parishioners, staying a day or less at each village. Both he and his escort were so taken up with preaching that we hear little about these who are now called the Pimas proper except for a general report of "abundant crops" and we are left to assume that since they were included in the same journey with the people of the San Pedro and Manje sums them all up together, they also had irrigation and raised corn, beans, pumpkins, and cotton. They and the people of the other two rivers, together, said Manje, had 920 houses and 4700 persons.[5] Among the gila people, we hear for the first time of

---

Bolton, 1936, p. 63.

[2] Causa Criminal contra Canito Parral, Archives, quoted in Bolton, 1936, p. 247, note.

[3] Bolton, 1936, p. 395.

[4] Bolton, 1936, p. 249.

[5] Bolton, 1936, p. 377.

2

eating mesquite beans,[1] and mountain sheep, whose horns were piled up in a heap overtopping the houses.[2] To the present day, among old fashioned Pimans, deer horns are piled in a special place as a mark of respect to the deer. They built for Kino a house of mats, like those of the Sóba Jípuris but the soldiers of his escort were entertained in a house of poles covered with reeds which was apparently the usual dwelling.[3]

Between the Gila and the Altar stretched two hundred miles of desert whose full length Kino traversed only twice. Here lived those Pimas who, at present, bear the name of Papago. Kino heard of them from the Gila Pimas who gave him guides, but the Desert People must have been in constant communication with the River People for, on the missionary's arrival they were prepared with the customary arches and crosses "although never in that village (kuhatk) nor in others of this vicinity and coast, had there entered another white face or Spaniard."[4] They were also in communication with the Sóba Jípuris of the San Pedro for they had just been down to help them in a fight against the Apache.[5] Kino noted that these people had abundant crops of maize, calabashes, beans and the unexplained melones.[6] He baptized the children and his official escort gave eight canes of office, a governor and three subsidiary officers to one village and a governor each to four more.[7] On two other occasions Kino dashed through the desert country, once giving a few more badges of office, once baptising and inquiring for the sick. He gives us the names of village sites but otherwise it is on Manje and the later recorders that we must rely for information about the Papago of the seventeenth century.

The villages are, at the present day, almost where Kino found them and they still bear the nickname bestowed by their neighbors, pápavi ó'otam, Bean People. Papago final syllables are whispered, so the Spaniards heard only pápav ót. In the succeeding centuries, they rendered it Papabotes, Papalotes, Papagotas, and finally settled down to Papagos.

The bean referred to was the aboriginal bean of the Southwest, now called tepary which is more heat and drought resistant even than maize and which, in dry summers, was the only possible crop. Manje mentions it at Sonoita, where there was permanent water and where he may have been justified in attributing the bean eating to laziness rather than hard weather conditions.

---

[1] Bolton, 1936, p. 373.
[2] Bolton, 1936, p. 372.
[3] Bolton, 1936, p. 373.
[4] Bolton, 1936, p. 397.

[5] Bolton, 1936, p. 398.
[6] Bolton, 1936, pp. 396—401.
[7] Bolton, 1936, p. 398.

"They gave us only beans for, although they have an arroyo and rich land with a ditch to irrigate it, they are lazy and do not get enough corn for the whole year."[1]

It seems to have been Manje himself who picked up the Bean People nickname and perpetuated it, for a little later he reports:

"We took a trip to the northwest to see the Papabotas"[2] and again: "These people are naked and poor for they are of the nation Pima Papabotas."[3]

As the Spanish occupancy went on, the nickname became official and Kino's successors say:

"I do not know why these rancherias have been given the appellation of Papagos."[4]

"The land in some places is somewhat sterile due to lack of care. The people there are called Papabotas. Their principal harvest is papavi (beans)."[5]

"Papagos is the name given by the Pimas to those particular Pimas who live in the desert as far as Tucson and . . . . . . . . . . up to the Gila, living on seeds, grass, rabbits, rats and wild fruits."[6]

"The papagos, or papabotas, a nation situated between Upper Pimeria (which must mean the Altar Valley) and the Gila."[7]

"To the north (of the Altar Valley) are the papagos, who also are pimas, but inferior. They have no water but live on the desert."[8]

"The Papagos are cowards and under the domination of the Pimas."[9]

"The Pimas of the North hold those of the West (Papagos) in little esteem and it is true that these latter, whether it be due to having less fire or to some other cause, recognize in the others some superiority and look up to them with a special respect which, although not amounting to subjection, remains a matter of knowledge."[10]

That is as far as the descriptions of the Desert People go and one imagines that most of them were from hearsay. But they establish that the Pimas who acquired the nickname of Papago lived in the desert between the Altar and the Gila, part of which is now in the Papago reservation. Their differences in culture were due to the exigencies of their habitat and when the Spaniards spoke of them

[1] Manje, p. 262.
[2] Manje, p. 262.
[3] Manje, p. 278.
[4] Afanes, p. 339.
[5] Velarde, pp. 2, 128.

[6] Doc. Hist. III, v. 4, p. 554.
[7] Alegre III, p. 291.
[8] Doc. Hist. III. v. 4, p. 838.
[9] Doc. Hist. III, v. 4, p. 892.
[10] Velarde, pp. 2, 133.

as "inferior" and "cowardly" they were referring to the frugality
and peaceableness which ultimately distinguished the Desert·
People in several ways from the prosperous, warlike and organized
Sóba Jípuris.

One other group was sometimes spoken of as Papago: the people
in the extreme southwest of Kino's country next the sandhills which
border the gulf. These were the followers of the great chief Soba
called Sobas as a group. The name is so similar to that of the Sóba
Jípuris that one imagines a connection, but they had small resemblance to the prosperous agriculturalists of the east. They are
the only people of whom agriculture is not reported. They were met
on a food gathering expedition, "the men without other ornament
than their innocence" and the women dressed in two deerskin
aprons,[1] which they had to take off to carry Kino's "little gifts" —
these aprons being all the clothing in the party. Other such poor
and skin clad Indians were to be found scattered through the
southern country away from the rivers. Further east Kino reports
120 of them scantily clad in rabbitskin,[2] and at another place two
women also with a slender covering of rabbitskin, dipping water in
jugs from a pool.[3] We may conjecture that those in the sandhills,
were the ancestors of the present Sand Papagos who now occupy
the arid region west of the Ajo Mountains, around the Tiñas Altas,
Tule Tanks and Papago Tanks,[4] and the vicinity of Dome. They are
still a nomadic people, the poorest of all the desert dwellers. But,
since all desert people are great travellers, they have had frequent
contacts with the Papago of our study.

We can summarize, then, five groups among the people called
Pimas. On the streams, there were the agriculturalists and irrigators: the "Pimas" in Sonora, the Sóba Jípuris in eastern Arizona,
the Pimas, called also Sóba Jípuris, on the Gila. In the desert
between the Gila and the Altar were the "Papabotas of the northwest" who had agriculture but without irrigation, and in the southwest the skin clad food gatherers who seemed to have no agriculture at all.

These people were in communication with one another for they
guided Kino all over the territory. They were not thoroughly
united for the Sóba Jípuris on the San Pedro had been fighting
one another and the Sobas had a feud with Kino's own village of
Magdalena, but occasionally they formed alliances against the

---

[1] Bolton, 1936, p. 276; Manje, p. 280.

[2] Bolton, 1936, p. 273.

[3] Bolton, 1936, pp. 274—5.

[4] Bryan, pp. 132—134; Hornaday, pp. 181—182.

Apache as did the Desert People and the Sóba Jípuris. They also had communication with other Indians, even at some distance. Sauer has shown that there was a well travelled Indian route all the way from Mexico City along the eastern edge of the Pima country and up to the Hopi.[1] Though this route would have been impassable to one who did not know the mountain passes and the flood seasons, the Pimas evidently followed it at least as far south as the Lower Pimas, where Fray Marcos met some of them in 1539.[2] The corn raising Lower Pimas and Opatas were so familiar with the Upper Pimas that Kino took them as interpreters and Manje employed them to teach the care of cattle.[3] The Opatas were thoroughly scornful of their less agricultural congeners and used to say when rebuked, "Do you imagine we are like the Papagos?"[4] It was the tyranny of an Opata cattle boss which precipitated the first feeble revolt of the "Pimas" against Spanish authority.

The Pimas evidently followed the trade route all the way to Hopi country. "They trade with a nation to the northwest, ten days journey on foot, who are white and clothed."[5] "The Sobaipuris have had communication with the Moquinos and have held fairs with them."[6]

The journey to the north was a difficult one, leading up onto the plateau in unfamiliar country which later was infested with Apaches. Much simpler was contact with the Yuman tribes living in the same desert country but further to the west. Kino visited many of these tribes with Piman interpreters and gives a map of them.

Going down the Gila, he passed into the villages of the Cocomaricopas without realizing that he had left the Pimas. In some of these western journeys, it is hard to decide in what territory he was, for "the principal ones came to see us from farther up and farther down and some .... from the Colorado. All were very affable, Cocomaricopas as well as those of the Rio Colorado, for although they are of a different language, there are always among them many Pimas and others who speak the Pima language very well."[7]

Kino sent messages to all the Yumans indiscriminately, both by Pimas[8] and Papagos[9], who seemed to be in constant communication with them. He was, however, aware of a feud which concerned the Opas, Yumas, and Maricopas, those of the west, the Yumas, having

---

[1] Sauer, Road to Cibola.
[2] RBAE 14, I, 356.
[3] Allegre III, 83.
[4] Doc. Hist. III, v. 4, 582.
[5] Velarde 2, 131.
[6] Velarde, 2, 139.
[7] Bolton, 1919, 1, 246.
[8] Bolton, 1919, 1, 237.
[9] Bolton, 1919, 1, 310.

always lived in very bloody wars with those of the east, the Opas (who, Spier says, were the Kaveltcadom) and the Maricopas. In this the Pimas of the irrigated valleys joined and at a fair they held yearly they exchanged, along with woven cloth and baskets, "the Yumas they have taken prisoner".[1] But the Pima-Yuma feud seems never to have reached the Papagos. The Yumas were actually their nearest neighbors. Kino used the Papagos of Sonoita as ambassadors to the Yumas,[2] and the Yumas reciprocated.[3] Years later Anza was doing the same thing. The Franciscan priest Garces in 1777 reported: "The Yumas are at war with the Pimas but friendly with the western Papagos."[4]

This gives a picture of constant intercourse toward the west, sometimes warlike and sometimes not, with the Yumas, Opas and Cocomaricopas, who in their turn knew the upland Yumas and the desert Shoshoneans, and the Digger Indians of Southern California.[5] All these tribes live in open desert country and among them obvious likenesses are found. Little is said about the Seri to the south, until they rebelled against the Spaniards and the "Western Pimas" helped suppress them.[6]

The picture of distant contacts over open desert country to the west is entirely reversed at the east. Here Pimeria is sharply bounded by the tongue of highland which stretches up from the Mexican Sierra Madre, and which formed part of "the very extensive Apacheria". No one knew in Kino's time how extensive but it certainly stretched up to the Hopi and down past the Opatà corn country as far as the Tarahumare. This was a roaming range with a few camps hidden here and there in the hills. From it raiding parties dashed out far into the fertile valleys, so that at one time Pimeria was almost surrounded with what was practically Apache territory.

This developed during the Spanish occupation. When Kino first arrived in the last ten years of the seventeenth century, the agricultural villages in the eastern end of Pimeria were existing undisturbed. There was a little talk of horse stealing which the Spanish authorities blamed on the Pimas themselves, but Kino on behalf of his charges finally fixed the guilt on the distant and mysterious Apaches.[7] Travelling to the northern part of his mission field, he was informed that it was not possible to go farther and reach the Hopis as had once been done, because the Apaches "for some years" had barred the way.[8] Kino's successor, writing about

---

[1] Orozco, 346.
[2] Bolton, 1919, 1, 310.
[3] Allegre, III, 135.
[4] Coves, p. 540.

[5] Spier, 41.
[6] Velarde 2, 138.
[7] Bolton, 1919, 1, 121.
[8] Bolton, 1919, 1, 198.

1720, says that the people on the San Pedro had had within his own time a quarrel with the Hopi which was never made up, because the Apaches prevented visiting.[1] Even in Kino's time assaults began on the eastern valley towns near to Apacheria. In 1697 one of the mission towns, Cocóspera in Sonora, suffered from what Kino refers to as the "first attack of the Jocomes (Apaches)."[2] The next year six hundred "Jocomes, Sumas, Mansos and Apaches" attacked Santa Cruz to the north in the San Pedro valley. The Pimas fought hard, gathering to pursue the invaders and killing on the second occasion cited 300 of them.[3] But then the Apache front was widened and the raids became constant over the whole eastern extent of Pimeria which was nearest to the hills and far up the Gila and Altar valleys to north and south. By 1750 the San Pedro which had once held 2,000 people was completely deserted. In the south, the Altar villages were depopulated and agriculture had almost ceased. Even the Spanish mines and ranches were being abandoned and the "total ruin of the province was feared."[4] This terrorism continued at intervals until the United States subdued the Apaches in 1874.

The Apache attacks were highly influential in producing the present distribution of Pima and Papago. As the comfortable river settlements were devastated, their Pima inhabitants fled or were killed and after more or less time the desert Papagos seeped in to take their places. The Sóba Jípuris after defending the San Pedro valley for years, finally abandoned it and settled in the next valley to the west, the Santa Cruz. Even this proved untenable and Bac which had had irrigation "more than the city of Mexico" became at last a Papago town and the first set aside as a Papago reservation. The same thing happened in the Altar valley where the irrigated towns, stocked by the Spaniards with wheat and cattle, were first depopulated and then repeopled by Papagos. "San Ignacio," a Spanish report said of one of them in 1750, "is more Papago than Pima."[5]

These movements produced the permutations which make it so difficult now to treat separately of Pimas and Papagos.

## Relations with Whites

The Spanish occupancy of Pimeria began with Kino's coming in 1687 and ended with the Gadsden purchase by the United States

---

[1] Velarde 2, 139.
[2] Kino, Colocacion, referred to in Bolton 1919, 1, 176; also Manje, 2, 83.
[3] Bolton, 1919, 1, 181.
[4] Bolton, 1919, 1, 155.
[5] Doc. Hist. III, v. 4, 892.

in 1853. In spite of this 166 years of influence, there did not occur in Pimeria either the dying out of the natives which happened in California or the almost complete Hispanization which took place in Sonora. White settlers were always few and white influence discontinuous, the reasons being the sterile nature of the country and the Apache raids.

When Kino arrived on the borders of Pimeria, the whole west coast of Mexico had been incorporated in the Spanish colonial structure from Mexico City up to the Sonora valley, the last but one before the Piman desert. Here there was already a military post and two mining towns with Spanish governors.[1] It was Kino's plan to gather the natives of all Pimeria into villages which should surround a church, which should have well stocked cattle farms and wheat fields, and which should act as supply stations on the road to California.

Kino was an organizer of the highest ability and he did all that one man could do to put the plan into operation. He established missions; he stocked them with cattle, horses, sheep, goats, and poultry, a herd of 500 horses and as many cows being nothing unusual. He taught the natives to build adobe brick houses for the priests and adobe brick churches; to sow and thresh wheat, lentils and vetch; to plow; and to tend cattle. He made fifty trips throughout the country, baptising and distributing Spanish names to localities and people. These first "entries" were an overhelming success and Kino's writings are paeans of enthusiasm over these people "so docile, so affable .. and industrious,"[2] who "in all places received us very kindly,[3] guiding and accompanying us with love, and, if the occasion demanded, coming to meet us with many jars of water many leagues journey."[4] They "listened with pleasure to talks concerning God, Heaven and Hell and told me that they wished to be Christians[5] and came fifty, sixty, seventy, eighty, ninety, one hundred or more leagues' journey, all for the purpose of asking and obtaining holy baptism."[6]

Many of these contacts were brief and the permanent "reduction" which was planned to follow them, proved impossible. Kino established three missions in Sonora: Delores, San Ignacio and Tubutama, each with several smaller places as "visitas". Caborca, to the west, never managed to keep a priest after the first one was killed, but Bac, across the international border, proved the most

[1] San Juan and Bacamuchi, Bolton, 1919, 1, 112.
[2] Bolton, 1919, 1, 120.　　　　　[5] Bolton, 1919, 1, 123.
[3] Bolton, 1919, 1, 172.　　　　　[6] Bolton, 1919, 1, 161.
[4] Bolton, 1919, 1, 189.

lasting of them all. Even in Kino's time they were not all manned constantly and afterward, there was an even greater fluctuation in personnel.

Beside the priest in charge of a mission, Kino, or the king's representative with him, appointed native officers. Even the remote savages whom Kino might never see again received discourses about the "two majesties" (God and the king of Spain) and their chiefs were given wands of office. The complete roster of civil and ecclesiastical authorities used in the more civilized pueblos seems not to have been attempted, but each large-sized town had an Indian alcalde (mayor), while the smaller ones had justices. There were, besides, local military captains who were given a horse and gun apiece and were to recruit their people against the Apaches. Carrying on the idea of organization, one captain general was appointed for the whole of Pimeria but this centralized government was unsuccessful for the captain general finally became overweening and organized a revolt.[1]

These appointees cooperated very willingly with Kino, hunting for offenders and bringing them to justice, carrying messages for him, and attending to church herds and farms. Those in his own river valley had contacts with him, but the others saw him only when he passed through their hamlets at intervals of a year or more. As for the Spanish officials to whom they were nominally subject, they were myths to the Indians and the Indians little more to them.

This was all to have been changed with time and Kino wrote urgently to Spain for more missionaries for this country, "which seems to give thanks to the Lord by offering such an opportunity for its conquest and conversion."[2] A few missionaries were sent. In fact there were by 1750 nine in Pimeria.[3] But the expansion which Kino had expected never took place. When the great organizer had died and the undermanned missions settled down to routine, the reports from Pimeria altered rapidly. "There are no Christians in the world who receive the doctrine more eagerly and understand it less than these Indians .. they forget it from year to year."[4] Nor did their agricultural education proceed much better The Indians at mission stations were supposed to work in the fields three days for the church and three days for themselves. But they "objected to working for themselves as much as for the church" and were "so lazy and wasteful that they had to be whipped to make them do anything."[5] The collapse of Kino's plan is clearly

[1] Allegre III, p. 290.
[2] Bolton, 1919, 1, 90.
[3] Afanes, 343, 359, 366, 448.
[4] Doc. Hist. III, v. 4, 592.
[5] Doc. Hist. III, v. 4, 594.

reflected as time goes on, in successive reports: 1716, the majority of the Pimas are still gentiles;[1] 1732, three new missionaries were sent, but only one stayed;[2] 1749, Bac (one of the stations) is more heathen than Christian;[3] 1750, the missionized pueblos have gone back to their ancient barbarism.[4] This last date is in the period of the most violent Apache raids, when the Spaniards themselves were talking of abandoning the country. It was the next year that the Pimas also revolted, destroyed two missions and killed the priests, besieged two other priests in their church and killed, according to one estimate, 119 Spaniards besides probably plundering other missions.[5] They were disciplined and promised to rebuild the churches, but they never did. A Spanish report after this states that there is no help for Sonora except to deport the Pimas who have returned to savagery.[6]

The Jesuit missions kept alive for eighteen years longer, but as Bancroft states: "The natives lived as they pleased, leaving their women and children at the missions for protection or coming in now and then to get food."[7] In 1767 the Jesuits were expelled from the new world. Their place in Pimeria after a year of inter-regnum was taken by the Franciscans, who remained until the war for Mexican independence in 1823.

This second mission period was one of devoted individual work without any attempt at the former large organization. The Apache terror was in full swing: funds were not availlable as they had been. The Franciscans confined themselves to two of the northern missions, Bac and Tumacacori, without any attempt to rehabilitate the Altar valley, which had been such a flourishing Jesuit domain. The devoted Father Garces made some mission journeys around the country and gave the people a chance to become reacquainted with the tenets of Christianity but after him the missions dwindled to a quiet death.

The contact with lay Whites during this time had been less than in almost any other part of the Spanish domain. Pimeria was a province of Nueva Viscaya and then of Sonora which meant that its Spanish governor always resided far to the south. There was, when Kino first arrived, one military post with fifty men just

---

[1] Velarde 1, 118—119.
[2] Allegre III, 245.
[3] Gallardo, quoted in Banc. V, 1, 534.
[4] Doc. Hist. III, v. 4, 614.
[5] Allegre III, 291; Keller, MS quoted in Banc. V, 1, 545.
[6] Doc. Hist. III, v. 4, 614.
[7] Banc. V, 1, 560.

outside the borders of Pimeria.[1] During the Apache raids frantic appeals brought two more,[2] and finally one in the Santa Cruz valley.

At these remote frontier posts one of the military escorts himself says: "The soldiers were lazy and rapacious."[3] They were continually streaming about the country in unsuccessful pursuit of the Apaches and often helped by the Pima, three hundred of whom sometimes went out with the Spaniards at once. This provided casual voluntary contacts but none that were permanent.

Ranches, in that difficult country were always few, the settlers complaining that the missions monopolized all the desirable land.[4] The Apache menace made large haciendas, such as existed in Cali. fornia, too much of a risk. In 1764 there were only two.[5] But the Spanish reports mention white men living far from any pueblo and owning a few cattle[6] and complain of the evil "Spaniards, coyotes and mulattos" who lead the Pimas astray.[7]

The most important contacts of the Pimans, outside the missions, must have been those with mining prospectors. The country abounds in thin deposits of gold and silver, reachable with a pickaxe, or in the river valleys through placer mining. In the Altar valley during the Spanish occupancy there were continual flurries of gold discovery, but no establishment of large mines like those farther south which set whole Indian populations to work. As a report to Spain in 1750 puts it:

"There is not a single regularly established *real* (mining camp) or settlement in Sonora or one having over ten permanently resident families. The population is scattered and constantly changing with the discovery of new mines...... poor miners struggle for existence."[8]

The Pimas themselves had made no use of the desert minerals and even Spanish miners did not push past the Altar valley until 1736 when a deposit of silver nuggets was found at Arizonac *(ari conacam,* having a little spring) in the middle of the desert country. For a while the country was flooded with "roving vagabonds called miners",[9] but the supply was soon exhausted. There must always

---

[1] Fronteras, in the Sonora valley.
[2] Bancroft, V, 1, 528.
[3] Manje, quoted in Bancroft, V, 1, 504.
[4] Salvador report, quoted in Banc. V, 1, 542.
[5] Doc. Hist. III, v. 4, 609.
[6] Salvador report, quoted in Banc. V, 1, 532.
[7] Doc. Hist. III, V. 4, 630.
[8] Gallardo, quoted in Banc. V, 1, 534.
[9] Banc. V, 1, 526.

have been a few individual prospectors wandering about the region but the majority were kept off by the sterile nature of the country, the expense of reducing ores and the danger from the Apache.

It was after the mission period that there began those changes which officially separated the Papago from the Pima. As has been mentioned, many of the former desert people had flooded into the irrigated towns, in the Altar valley and up the Santa Cruz. But those towns were still within Apache country and out of the way of travel. The Pima on the Gila had never been forced to move nor been replaced by Papagos. Little by little, as the United States expanded westward, the route along the Gila became known and with it the Pimas resident there. When the United States made a purchase of territory from Mexico in 1853, this Gila Valley was included. There was also included a stretch of desert to the south of it which had the effect of cutting the old Pimeria practically in two. The Altar valley, which had bounded Pimeria on the south, remained in Mexico. The desert dwellers who had always had more affiliations with that valley than with the Gila kept their connections with it.

Thus as the stream of white travel touched the River People more and more constantly, the Desert People remained unknown, their contacts still in Mexico. There was some attempt to regulate all the territory of the Gadsden purchase from Tucson but in 1870 a reservation was set apart at Sacaton and called Pima. When in 1874 a little land was reserved to the Indians around the old settlement of Bac, this was called Papago.

White ranchers and prospectors were now beginning to settle on the Public Domain which had been Papago land and it became obvious that the Indians must have protection. There were set aside in succession, first 10,233 acres at Gila Bend, then eighty at Sells (with eighty more at San Miguel for Presbyterian and Catholic missionaries) and finally the large reservation established in 1917 and enlarged in 1921 and 1933 until it now contains 2,636,615 acres. It was the last reservation to be established and its provisions contained a ruling not made with other reservations, to the effect that the Indians' right to the land did not include a right to the minerals. The Indians were considered to have, under the United States, exactly the rights they had had under Mexico and, since they had never done any mining, mining rights were not included.

From this time the process of Americanization proceded as on other reservations. By 1931, the reservation had four government schools and nine mission schools, with 974 pupils. There was a hospital at Sells and a tuberculosis sanatorium being built at San Xavier. There was an Indian policeman paid by the government and minor offenses were heard before Indian judges and punished in the reservation jail. An Indian stockman, paid by the government, superintended the sale of Indian cattle to the best advantage. Deep wells had been drilled at several of the summer villages so that the people need not use an insanitary pond nor fetch water from a distance.

The Papago were still supplementing their earnings by working for the Pimas and the Mexicans of Sonora, but a settlement of them had grown up in Tucson where they worked as house servants and gardeners for the Whites. At Ajo, just off the reservation to the west, there had grown up a copper mine where as many as 600 of them were sometimes employed at one time. They were still reported as agriculturalists, most families on the reservation raising enough for their own use and some having a surplus for barter at the store. Cattle raising had taken the place of hunting and at the south, where cattle had been longest known, there were several large ranchers. Other families had ten head or more and the total number of cattle was very roughly estimated at 20,000. Every man, if possible, had a riding horse, many had wagons and there were perhaps, one or two automobiles.

The government had dug deep wells at some of the larger villages so that the constant need for water had been alleviated and, with it some of the movements of the population. The young people spoke English after a fashion though few over thirty spoke other than Papago with a few words of Mexican. They wore Mexican clothes: cowboy regalia for the men, cotton frocks and mantillas for the women. Their houses were the one room structures of wattle and daub so common in Sonora.

In 1933, the leisurely progress of the Papago toward Americanization was suddenly speeded up. Emergency Conservation funds were appropriated for the improvement of the water supply by the drilling of deep wells, installing gasoline pumps, improving springs, digging reservoirs. Trails and truck roads were to be built to make these accessible. Papagos were employed at the work and taught stone masonry, carpentry, machine operating. Almost every man had a chance at day labor for a few months, at the standard pay given to Whites.

In 1935 the Indian Reorganization Act was presented to the Papagos who voted to accept it and produced a constitution. The election of officers is in process at the time of this writing.

It is not the purpose of this paper to follow in detail the rapid and complex changes which are shaping the reservation under White influence. Those changes can be better studied after a few years have defined their course, but they can hardly be evaluated without a clear understanding of the culture which formed their background and which is rapidly disappearing under the new stimulus. The following pages present as clear a picture as could be formed in the time available, of the old culture which had remained almost intact for many centuries. The description is in the past, since the extent of its preservation differs from village to village. In many places, it seems almost untouched; in some it has disappeared. The simplest method seems to be to describe it as in the youth of which most informants were telling and to indicate briefly at the end of the paper the direction and the amount of change.

# KIN GROUPINGS

## MOIETY

The Papago are divided into patrilineal moieties, whose totems are Coyote and Buzzard. In consonance with California belief, Coyote is thought to have a white heart, while Buzzard's is red.[1] As subsidiary totems, the two moieties have white and red ants, actually a form of wingless wasp. The bear is sometimes mentioned as having a white heart and befriending the Coyote people, while mountain lion befriends the Buzzards.

But the moieties are actually remote from Papago life and many people do not know to which they belong. No moiety exogamy is now practised and only three informants had heard a tradition of such a thing. Most of them laughed at the idea; "We're all just the same. Those names don't matter." The marriage rule, in fact, is that of a bilateral system, which forbids marrying relatives on either side of the house. The kinship system is in accordance with such a rule since it gives equal weight to the paternal and maternal lines and calls cross and parallel cousins by the same terms. It is a terminology which takes no cognizance of moiety.

Moiety functions only in ceremony.[2] It was with some difficulty that the traces of this were unearthed but, from the impressions of the oldest informants, it would seem that there were many more at one time than now. At the wiikita, the harvest festival held in the northern part of the region every four years, two girls and two boys scattered sacred cornmeal. They impersonated four children originally sacrificed to prevent a flood and there must be a boy and a girl from each moiety as there had been in that legendary case. At the final purification of an Enemy Slayer, old Slayers sang and

---

[1] The Pima tradition makes the red people the descendants of the former inhabitants of the land (Russell, 179), while Papago narrators say that these inhabitants were driven south.

[2] Herzog, G, AA vol. 38, no. 3, pt. 1, p. 520, reports Pima moities as once taking sides in games. With the Papago, the game unit is now the village or the group of related villages, all of whom descend, theoretically, from the same patrilineal ancestor. If we conclude that women were married into these related villages, which thus came to be thought of as groups of cross cousins, we should have to disregard the Papago rule which forbids all marriage between relatives. With the Papago, the village has long been the functioning unit and even the selection of kin which constitutes it is coming to have less and less importance.

blew tobacco smoke over him. These smokers held in their mouths a different herb according to the moiety of the man to be purified: a sweet grass for the Coyote moiety and *yerba mansa* for the Buzzard. At the corn dance, which is now only a tradition, Coyote people painted their bodies with white splashes, Buzzard people with red.

Moiety influenced a man's choice of guardian spirit and his dreaming of songs. A Coyote man would be very likely to dream of Coyote, though other animals would be possible. He would never dream of Buzzard, who helps his own "partners".

The Coyote moiety is numerically in the majority as may be noticed in the list of informants. In fact it was difficult to find enough Buzzards to be sure their side of the story would be heard. In songs and chants the expression "our partner" is taken to refer to Coyote without further description, while Buzzard rarely appears.

However, every one is still aware of his moiety (with the exception of one clan to be mentioned below). People use the knowledge principally to taunt one another in joke. This may be done privately but is also much in use at festivals, where it seems to be semi-ceremonial.

"Two women, a Buzzard and a Coyote, came to a pond where a coyote had been drinking. 'Oh, how had it smells!' said the Buzzard woman. 'That is your partner.' 'Your's smells worse,' said the Coyote woman." (22)

"The Buzzard people, seeing a buzzard in the air, will say: 'Our partner is always dancing.' Coyotes reply: 'He has to stay up there. He smells bad.'" (22)

"'Your partner steals,' say the Buzzards. 'Well, yours eats dead things' the Coyotes reply." (22)

A Coyote man would never kill a coyote. If the animal pilfered from his garden, he would simply submit. "We can't chase away our partner." In killing a deer he would leave the entrails and perhaps a piece of meat hanging on a tree, saying: "Here, partner. This is your share." A village called "Coyote Lives There" once contained a tame coyote, which informants think must have been kept by a member of the Coyote moiety. "It would not stay for a Buzzard." There are fewer stories about the treatment of Buzzard, whose cult seems to have lapsed.

## SIBS

Five patrilineal sibs are known, with a legendary sixth and seventh. They are:

| Coyote | | Buzzard | |
|---|---|---|---|
| aapap-kam | aapap people | maam-kam | maam people |
| apki-kam | apki people | waahw-kam | maam people |

| Uncertain | | Legendary | |
|---|---|---|---|
| o'kari-kam | o'kari people | a'to-kam | a'to people |
| | | si paṭ-kam | bad people |

The distinguishing characteristic of these sibs is that a father is called by his children, not by the ordinary word for father, but by the stem of the sib name: aapap, maam, etc. This is similar to the custom in Yuman tribes of calling the women of one sib by a common sib title.[1] The father term is used to every father in the sib by both male and female children and women do not cease to use it on marriage. Therefore no Papago can be unaware of his sib, though all its functions may have been lost.

The placing of the sibs in the moieties is not entirely clear. All informants agreed. that the aapapkam were Coyote and the maam-kam Buzzard. In fact these main sibs were sometimes used as synonymous with the moieties and many had never heard of any others. When they had, they assigned them a subsidiary position. For example, apkikam is the youngest clan (12); waahwkam is slave to the others and has no real partner, but looks to black buzzard who is slave to yellow buzzard, the moiety totem (20).

It was the common opinion that, four being the ceremonial number, there ought not to be more than four sibs and informants tried to explain away one or another, the omitted one being little represented in the speaker's neighborhood. Thus some informants thought that apki was merely a variation of aapap and that the two constituted one sib (5). Others thought the waahwkam existed only among the Pimas (20). The writer is inclined to agree with the greater number who were convinced that the o'korikam were not a sib at all (12, 23, 16). The proof was that most informants did not know to which moiety the o'korikam belonged and some o'korikam (35) had the same difficulty. Most of this sib have come from below the Mexican border where there has been more fighting and scattering than at the north. They may have been people who had lost clan affiliation and had taken the ordinary word for father, ok, and made a diminutive. The legendary sib, á'tokam, was said (10) to have been that of Elder Brother himself which came up from underground but went back at last, and he with it. The sipáṭkam were bad people who never joined the others in the expedition above ground (25).

[1] Forde, 143; Kroeber 1919, 741,; Spier 1933, 187.

3

There is no tradition of sib exogamy and, as has been remarked of moiety, such a rule would be in direct conflict with the kinship terms and the present marriage regulations. Every Papago, if he uses the old father term, must know his own sib but so little has it to do with daily life that he rarely knows the sib of another. Informants, asked for such information had to try to remember hearing the individual in question address his father. If they could not recall this, they did not know the sib, even of their own mothers. In the census of old settlements appended to this paper, sib is omitted because it could be obtained in less than half the cases.

The few sib functions which persist are ceremonial like those of the moiety. In fact, as has been mentioned, some functions are ascribed to the pricipal sibs, aapapkam and maamkam, which may be historically moiety functions, since no mention of the other sibs is made. Thus at Pisinimo, when the men take their places for the drinking ceremony, the maamkam sit at east and south, the aapapkam west and north (1). When a deer was killed for the deer dance, an aapapkam ran home with the tail, a valued ceremonial object, while a maamkam must always carry the meat. The meat must be cooked by old women belonging to both sibs. A tradition which takes cognizance of four or more sibs is that which says that at the singing which precedes the ceremonial drinking, there should be four dancers at the head of the line, one for each sib (1).

There are indications that the sibs may once have been localized. Though at present members of all may be found in any locality, there is a preponderance of maamkam at Pisinimo and Kaka and of aapapkam at Archie, while the o'korikam are grouped near and across the Mexican border. This is similar to the southern Shoshoneans whose sib names, when translatable, often refer to localities.[1] The Papago names which are untranslatable, all but that of the legendary "bad people", may have had similar connection. In that case, however, the localities referred to must be past and not present habitats, since the Pima, in a different geographic location, have the same sibs.

## KINSHIP

In practice, there is little feeling that a man's sib mates are nearer to him than the members of other sibs. The important grouping is that resulting from the kinship system which is bilateral. The close relatives are "the down on his legs", "the other end of his navel string", and these are on both sides, often in several sibs.

---

[1] Strong, 330.

## KINSHIP TERMS

Prefaced in address by the possessive pronoun *nyi*, my.

b brother, c cousin, ch child, d daughter, f father, gp. grandparent, m mother, mn man, o older, p parent, s son, sb sibling, si sister, wm woman, y younger, sp speaking.

### Parent Class

| *Term* | | *Reciprocal* | |
|---|---|---|---|
| sib term (in address) | f | árita'k | ch |
| o.k   (descriptively) | f | | |
| tcï'ï | m | maṭ | ch |

### Grandparent Class

| | | | |
|---|---|---|---|
| wo.s'k | ff | wó.somaṭ | mn s ch |
| wo.s'k kï.ri | ffb | wó.somaṭ | mn b s ch |
| wo.s'k o'ks | ffsi | wó.somaṭ | wim b s ch |
| kaak | fm | ká'amaṭ | wm s ch |
| kaak kï.ri | fmb | ká'amaṭ | mn si s ch |
| kaak o'ks | fmsi | ká'amaṭ | wm si s ch |
| paap | mf | pá'amaṭ | mn d ch |
| paap kïri | mfb | pá'amaṭ | mn b d ch |
| paap o'ks | mfsi | pá'amaṭ | wm b d ch |
| huhuri | mm | móos | wm d ch |
| huri kï.ri | mmb | móos | mn si d ch |
| huri o'ks | mmsi | móos | wm si d ch |
| | | | |
| wi'kori | ggp | wícaṭ | ggch |
| wi'kori kïri | ggp | wícaṭ | ggch |
| wi'kori o'ks | ggpsi | wícaṭ | ggch |
| cïpi'tc | gggp | siis | gggch |
| cïpit'tc kïri | gggp b | | gggch |
| cïpi'tc o'ks | gggpsi | | gggch |

### Sibling and Cousin Class

| *Term* | | *Reciprocal* | |
|---|---|---|---|
| siis | o sb, cousin[1] of senior descent | cïpi'tc | y sb, cousin[1] of junior descent |
| wï.na'k | sb (descriptive) | | |
| u.wika | mn si or female cousin[1] (descriptive) | | |

---

[1] Herzog, G. AA vol. 38, no. 3, pt. 1, p. 529, quotes a Pima term for cross cousin. This is the word used by the Papago in describing moiety totems and, by them, translated *partner*. It is applied also to related villages whose members are assumed to be, not cross cousins, but men of the same patrilineal stock. Cross cousins are called siblings like parallel cousins.

3*

## Uncle Class

| | f o b | tcutcuht | mn y b ch |
|---|---|---|---|
| father term | | | |
| ather term plus kïri, (old man) | | | |
| father term plus oks (old woman) | f o si | tcutcuht | y b ch wm sp |
| tcï'ïs | m o b | mat | y si ch mn sp |
| ta'a't oks | m o si | mat | y si ch wm sp |
| haki't | f y b f or step f | hakimat | o b ch or step ch m sp |
| wowoi't | f y si | hakimat | o b ch wm sp |
| tahtari | m y b | ma'i | o si ch mn sp |
| tciisk | m y si m or step m | ma'i | o si ch or step ch wm sp |

## Affinal Relatives

| kun | husband | honyi'k | wife |
|---|---|---|---|

A co-wife was addressed by the kin term. If not related, the first wife still called the second younger sibling, while the second reciprocated with senior sibling, as though married under the junior sororate. In joke, wives alluded to one another as nyi hï'ïhk; one with whom I have a relation of jealousy. The same term was applied by either spouse to an illicit lover of the other.

Affinal relatives are considered kin only as they are in the direct lineage of a child who is also in the speaker's lineage. Thus, father-in-law and son-in-law would address one another as "Father of my daughter's child" and "Maternal grandfather of my child." Until a child is born they allude to each other as "that old man", "that young man" and, in address, say "friend." Other relatives, in choosing the child through whom they will count relationship, select one in the father's line if possible, even though the connection is more distant than that of one in the mother's line.

There are a few cases in which a term seems to be "frozen" as in the word for father-in-law, which is identical with that for son-in-law and actually means: father of my grandchild through a daughter, man speaking.[1] Otherwise there is only one independent affinal term kihï, brother-in-law, which is said by some Papago to be an adaptation from the Mexican *cognato*.

---

[1] Parsons (1929, p. 449) quotes a set of affinal terms for the Pima but these exceptions, show the teknonomy cited above though with a number of frozen terms. Since the orthography used here is different from that of Dr. Parsons, I quote both.

## Step Relation Class

Step relationship might occur either with the marriage of several women to one man or with the remarriage of a spouse after the death of a former one. In either case, the terms used were the same. Step parents and children and step siblings might already have been related and, in that case, they called each other by the old terms. If they had not been related, terms were established as though the new spouse had been married in accordance with junior sororate and levirate. i. e.

| | *Term* | | *Reciprocal* |
|---|---|---|---|
| hakit | step f | hakimaṭ | step ch mn sp (or, collo- quially, wokca, arrow quiver) |
| tcisk | step m | ma'i | step ch wm sp |
| siis | step sb, senior descent | cïpitc | step sb junior descent |

These three terms make no provision for other procedure than the junior levirate, the step parent being called by the term for younger brother or sister of the dead parent, step siblings by the term for real sibling. The colloquial term which has come to be used for step child means "arrow quiver".

Other step relations are called by the term of previous kinship.

## Extensions

The use of extensions should theoretically go to the fifth remove in both directions, for the Papago statement is: "The great great grandparent is the last relative. After that, we are no kin." As a result, any descendant of the great great grandparent should be given his proper place among the extensions while the more distant connections would be called not "my relative" but "relative of my father, my grandfather" or some one within the required five generations.

| *Pima term* | | *Papago term* | |
|---|---|---|---|
| vosamajik | d-in-law, mn sp f-in-law, wn sp | wo.somaṭ tcï'ï | m of gch through d, wm sp |
| kaamejik | d-in-law, wn sp m-in-law, wn sp | ka'amaṭ tcï'ï | m of gch through son, wm sp |
| nyipahamatak | s-in-law mn sp f-in-law-, mn sp | nyi pa'amaṭ o.k | my f of gch through d, mn sp |
| moi ak | s-in-law, wn sp | mo·s o.k | f of gch through d, wm sp |
| chuchumi | m-in-law, mn sp | | unexplained |

In practice, however, the Papago is not very assiduous in reckoning relationship. Those kin who live in the same village will be kept track of and called by the proper term but the distant ones seem to be lost to sight after the third remove, often the second. Marriage is forbidden between relatives, supposedly those within the five removes but when I inquired for examples of projected marriages stopped because of kinship, I found that the offenders were second cousins or uncle and niece. Inquiring about more distant kin, I was told: "No, we could not marry them. *If we knew we were related.*"

But at least as far as the speaker's second cousin and sometimes his third, the relationship was kept track of. These cousins were called siblings, younger or older according to their descent but, when necessary, they could be further distinguished. For a blood sibling, the term was prefaced by si (very much) for a first cousin, by miah (near) and for second or third cousin by mïhk (far). The same qualifiers could be used for all the other terms, or the relationship could be otherwise defined as "my sibling, the son of my very own uncle" etc.

This terminology is entirely lacking in such emphasis as would reflect clan and moiety. There are the same number of terms for relatives on each side of the house and they have the same general significance. All cousins, cross and parallel, are known as siblings. The fact that the affinals have no status until the birth of a child is further evidence to this effect. There can be no classing of certain kin as possible spouses, since no kin are possible spouses. Therefore neither line is weighted with an unusual number of terms, as may happen in unilateral systems.

The other points emphasized appear in some generations and are lost sight of in others. For the great great grandparents and the great grandparents we have only an undifferentiated term. With the grandparents, there is noted the sex of the relative and the difference between the father's and mother's line. With the uncle class, these two distinctions are still present and, in addition, the factor of seniority, not of the relative himself but of his ancestor in the direct line. With Ego's class, all distinctions disappear but seniority and cousins, male, female, cross and parallel are siblings, either junior or senior. In the nephew class, seniority remains and there is added the distinction between father's and mother's line but the sex of the relative is still absent. The grandchild terms are reciprocals of the grandparent terms, which mark the difference between father's and mother's lines and the sex of the grandparent but not of the grandchild. The great grandchild and the great great grandchild terms, again, are single and undifferentiated. Affinals play a small part in the system, though a logical one. They are not related at all until they have children to connect them with the blood kin and then each is known as parent of a certain child.

We have, then, an emphasis on seniority, not of the individual but of his line. We have a distinction between the father's and mother's line and the sex of the relative, all appearing in some generations and disappearing in others. It seems a disjointed view of relationships and the seniority is particularly hard to explain since, in Papago life, there is no inheritance either of office or of goods through primogeniture.

But from one viewpoint, the terms are logical. Let us consider seniority emphasis as reflecting the junior levirate and sororate and let us look at the generations from that of Ego, an immature child. We must begin with the three generations with which Ego is most concerned, his own and those immediately above and below it. It is in these that marriages are occuring during Ego's lifetime, while the remoter generations being more static do not call for terms having to do with marriage.

Ego has a word for father[1] and a word for mother and they have reciprocals for him which naturally express their sex and not his.

In the uncle and aunt class, Ego needs to differentiate younger brother of my father, who may become my stepfather and is called by the same term and similarly younger sister of my mother who may be a stepmother. Seniority, line and sex of the relative are all needed in view of the levirate and sororate. But in an efflorescence of terms Ego goes to the logical conclusion and makes these distinctions for all the uncles and aunts.

In Ego's own class, none of the relatives can be his spouse, so they are all called siblings. If Ego were an adult, he would make sex distinctions, since either younger sisters or younger brothers might some day be entering his own household as step parent, while the opposite sex would not. But it is not Ego's own relation to the marriage rules which is considered but that of his uncles and aunts. Ego calls his siblings simply older or younger without regard to their future marriages and he thinks of his cousins as descendants from the uncle class and calls them younger or older according to the age of their parents, the main figures in his scheme.

Toward the nephew class, Ego's point of view must necessarily be that of an adult and not a child and here, for the first time, his own marriage is considered. He calls his nephews child of my senior and child of my junior but he also distinguishes the sex of the

---

[1] The father term carries a sib connotation which has been considered elsewhere and which is inoperative in Papago daily life.

sibling as he did not do in his own generation. He says child of my junior sister or junior brother, senior sister or senior brother, as do those who consider the effect of levirate and sororate on their own households. There is a reflection, here, of the same efflorescence we found in the uncle class for actually, a man would need to distinguish the ages only of his brothers and a woman of her sisters and other systems have this practice. But the logical completeness found in the uncles class is here also.

These three generations, then, have terms which might very logically be used by a society which made junior levirate and sororate its main consideration in the ranking of kin and which considered relationships as far as possible from the point of view of the child, not the adult.

In the remoter terms, all reference to seniority is absent. If the ranking of Ego's cousins according to seniority of descent really had reference to primogeniture, it would be worth while to know whether his grandfather were an oldest son and therefore the chief of the line, but the terms have no reference to it. Ego differentiates his four grandparents as to sex and as to relationship with father or mother. The distinction can be explained on a household basis since his grandparents are his mentors and nurses in childhood, with decidedly different sex functions. One couple, however, will live in the same camp with Ego and one in a distant camp, according to residence is matrilineal or patrilineal and therefore the distinction of line is necessary. The grandchild terms are reciprocals of the grandparent terms, expressing therefore the sex of the grandparent and not of the grandchild. Two terms have been added in this generation which have no reciprocals. The grandchild sometimes distinguishes his grandparents' siblings from the ancestor himself by adding to the grandparent terms the words old man or old woman, but these great aunts and uncles reply merely with the term grandchild. This differentiation does not occur in all groups using the terminology and is a convenience for keeping the main line separate from the collaterals.

The great grandparents and the great great grandparents are probably not alive in Ego's generation and their figures are too dim to require more than a single inclusive term. After the last there are no further kin terms and the relatives themselves are called siblings "as if they began a new line backward." The whole ancestral line thus seems to be viewed in segments of nine generations with the great great grandparents as the connecting link. This terminology shows the Papago as making use of a kinship system apparently worked out by a group with bilateral descent and strong emphasis on the levirate and sororate. It is the system used, in one form or another, throughout the desert area, the Basin and Plateau, and it would be strange if the Papago had departed from it. There was nothing in their customs to force them to do so since their family was bilateral and the levirate and sororate were practised though not emphasized.

But the Papago were not given to hard and fast rules. It may have been their frugal and difficult existence which forced them always to consider economic convenience first, but certainly the sororate, was practised only if the husband was a good provider and relatives were intimate or not according as they were of economic use to one another. In fact, given the above kinship system as a starting point, the different relationships took on validity for economic and geographic reasons rather than from set ceremonial usage. Consequently the points most important in behavior are not reflected in the terms.

In order to study actual kin behavior, before the days of White influence, a census was made of the families living in eight different settlements between the years 1850 and 1900. This list, contained in Appendix I, notes the constitution of each family group and their economic arrangements for cooperative living, land sharing and gift exchange. Sib was not noted, since it was so rarely known. From this data, we may attempt a picture of actual kin behavior.

# KIN BEHAVIOR

## THE GROUP

The relationships of the ancient Papago, economic and social, were almost all within the kinship circle. "We love our relatives." "We would do anything for our relatives." "A purified scalp works for you like a relative." "We like to go to feasts *to see our relatives*." Address by the kinship term was the regular greeting, the regular form of applause and the final rite for receiving a neophyte back to daily life after purification. White residents, critical of Papago self-government remark: "A Papago elected to office will consider no one but his relatives."

Anciently, the only standardized relationships were within the extended family. People outside it should not be chosen as friends because they could not be relied on. Any exchange of gifts made with them should be in the nature of a trade, with full payment immediately and no credit. Even though near neighbors, they remained in an outer sphere unless they were judged desirable connections in a marriage alliance. Then they were investigated, approached and finally drawn within the active circle of kin, to have their share in companionship, service and gift exchange. Within this kin circle, there were no rigid rules. Papago had no avoidances and no joking relationships. The marriage regulations were tempered with economic convenience. The particular group of kin to whom one owed constant duty was not the nearest in blood but the nearest geographically.

This pragmatic use of a kinship formula was in agreement with the Papago mode of life. Villages were scattered over an immense desert country where travel was difficult, because of the absence of drinking water and a relative removed to another village became almost inaccessible. But relatives close at hand must be a constant reliance. They were the people called on for cooperative labor in house building, ditch digging, planting, harvesting, spinning, arrow making. A family's actual existence might depend on cordial relations with them. "We would do anything for our relatives" had the connotation "And our relatives would do anything for us." The cordial relations were an economic investment

Such an investment was rarely made in non-relatives, since they could not be trusted to repay, having their own more intimate obligations. But a relative valued his kin status and would pay, either in goods or services, now or later. So one turned to any relative at hand. The Melanesian, walking across an island to carry a ceremonial gift to his sister, would be incomprehensible to a Papago. In the practical scheme of the Desert People, a sister received gifts when she was present, none when she was absent.

The geographic grouping of relatives depended on land. The desert country contained innumerable small patches, near the mouths of washes, where flood agriculture was possible. Each family must have such a patch where it could plant in the summer, migrating in the winter to the mountain springs. But the patches within walking distance of any village finally became exhausted and then one of the younger men would decide to move. It was unthinkable that he should go alone to his new home, both because of the fear of enemies and because neighborly help was a constant necessity. So he looked for others who needed land and, of course, he looked among his relatives. The records show no examples of unrelated people joining in such a move. But, given the passport of relationship, circumstances might bring together kin of almost any degree. The five new settlements recorded, show the following relatives each with his immediate family.

Appendix I. 3   Ego
> Ego's full sister and two half sisters, all married to the same man.
> Two other full sisters.
> Ego's mother

I. 4   Ego
> Two nephews
> Three classificatory paternal uncles
> Five cousins of the uncles, kinship to Ego not known

I. 5   Ego
> Mother
> Four brothers
> Dead wife's mother's brother
> Dead wife's older brother's son

I. 7   Ego
> Brother
> Widowed sister

I. 8   Ego
> Two brothers
> Three sisters

(Group I. 5, contained a nephew of Ego's dead wife, who had moved because he needed more land. But having joined, for economic purposes, with a group of his affinals, he proceeded to have all his intimate relations with them and, even in winter, when he moved back near his blood kin, his relations were with the new group, not with the old. It was propinquity which determined intimacy.)

An old village was larger and contained more unrelated families but it was generally segemented into groups of kin who continued to build houses near each other and to unite for work sharing, almost as though they were a separate village. The selection of these groups was as dependent on economic chance as that of a new village for, though usually close kin kept together, some of them might, for reasons of land or housing convenience, become attached to a group of more distant relatives. Then they would throw in their lot with these new neighbor-kin and have their closest relatioships with them rather than with the old group.

Kin groups recorded for old villages are as follows:

Appendix I. 1　Ego
Three brothers
One sister
(A group of paternal relatives lived elsewhere in the village)

I. 2　Ego
"Near sibling" i.e. first cousin, side of house unknown
Father's younger sister
Father's mother' daughter's son to Ego's wife
Father's father's brother's son to Ego's wife
Two brother's of Ego's wife
Two father's father's brother's sons' daughters to Ego's son's wife
(In another part of the village lived relatives who were actually closer to Ego, i. e. two daughter's of Ego's younger brother with other relatives of his wife.)

I. 6　Ego
Younger brother
Younger sister
Younger sister's daughter

Each biological family in a group worked its land in common, (at least until the death of the father) but on special occasions, such as planting and harvesting, they called in the neighbor kin and were called by them in turn. Every one who worked received a share of the harvest commensurate, not with his work but with what the owner could spare. The more an owner gave, the higher his repute and the greater his assurance of getting service in his turn. For other activities, such as house building, the workers received only their meals but again they had the assurance of future help.

Work sharing may be considered the basis of the whole arrangement but the group having been formed for this purpose, was kept in running order by constant exhibitions of goodwill. These took the practical form of gifts and gifts of the one commodity which the Papago ever possessed in excess of their need: food.

When a hunter brought home a deer, he went to each main house and presented a portion proportionate to the size of the family there. If there were hunters in that house, his family would soon receive a similar gift: if not it would be any other food they could afford. But with such relatives, there was a distinct obligation not to cease giving even though there should be no return. The investment was a long term affair to be realized on in the future if not the present.

The women treated each other similarly. Whenever a special dish was cooked in one house, children would be sent around to carry portions of it to all the others. Some groups went so far that they interchanged such food gifts every day at the evening meal, the only heavy one. (App. I, 3 C and D. I. 8. C. D and E) "So you were never hungry. Even if you didn't cook one day, a dish would be sure to come in from some of the relatives." As the groups grew larger, not every house could be so treated. (I, 8, A & B). Then a woman would give regularly only to her husband's siblings (I. 3. A. 2; I. 7) with, perhaps, some old people who needed help. Or there might be family cliques and favoritism. (I. 3; I. 9). One woman, who happened to have both brothers and sisters nearby, "always gave to her brothers for she thought the sisters could cook for themselves." But even if certain families were not often included, a gift must be sent to them now and then to keep up good feeling. (I. 2. A; I. 4. A; I. 5. A).

The geographic group had ceremonial obligations as well as economic ones. Every Papago youth was expected to become a "ripe man" through the performance of certain ceremonial acts which conferred a blessing but also subjected him to supernatural dangers. In both danger and blessing the kin were thought to share and therefore, while the youth fasted and bathed to purify himself, the kin abstained from salt and bathed also. When I inquired what kin shared the hero's lot in this way, I was given an incredible list extending, in some cases, to the above mentioned five removes — and on both the man's side and his wife's. Such wholesale purification would have disrupted the life of several villages but, on further inquiry, it appeared that those at a distance "felt the power would not reach so far." A second cousin, or even a third, living in the same village would "think it safer" to bathe and go saltless but a sister who was far away might take no precautions at all.

The same considerations applied to the gift giving. At the war purification an elaborate dance was performed by paid dancers, the pay being furnished by the hero's kin. There were no stated obligations." "If his father had nothing to give, an uncle might do it all." Or even a "distant uncle" *if he lived near*. The underlying idea seems to be that this payment was an investment in blessing. The hero, when he became a "ripe man" would enjoy a material success, either as a hunter or as a paid singer and his neighboring kin would naturally share in the proceeds. The one who had given most would be repaid accordingly.

We have pictured the geographic group, selected by circumstance and economic necessity, as the most important one. But the duties toward this group did not preclude relationships with other kin and these were kept up, often under great difficulties. Ties with the nearest kin, such as parents or children, were not allowed to lapse no matter what the distance and other relatives when they became neighbors, were immediately included in the gift giving circle. (I. 1. D; I. 4. B, I. 6. D. 2; I. 7. B. 2). But there was a general range of duties to be observed toward any class of relatives, geography permitting, and these may be taken up for each class separately.

SIBLING CLASS. Siblings were brought up in the same one-room house but a sex distinction began very early. Boys followed the men, learning to hunt and to till the ground, girls kept with the women, gathering food, fetching wood and water, grinding corn and making baskets. The fear of the menstruating woman caused a separation between the two groups so that even husband and wife were seldom together during the day. Boys played together and, when they wanted more companionship, sought out their male cousins who generally lived near. Girls formed a group with their female cousins.

Between brother and sister as between the remoter "siblings" of opposite sex, there was a mild respect relationship. No brother and sister would stay alone in the house at night or be seen out together. Any sister had a special duty to prepare food for her brother, even more than for the other male relatives and he, at need, would hunt or till the land for her. But the relationship was one of help without intimacy.

The close tie with siblings of one's own sex and respectful help to the opposite sex, continued into adult life. The brothers, during their father's lifetime, worked together under him, often living in the same house and bringing their wives home to share it. On the father's death, they built themselves separate houses but often they continued to share the land and its proceeds, their wives cooking together in a common kitchen. (I. 2. A; I. V. A and C).

Even if the brothers divided their land, they acted in many way as an economic unit. Ceremonial payments falling upon one member were made by the whole group or by that member who could best afford it. Vengeance for murder — a rare occurence — fell on any member of the group who was available. Dependant relatives were billetted in any of the houses as convenient and the young people of the group worked for any member as ordered. The junior levirate was strongly in force and an older brother, dying, would be replaced in his household by one of the younger ones.

The companionship of sisters somethimes lasted equally long. After sleeping on the same mat through childhood two of them, or even three or four, might be married to the same man and continue to share their tasks till death. Even though they were not co-wives during life, the younger might marry her sister's widower and care for her sister's children.

But when the sororate was not convenient, the connection of sisters with all their siblings temporarily lapsed. A woman was always expected to marry into another village so as to avoid her blood kin, and in her husband's household she became part of a new female group, composed of sisters-in-law married to the sons of the family. Often she was too far off for her siblings even to send her gifts, for only one gift exchange between such a brother and sister is mentioned (I. 3. B). If her brothers went through ceremonial purification, she might not know of it and would be absolved from bathing and fasting. She would go through these rites with her new family; her husband and his resident brothers.

But this separation, dependent on geographic limitations, was often only temporary. If the sister's marriage was broken up by death or divorce, she immediately returned home. (I. 3. B). If she were too old to remarry, her brothers would provide for her as suited their arrangements: either in a house with one of them, in a separate house, with a field of her own or with produce from the common field. If she was still young, it was their duty to find her another husband. "My brother found a man for me. I did not want that man but I could say nothing against my brother," (26). The males of the group were in authority and their responsibility for the sister was resumed as soon as her connection with the distant village ceased.

This sometimes happened without her losing her husband. For various reasons, listed elsewhere, she might find it convenient to return with her husband and share the family land. No objection was ever made to this practice and for three groups of brothers only, there are five groups including one or more sisters. (I. 1. A. B. C. D. E; I. 3. B. 5. 9. and 12; I. 6. A. B. C. D; I. 7. A. B. C; I. 8. A B. C. D. E). In such a case, the sister's husband was given exactly the same status as a brother, sharing land, services and payments. But the sex division continued for even adult men should not converse too freely with their sisters. It was the sister's husband who received intimate treatment, while the sister joined the group of her brother's wives.

Outside the group of blood brothers and sisters, were the "distant siblings", the cross and parallel cousins on both side of the house with whom marriage was forbidden. But the relationship was sometimes rather vague if the relative lived in a distant village. "They married me to one whom I called elder brother but he was very distant. And he lived in another village so we thought there was no harm" (26). In childhood, if cousins were the children of brothers, they might live very intimately but as they grew up, they formed their own sibling groups and were cut off from their former companions. Still, they were thought of as potential intimates and, whenever the geographic difficulty could be overcome, they were accepted into the circle. "I heard this story from my father's sister's daughter's daughter's daughter. She was living with us that winter" (26). In cases of necessity, also, duty to a sibling had to be done at all costs. I. B. 1 was an old man with three wives but when his distant senior sibling died and there was no one to marry the widow I. B. 1 became her titular husband although neither he nor she cared to have her live with him.

It may be of interest to note whether Papago behavior shows any emphasis on seniority outside that involved in the levirate and sororate. Very little is apparent for, although in the origin myth, the supernaturals strove for the title of Elder Brother, no modern informant could explain why the title was important. Such a title is usually connected with inheritance of property or office but Papago sons inherit the father's land equally, sometimes without dividing it. I. 1. 8. B. 1, an oldest brother, voluntarily absented himself and left the inherited field to the others. Ceremonial and secular office were handed down by the father, not to the oldest son but to that one fittest to receive them. "I started teaching my ritual to my oldest son, but it seemed he couldn't learn. Then I tried the second but he was always away, working for the Whites. Now I must get a nephew," (2). The father-in-law of 21 tried teaching the calendar stick to his son, found him a poor memorizer and gave it to his son-in-law. Thus the eldest does not inherit property or office nor does he, apparently have authority. (I. 1. A an oldest son and II 1. 8. A. 2, an oldest daughter, took authority in their groups, but this was rather by virtue of character than seniority.) It is true there is authority in the family but it is exercised by the brothers in a group over the sisters, not by one oldest son.

Seniority would seem to be referable only to sororate and levirate, which dictated the kinship terms and we may question whether its appearance in the myth is not also a heritage from some of the other cultures where the same myth is found and where the older brother may have more importance.

Sibling behavior according to this data matches sibling terminology in those points emphasized by the terms, which are points having to do with marriage. Cousins on both sides of the house are considered equal and are impossible as mates while their age status is important because of junior levirate and sororate. But in daily life there appear two other important factors, not reflected in the terms: sex of the relative which conditions social behavior and geographic situation on which all kin behavior is contingent.

PARENT CLASS. Probably the most intimate relation in Papago life was that between father and son. The father was the head of an economic unit, with his sons as his working staff. He directed their labor and arranged for the sale of the produce. If new equipment was needed for any member of the family out of the common supply, he decided upon it. He was responsible for the behavior of his sons and, long after their marriage, he continued to direct them by moral discourse. He, with the mother, decided upon the marriages and received the brides under his protection. When the sons underwent ceremonial purification it was he, first of all, who should make the payment and receive the consequent blessing. He continued as their protector and advisor until his own death, and began very early to train one of them to carry on any office he might hold or to practice any skill. Hunting or weaving, therefore, ran in special families, where the father passed on his knowledge to his sons.

Although the father was so definitely the head of the family, he ruled, as did the chief, by moral suasion rather than by force. He and

4

his sons formed a friendly group in which custom demanded that his should be the deciding voice. But if a son was recalcitrant, no father would take such strong measures as to oust him from the family land or otherwise discipline him. The attitude of most fathers was one of extreme protectiveness: "My son has moved away to get more land but I'll be watching him. As soon as he has any trouble, I'll be right there. I have to help him: he's my child" (2). The Papago attitude toward a son is so different from the Hebrew attitude of proprietorship that a Papago being told about the atonement protested: "A God who would let his own son be killed cannot be my God. No father should do that."

A father's attitude toward his daughter was far less intimate, for she was part of the female group and received her instruction from her mother. But she listened to his moral discourse at night and was lectured on important occasions. It was his responsibility to see that she was a desirable citizen and one informant thought that in old days a father who failed to see that his daughter was segregated at the menstruation period would be whipped. The father, with the mother's help, selected a husband for her and made the proposal. After that he handed her training over to her father-in-law. Sometimes he retained his protective attitude toward her, summoning her at harvest to help herself from his field, (I. 4. A. 1) and sometimes carrying her gifts. (No. 2 takes meat seventeen miles to his married daughter whenever he kills a beef.) If she was widowed or divorced, she returned and he again assumed responsibility for her (I. 2. H. 3). But also, if he had no sons, he might call on his daughters' husbands to help him and even if they had lands of their own, they and their wives did him service (I. 7. C).

This responsibility of the father for the patriarchal family had not, in the memory of informants, any connection with the sib as a whole. Yet the sib term, used instead of a father title, might indicate that he was a sib head, even embodied the sib like the MacPherson or the O'Donohue. But we have mentioned before how little connection the sib has with Papago life. The use of a sib title in the kin terms is in direct variance with the system of terminology. There are traces here of two incompatible customs and Papago usage seems to correspond with the majority of the kin terms in ignoring sib.

The mother, who was the head of the female group, had her most intimate companionship with her daughters. She and they were constantly together until the daughters married and their place in the female group was taken by daughters-in-law. Her sons were always occupied with the men but they were members of the home group and she cooked and cared for them perhaps until her death.

If she was widowed, her husband's house was torn down and she lived with one of the sons. The most responsible of the latter then headed the family group and she, like the daughters accepted his decisions. When informant 26 was married against her will her mother took her side but "could say nothing against the men" her son and cousin. Again the difference in sex, which is marked in Papago life, is only partially expressed in the terms.

STEP PARENT CLASS. The step parent is assumed to be the junior aunt or uncle and is called by that term while he uses the reciprocal. Step parents are received very easily into the family. If not actually relatives, real or classificatory, they are still treated as such and given the corresponding place in the family group.

UNCLE CLASS. Tradition picked out the senior uncle as a special guide and mentor. The ceremonial guardian of a man undergoing purification called his protegé by the same term as would a senior paternal uncle or aunt and in rituals where the raingods are represented as addressing human beings, they also use the term. It would seem to point toward a specially protective attitude of the senior uncle and perhaps to his being chosen as a ceremonial godfather. At present there is no such practice nor remembrance of it. Behavior toward the senior uncle, who may once have been a godfather, and the junior uncle, who might be a stepfather, show the same intimate respect and if a maternal uncle or a distant uncle happened to join the family group, this behavior would be extended to him also (I. 4. B. and C; I. 1. F).

All uncles felt it their duty to admonish a child. "When I am with my uncle he always talks serious, telling me how to behave," (27). "If an uncle is left alone with a boy, of course he preaches to him. That is what he has to do" (22). "In the old days, people knew what was right because, besides their fathers. they had all their uncles to talk to them" (5).

An uncle took this leading position even if he was no older than his nephews. I. 8. E. 1 had nephews even older than himself but acted always as their head and protector. He looked after their cattle when he was six and they ten. When his older siblings went to cactus camp, he was the one left at home to take care of their children. He arranged the chores for his nephews and stopped their quarrels by a mere command. His status continued into adult life.

The same obligations might fall to a maternal uncle or to a distant uncle if he happened to form part of the family group. I. 8. E. 1 arranged a marriage for his classificatory niece with a man as old as himself and this man has respectfully taken his orders ever since.

Nephews owed an uncle help and support almost as if he were a

4*

father. The younger brother of informant 22 lived permanently with an uncle who had no son to tend his field and had commandeered a nephew. If an uncle, for some reason, had no land, he assumed the right to share that of nephews or nieces on either side of the house (I. 1. F; I. 6. D. 3; I. 5. E. 1). An aged uncle, with no near relatives would expect to be cared for by a nephew or niece. Informant 22 lives with his younger sister's daughter part of the time and part with a female cousin, exact relationship unknown.

On the other hand, a nephew could expect support and help from an uncle almost as from a father. If his parents died, he naturally entered the house of one of his uncles in the same family group. Even when adult, if he had no group of his own, he would seek that of an aunt or uncle and be accepted like an own child. (I. 6. D. 2). When ceremonial payments had to be made for him, it was his uncle, quite as often as his father, who provided them, (payment was made for I. 1. A. 1 by a father's younger brother).

When uncle and nephew were not in the same group, a gift-giving relationship was often maintained between them. This depended, apparently on their distance apart and the number of other obligations upon each. A distant uncle might invite his nephews to harvest for him and take a share of the produce (I. 1. I; I. 1. A. 2) or he might visit periodically, bringing gifts. (I. 1. I)

Aunts usually lived at a distance, since they were expected to marry into another village, but there were many exceptions. A mother's younger sister was often the father's co-wife and treated very like the mother. Any sister of the father's might have returned to use the ancestral land and then would be an intimate member of the group, taking almost as much responsibility for the girl as did her mother. When cooked food was distributed, a child might make daily trips to the aunt's house with a food bowl, receiving gifts and instruction (I. 1. A. 4; I 8. E. 7).

Aunts admonished their nieces and nephews much as uncles did. Just as ritual points to the senior paternal uncle as a ceremonial godfather, so the senior paternal aunt is a godmother. However, the office is not legendary but was in use a short time ago at the time of a girl's puberty. At this period, a girl was secluded for four days in the company of an older woman who trained her in industry and lectured her on the duties of marriage. The oldest informant, though she knew of no rule for the selection of this woman, remembered that the person chosen was her senior paternal aunt (26).

As with the uncles, even a distant aunt or one younger than oneself was entitled to respect. "Lupa, older than I, is my distant niece. At a fiesta, she always comes to speak to me, knowing it is not my place to speak to her" (32).

GRANDPARENT CLASS. The four words for grandparent indicate an equal importance in all four individuals, subject to the determining factor of propinquity. The grandparents in the male line were normally the leaders and teachers of the whole family group, parents and children alike. The young parents were often away from home, on the active tasks of food getting and it was the grandparents who trained the children in crafts and in moral behavior. A Papago, in looking back on his early education, thinks not of his father but of his grandfather. The loss which would disrupt his home in early life would be that of grandparents, not parents.

The grandfather, in particular, was the moral mentor, talking to the children nightly and waking them before dawn with homilies on virtue and industry. It was he who recited the myths in the proper season and, if there was ritual knowledge to be passed down in the family, he often selected the grandson to receive it.

As the grandfather grew older, he benignantly abdicated his post of family head and the most energetic of his sons managed the family business. The grandfather now became the constant companion of the children and even at present, it is he who normally sits holding the baby while the younger members of the family are at work. When he grew older still, it was the grandchildren who waited on him while the parents did harder tasks. In rare cases where a grandfather happened not to live with the family group, children were detailed to stay with him.

Informant 23 lived in a village from which all his sons had moved away. When he grew too old to work his fields his grandsons in the male line were already grown and married. He rode to his daughter's house and asked for a boy to live with him. "She and her husband didn't say anything. They just told the boy: Get your things and go with your grandfather." Informant 43 was sent regularly during the dry season to live with her paternal grandfather's sister and fetch water for her from the spring a mile away.

The paternal grandmother directed the women of the home group, as the grandfather directed the men. Little girls generally slept on a mat with her and it was she who taught them cooking and basketry while their mothers were out food gathering. She cared for the children while their mother was in the segregation hut, at menstrual periods and childbirth. Moreover, a young father was sure to undergo several periods of ceremonial purification, during which his wife was secluded also. Then the grandmother cooked for the children, instructed them in behavior and gave them their ritual baths. She remained in the home group until her death and if, her husband died first, would be taken into the family of one of her sons where she would continue her duties (I. 5. B. 1; I. 1. A. 3).

Any sibling of the grandparents was treated much like a grand-parent, provided he lived in the home group. Many houses have several dependent old people of this sort addressed briefly as grand-parent, without the suffix old man or old woman which indicates a grandparental sibling. In such a case, it is almost impossible to tell by behavior which is the grandparent and which a collateral.

The grandparents in the mother's line normally lived in another village and could be seen only on visits. But these visits might last a long time (I. 1) and also there were many reasons why a mother might return to her own parents. Then these would take the same position as teacher and nurse which was normally occupied by the father's parents (I. 3. C. 5).

### Great Grand Parent and Great Great Grandparend Class

The more ancient relatives existed only as dependents, cared for in any family which could find room for them. Their unimportance is expressed by the fact that, in their titles, no distinction is made as to sex or line and the remotest, the great great grandparents, are called by the children "younger siblings" in allusion, one informant thought, to their second childhood.

### Spouse Class

Though the man was the head of the family and residence was at his village, there was much emphasis, in daily life, on the equality of the spouses. Each was supreme in a special field of activity and, in many phases of ceremonial life, one could not participate without the other. At home labor, the patriarch directed the men and his wife the women. He disposed of gifts of meat and cultivated crops; she of cooked food and wild crops and the relatives of both shared equally in the distribution, subject to the factor of propinquity.

Co-wives were not frequent except with older men who had acquired the goods to support them. They were usually sisters and, in that case, there was no formal precedence of the older. They arranged their work and distributed gifts in committee and the husband accepted their joint decision. Wives who were not related were expected to fit into the sister pattern although the colloquial term "she of whom I am jealous" shows that they did not always do it. But there was no hard and fast rule for precedence of the senior wife. The women of the household were left democratically, to settle their troubles between them.

Though women had few ceremonial duties of their own, the obligations of a husband often reflected on his wife, or wives, automatically, thus emphasizing the unity of the spouses. When a man was ceremonially purified, a wife went through the same ordeal mitigated only slightly because of her sex. At its end, she had the title of "ripe". Her relatives automatically shared her blessing and her danger and, to protect themselves they abstained from salt and bathed every four days. A list of affinals purified with I. 1. A. 1 is as follows: wife, wife's parents, wife's father's brother, wife's siblings in another village, with their spouses and children. The others were far away or "they would have been purified too."

Yet this close relationship depended on the birth of a child to the young couple. After that event, the new spouse was known by affinals as "father of my grandchild", "mother of my elder brother's child", etc. In the absence of a child there was no word available but "that young man" or that "young woman."

Death or divorce did not prevent the use of kinship terms, since these depended on the child, but they often broke up economic relationships and the ceremonial ties which derived from them. On the death of a spouse, the levirate and sororate might come into play and then all relationships remained unchanged. But these rules were by no means inviolable. If a wife died and her sister did not replace her, the children normally remained in the husband's home group, cared for by his parents. If a husband died, the wife returned to her own home group taking, at least, the young children. But if she were old and her sons able to care for her, she might remain where she was.

Gift giving relationships with the affinals depended on whether the widowed spouse was within geographic reach. One family group shows the dead wife's relative as being within the intimate economic circle since they had land there. (I. 5. D. E). No purification is recorded for this family so we cannot tell whether a ceremonial tie was felt also.

There is no record of gifts to geographically distant affinals after a spouse's death but relatives would, if possible, remember the children and visit them occasionally. Such children could come back for help if they failed to get any group of their own. In divorce, conditions were much the same. The woman left the man's house and probably married into a new family group so that the old economic arrangements were necessarily broken up. All her ties, economic and ceremonial, were with the new group.

These instances show that, in Papago kin behavior, sex is always important since men and women work and play in sex limited groups. Degree of kinship may determine economic behavior toward any relative but social behavior depends very much on the sex of the two concerned. A kinship terminology which reflected general behavior would need to note the sex, both of the relative and of the speaker.

# VILLAGE GROUPINGS

A Papago village official addressed his speeches not to "my fellow townsmen," but to "my kinsmen." For applause, each one called him by the kinship term and it was rarely that anyone had to substitute "my friend." A village was a settlement of kin and others entered it only by invitation or by marriage.

But a village was not a constant unit, for desert conditions, before the digging of government wells, did not permit of year-long residence in any one place. In the summer, when rains filled the shallow reservoirs scooped out with blades of wood and stone, the people could live in the flat country whose name is the same as that for "land" and "ground" and here they could have their fields near the mouths of washes. Such a farming settlement was known not as a village but as Fields, since these were the important thing.

The fields could be occupied only during the summer rainy season and as long afterward as the water lasted in the reservoir: then the people must move to the foothills where there were springs. Each Field had its foothill camp, known as the Well where its residents kept duplicates of the objects they could not transport, such as metates and water jars and where they had at least the posts for a shelter. Sometimes one Well would not accomodate all the Field people and then they had several. Sometimes two related villages used the same Well, but then they kept apart and established no gift intimacies with their new neighbors. When one changed his Field village, for good reason, he was still not expected to change his Well village. Relationships in each were permanent.

The result was that each village had a dual existence, in summer at the Fields, and in winter at the Wells. Many censuses have come to grief over this difficulty. But Field and Well together were part of a larger group. In the course of time, the villages had proliferated, sending out one group after another to look for more land. The new settlement thus made might be only a suburb of the home village, obeying its officials and coming home for ceremonies But sometimes the daughter village was so large or so far away that it needed a leader of its own. Then it appointed one, but considered him always subsidiary to the leader of the parent village. The new hamlet might also, in course of time acquire a fetish and hold a few ceremonies in imitations of those at home. But, on great ceremonial occasions, all daughter villages returned in a body to the parent village. If intervillage games were held, it was understood that all played and bet on the same side. If one went on the warpath, the others were notified and asked to join. Modern interpreters speak of these related villages as "partners". We shall refer to the whole group of mother village, daughter villages and Wells, as a village unit.

The three reservations number eleven such village units whose location has changed very little in the two hundred and more years since Kino visited most of them. The reason is obvious. They were placed in spots which were, then as now, the best for cultivation. Usually, the main villages are found in the middle of the north-to-south valleys, with their daughter villages stretching along the valley in both directions and their Wells perched in the mountain walls at either side. Sometimes a village has made two or three short moves to get better water and it may have carried its old name with it to each location, but all the sites are easily identified and generally the history of the moves is preserved in tradition.

Our knowledge of the daughter villages dates only from 1860[1] and it is possible that their settlement is recent and due to the cessation of Apache raids. Kino, who visited several of the mother villages, says nothing about the daughters and we do not know whether the three hundred and seven hundred people who greeted him[2] lived in town or in the environs. But we know that, during the eighteenth and most of the nineteenth century there could be no daughter villages. That was the time of the Apache attacks, when the people were obliged to concentrate and, no matter how far away their fields were: "They could not live far apart. They were afraid." (26)

But when the Apache ceased to trouble, toward the end of the nineteenth century, the large villages began to break up and groups moved out, either to the fields they had been cultivating, or to new ones. Several villages recorded in the appendix were founded in the last two or three generations and the movement is still going on. In the last few years there has appeared a factor which will influence residence even more than freedom from attack. This is the digging of government wells. Already these have given some of the large Field villages a permanent water supply so that movement in the dry season is unnecessary. As more of the Fields are supplied, we may expect some of the Wells to be abandoned while others, if conveniently located for cattle raising, may grow into

---

[1] Hoover, 1395, p. 259.
[2] Bolton, 1936. pp. 397, 398.

permanent villages in their own right. Certainly the yearly migration of the population and its dual residence, will become a thing of the past.

The eleven village units form the outstanding divisions in the Papago country and the loyalty of each individual is above everything else, to his village and its "partners". But the units are gathered into dialect groups, each with very different affiliations. The groups have no governmental or ceremonial significance and their members intermarry, though generally they prefer not to do so on account of divergent customs. The differences between them are fast disappearing and to find the points presented here required a long search. Many of the influences which have caused differentitation may be recent but it is not impossible that some of the lines of cleavage are very ancient ones and reflect a difference between the early Hohokam and those who accepted Pueblo acculturation. There follows a list of the dialect divisions, with their component village units and such historic data as are available for each. This list is in substantial accord with the excellent map published by Hoover[1], who has done painstaking work in tracing village descent. At the end of the chapter is a condensed chart, giving the names in common use (which may be Spanish, English, or adapted Papago), the Papago names and translation.

## PAPAGO-DIALECT GROUPS AND VILLAGE UNITS

### 1. ARCHIE DIALECT GROUP

These are the Papago proper, the people on whom the name of Bean Eaters was originally bestowed. They have an opprobrious nickname, totokuanyi (loose gee string) never used by themselves. For clarity, they may here be spoken of as the Archie group, Archie being their oldest and most important village. It is this group which, tradition says, came up from underground and followed Elder Brother, finally planting their prayer stick on the site of Archie and thence populating the land. They are the people whose ceremonies show the greatest amount of Pueblo influence. The Pima, with whom they are closely associated, would seem to have provided the channel.

This group occupies a long north-and-south valley in the eastern part of the reservation, not far from the Pima. Their dialect is more like that of the Pima than are those of the other divisions and such of their customs as can be compared with the Pima show a

---

[1] Hoover, 1935.

close resemblance. Comparison however, is difficult since the Pima have undergone such rapid acculturation in recent years. Kino, visiting these people in 1689, before they had received the name of Papago, found them in close communication with the people of the Gila[1] from whom, apparently, they had learned to receive him "with arches and crosses." This communication continues, many of the Archie people having relatives in Pima country and going there regularly to help in the harvest.

The Archie group was the one furthest from Spanish influence and acculturation has been slower there than in the south. Few of the people speak Spanish and few over forty speak any English. They did not begin to keep cattle until long after the southerners. Basketry still flourishes among them and even the old plaiting technique is occasionally found. They retain many of the old ceremonies abandoned elsewhere. The important Puebloan ceremony of the Wiikita "belongs to them because it is they who have the songs and the scraping stick." They have also, in every village, the old ceremonial leader, in addition to the modern "governor" and have usually an ancient round ceremonial house. Aapap and apki sibs predominate and are the ones featured in ceremonies.

The Archie division includes four village units, that of Archie itself, Mesquite Root, Akchin, and Komelik. These have a closer approach to federation than have any of the other villages, acknowledging the Archie chief as their leader, much as the Pima acknowledged the chief at Sacaton. Their statement is that all of them "the true Papago" settling at Archie scattered seed which blew down the valley as far as Mesquite Root, thus establishing their claim to the land. Komelik, which is even farther away was a later offshoot.

### Archie Village Units

Archie (aatci, the Narrow Place)

> At the head of the Santa Rosa Valley. Oldest settlement of the Papagos proper, and head village of its dialect division. Locale of the quadrennial harvest fest which is performed only by the four village units of this division. The village was visited in 1698 by Kino who found seven hundred people there and called it "the great rancheria of Adid" which he re-named San Francisco.[2] Archie's present Well is Cirenaca (siri nakia, saddle hanging) or San Lorenzo, and a few people have Fields at Beebhak.

---

[1] Bolton, 1936, p. 396.
[2] Bolton, 1936, p. 398.

Bac (vahk, the hollow place)
   The large and important village of San Xavier del Bac, once
a stronghold of the Sóba Jípuris, now ranks as a daughter
village of Archie, having been settled by its people as the
Sóba Jípuris died out. Bac is the only one of the old irrigated
towns now on the Papago reservation. In Kino's time, while
the Sóba Jípuris still held it, the Father Visitor thought its
irrigation compared favorably with that of Mexico City itself.[1]
But during the eighteenth century, the Sóba Jípuris died out
of some contagious disease and the desert Papagos seeped in
to use the fields. The writer was able to find no traditions
among them which differ from those current on the reservation,
but Bac has long been under intensive White influence and all
native traits are fast disappearing.
   The village was given a missionary in Kino's time and continued to have one, at least intermittently, until Mexico's
separation from Spain. It was the only town above the Mexican
border to have this intensive Spanish influence and it may
have been for that reason that the Sóba Jípuris remained
there when they left the other Santa Cruz villages. The church
founded by Kino is still there and the people are definitely
Catholic.
   The present Bac people are largely from the Santa Rosa
neighborhood. Many of them retain their old fields and
vibrate back and forth.

Santa Rosa (kaitc mïhk, Burnt Seeds) is an offspring of Archie
   which has far outgrown the parent village and now has
   a chief and ceremonial leader of its own. It uses several
   wells. Covered Wells is the largest and oldest, a place where
   water could be feached through the gravel of a sunken stream;
   others are Comobabi (shared with Akchin), Cobabi (Badger
   Well), Noipakam, and o'ot wahwia (Sand Wells). Offspring
   of Santa Rosa is the village across the wash, really an extension
   of the parent village and called kokomat kïhk (Palo Verde
   Standing), also sikorhimatk (Where Water Whirls Round), on
   the road to Sells. Bolton thinks that a delegation which
   visited Kino at Mesquite Root may have come from this last
   place.[2]

Akchin (ak tcinyi, Mouth of the Gap)
   In the valley with Archie and Santa Rosa and so close that
   the three act practically as one, though having separate go-
   vernments. All three join, with Anegam in the harvest feast and
   the drinking ceremonies. Kino visited Akchin in 1698, was
   welcomed by four hundred people and baptised sixty one

[1] Bolton, 1936, p. 268.
[2] Bolton, 1936, p. 399 note.

children.[1] He was told the name was Actum Chico, Little Akchin or Mouth of the Little Gap, and he re-named it San Serafin, a title now forgotten.

Half of Akchin uses Comobabi as a Well and half goes to Sand Wells, both shared with Santa Rosa. Hoover[2] says that Cirenaca, Sand Wells and Worm Pond are all offshoots of Comobabi. A further recent offshoot is at Fresnal Ranch, south of Comobabi where some Indian families use the ranch water all the year and have formed a settlement called tciauri tak, (Devil Sitting).

*kuitatk* (Mesquite Root)

The long valley in which Santa Rosa, Akchin and Archie are situated, extends south to this abandoned village at the southern extremity of Quijotoa Mountain (kiho toak, Carrying Basket Mountain). Being in the foothills, it is properly a Well and not a Field village, but it was the chief one of its group, perhaps because it was a point for defense against the Apache. In Kino's time, before the Apache raids became so frequent, it was in a slightly different location, near a pond and was called Batqui (watcki, the Pool). Kino counted two hundred people there. The pool dried up and the village moved to Mesquite Root[3] where a stone compound was built for refuge in case of attack. The Apache destroyed the village in 1852 and it was never completely repopulated. Nevertheless it was, during the nineteenth century, one of the most famous of the Papago villages, its chiefs having close connections with the authorities, first of Mexico and then of the United States.

After the Americans took possession, a silver mine was started in the nearby mountains and a water system put in, the location of this novelty being called by the Papago, wainam kïhk, (Iron Stands Up, or Iron Pump). It was soon abandoned and some people from Mesquite Root moved in. But even this settlement did not last and the whole locality is now deserted. The sacred basket has been taken to Big Fields, which was always the Field village, but it is returned to the old home for ceremonies. Big Fields does not even use Kuitatk as a Well any longer but goes to Noric.

People from the old Kuitatk village scattered south and east and, since the danger from Apache attacks was over, formed smaller hamlets. The first was at Coyote Village (pan tak, Coyote Sitting). Some families had always had fields there and now they dug a well and planned to remain the year round. But the well was not enough for many; so a few moved to San Pedro (wiuhpuri, Tobacco (Mountain)) and dug

[1] Bolton, 1936, p. 399.    [2] Hoover, 1935, p. 261.
[3] Father Bonaventura.

another well. Others went to wahw kĭhk, (Standing Rock) abandoned that, and moved across the road to San Isidro (havanyi nakia, Hanging Crow). All these offshoots considered themselves under the governor of kuitatk, while that village still existed and ultimately under the governor of Archie. However, they had a subsidiary governor and a ceremonial leader of their own, located at San Pedro but they have grown so fast that they are considering a governor at San Isidro also.

Other offshoots of kuitatk are: Santa Cruz, Rincon Jeowic, Alamo, Chuapo, Artesia.

### Komalik (komarik, Flat Place)

This is the southernmost of the Archie village units, near the Mexican border and under the shadow of the Baboquivari Range, the dwelling of Elder Brother. It is the rancheria of Baggiburi, reported by Kino to have five hundred inhabitants.[1] It acknowledges relationship to Archie but is too far away to join in the quadrennial harvest feast. Its neighbors, some of them interspersed among the Komalik Wells belong to the southern or Mexican dialect division and are considered almost as foreigners by the dwellers of Komalik who still have the speech of the north and many of its rituals. Komalik has moved slightly from its former position at kom wo'o (Mulberry Pond) which was too open to the Apache. Its present Well is Bear Well.

Its oldest offspring is the neighboring village of Chulic, whose inhabitants are said to have been frightened out of Komalik by the Apache. Chulic also uses Bear Well.

Topawa is another offspring, originally called koks mĭhk (Burnt Dog). Its present name is also Papago, a White corruption of the Papago words ṭ pawi, it is a bean, used in answer to a question as to their crops. Topawa is headquarters for the Franciscan missionaries. It uses a well at Fresnal, although Fresnal is Koloti property, while its own well is called pi-t-oikam, (their special well).

### 2. KUHATK DIALECT GROUP

Kuhatk, meaning something dried and burnt, was spelled by the Spaniards *Quajote*. The name applies to a small strip of territory at the north of the reservation, between the Archie group and the Pima. It figures largely in the tale of conquest and it was here, in the early days of settlement that the best warriors were said to live. The Bitter Man at Kuhatk was leader in battle for his own group and for Archie.

---

[1] Bolton, 1936, p. 399.

Archie legend says that the kuhatk people moved to get better land and thus came closer to the Pima than to Archie. Certainly they were in close communication with the Pima when Kino found them. Their land was, for some time, included in the Pima reservation and it was not returned to the Papago until 1933. In the meantime, they had intermarried largely with the Pima and had also undergone much White influence. Though they may have once felt themselves a part of the Archie group, they now speak somewhat differently and are regarded as a separate unit. Still, it is obvious that Pima, kuhatk and Archie, form a group similar in dialect and customs and that later distinctions have been arbitrary.

Among the kuhatk, aapap and apki sibs predominate, as at Archie. There is the same conservatism in material culture as among the neighboring groups, but during the Pima connection, much kuhatk land was allotted, acculturation necessarily proceded faster, and many old ceremonies were lost. Anegam, the kuhatk village nearest to Archie, always remained part of the Papago reservation and being cut off from its congeners, joined with Archie in ceremonies. But it kept a certain connection with the people of hunuhra, the dialect division to the west, which sometimes shared the Anegam Well. The result is a feeling of foreignness between Anegam and Archie, resulting in mutual ridicule and frequent quarrels between their children in the government school.

### Kuhatk Village Units

Anegam (ánkam, Having Willows)

This is the first of the kuhatk towns, a close neighbor of Archie and Santa Rosa, joining with them in ceremonies. The village was in the same general locality in 1698 when Kino passed near it and sent its chief a wand of office.[1] Later it moved to ohn k wahwia, Salt Well, but this area, when the Papago reservation was formed, was left outside it so Anegam moved in close to Santa Rosa. The Wells it uses now are Montezuma Mine, Copperosity and kïh wahwia (Big Wells). While Salt Well was still in use it was often shared with the people of Kaka, in the huhuhra division and many Anegam people are said to be huhuhra:

Quajote (kuhatk, Dried and Burnt)

This village, with those to follow, was in the strip left outside the reservation and not purchased until 1932. Its communications, therefore, have been with the Pima and many of its former residents are now on Pima land. Quajote received

---

[1] Bolton, 1936, p. 398.

Kino in 1698 and sent runners into the desert to bring him water long before he arrived.[1] Kino gave to this village and to its near neighbor sihw oitak (Bitter Fields) the name of San Bonifacio and in the two together he found more than three hundred people. A cane of office was bestowed on the chief who accompanied Kino nearly to Archie. Communications at that time were close, both with the Gila Pimas who had sent word of the missionary's coming and with the Sóba Jípuris of the Santa Cruz, whom the Quajote people had just been aiding in a fight. Quajote Well is Bitter Well.

Other villages in the Quajote area are Chuchu (tcïhtcïh: caves) Kokomelik, perhaps visited by Kino and called el Cubit Tubic[2] and Wotum (Cockleburr) which was certainly visited. It was the nearest village to the Gila Pimas and apparently in close connection with them for it knew how to welcome the missionary with arches and crosses though no Spaniard had visited it before. Kino baptised five infants and a sick adult here and called the place San Angelo.

### 3. HUHUHRA DIALECT GROUP

Huhuhra means grandmother's children, *i. e.*, orphans and was bestowed on the people of Káka[3], one village of the group because they had no Well and wandered about sharing those of other village units. The huhuhra area is at the extreme west of Papago country running south into Mexico. Further west are mountains and uninhabitable desert which preclude expansion in that direction. The legend is that these people did not "come up from underground" but are the original inhabitants of the land, driven out by the Archie people. The site of magical events said to have taken place before the emergence (such as the death of the monster eagle) is placed in their territory. For this reason, huhuhra people are all rumored to have magic power and are looked on somewhat askance by the other groups. Some corroboration for the legend can be found in the fact that the huhuhra do not have the Puebloan ceremony of the Wiikita, though they have the Mexican ceremonies of the drinking and the cleansing feasts. Their dialect is more like that of Archie than like the Hispanized speech of the south but it contains many incomprehensible words, said to be ancient. The huhuhra are the most primitive of Papago groups and the most conservative, having kept the old brush house long after it was abandoned in other parts of the reservation.

---

[1] Bolton, 1936, p. 397.  [2] Bolton, 1936, p. 399.
[3] Father Bonaventura.

5

### Huhuhra Village Units

Kaka (the Cleared Land) is the village which earned for its whole division the name of Orphans. Its people wandered about in the dry season. The spring now called Isabel Mine, which they used to share with Anegam dried up but a new one, sihw wahwia, Bitter Spring, burst out on Quajote land; so they went there. Kaka itself, however, has long been in the same place, for Kino in 1698 sent a wand of office to its governor while he was visiting Archie. The Spaniards spelled the name *El Gaga*. Kaka has outlying fields called kuitcit watchki (where there is a big pond). When it dries, they go to capitchk (a narrow wash). They now draw water from the pump at the government school. Before that, when the plant was owned by the rancher McKinney, he supplied them with water; so they have not migrated for some time.

A present connection of Kaka is the Papago village near Gila Bend, called siri mihk, Burnt Saddle. This is said to be a recent camp of men who were employed in the building of the Southern Pacific Railroad and afterward settled in the vicinity. However, it was an old village of the Gila Pimas and may be another example of the seepage of the Desert People into deserted villages of their richer kinsmen. Kino, going east along the Gila in 1699, passed several villages of "Cocomaricopas" and then, at the bend the first village of Pimas called Oydabuise (oitak, field, buise ?) and containing one hundred and fifty men who welcomed him with their usual arches and crosses. We have no history of the place until recent years when its chief was appointed from Kaka.

### Perigua (Papago hikiwanyi)

The inhabitants of this unit are nicknamed kikimai, fat or rich. Old Papagos say the town was once as big as Santa Rosa, and Kino, in 1698, found two hundred eighty Indians there, raising maize and calabashes. Very recently some of the inhabitants have branched out and founded the settlements of Imikah and Toabit though the others offshoots may be older. Each of the last two has a chief appointed by the Whites and considering himself subsidiary to the chief at Perigua. Red Well was once the only well and the people kept a sacred basket there as well as at Perigua. Now they use Poso Redondo which was dug by the Spaniards and some even move down into Cubo territory.

The valley in which Perigua is situated continues south to Cubo and then on across the Mexican border, almost to Caborca, the home of the primitive western Pimans mentioned above. This valley, in Kino's time, was flourishing, for he mentions 1000 inhabitants.[1] The principal towns were El Comac (Ko-

---

[1] Bolton, 1936, p. 435.

maki, (gray mountain) famous in Papago song, and Actum Grande, the Mouth of the Big Wash. With four hundred inhabitants Actum Grande had an offshoot — Gubo, the modern Cubo (kï wo'o, Big Pond), but in time the big pond disappeared, the whole valley became depopulated,[1] the Perigua people were invited down to repopulate Cubo, which therefore has an intimate connection with the older village. Its wells were below the border, Foam Well, Ground Owls and Sweet water. The small settlements around Camote, which was really only a field for gathering roots, use Molinitas, which is Tecalote's well. The northern ones used Red Well, until they themselves dug at Walls Well.

### 4. KOKOLOLOTI DIALECT GROUP

This division represents the extension, into American Papagueria, of the Hispanized area to the south. The Jesuit missions to the Pimans were, with the exception of San Xavier, all in what is now Mexico, on the Altar and San Ignacio rivers. But they had frequent communication with the heathen Pimas who came to stay for long periods working for their food and receiving religious instruction. There is record of Pimas from the Gila making this sort of visit but it must have been much more common among the southern Papagos, only a few days journey away, as are the villages on both sides of the present border.

Tecalote was one of those villages, with territory on both sides of the border. Its old Papago name tcukuht kuh, (owl cry) became translated into Mexican Tecalote (Nahua tecalotl, owl) and its people, by a doubly reduplicated plural are called kokololoti.[2] All its connections are with the river valleys of the present Mexico. Its dialect shows the influence of Spanish since it is not only interlarded with Spanish words but has lost the constant aspiration of the northern speech and substituted a lengthened vowel more in consonance with the Romance languages. The dialect is much ridiculed by the Archie people who profess not to understand it.

Most Tecalote people still speak Spanish. From the well stocked missions to the south, they learned the raising of cattle and began to own them and to ride horses long before either was custom reached the north. They were frequently called on for help by the Spanish and Mexican soldiers and many of them served as scouts and acquired guns before the northerners.

---

[1] Father Bonaventura.

[2] Papago words are all accented on the first syllable and since the language could not accept a word accented in the middle, it split it into two, *teca loti* and reduplicated both. The *te* got lost in the process.

Their native government, as far as it persists is modelled on the Spanish colonial regime with a secular governor and a whipping post to punish transgressors. They all profess Christianity, the majority Catholic but a fair number of Presbyterians. None of the old ceremonies are now held but a few have been amalgamated with Catholic ceremonies to form a new ritual.

The Kokololoti and the Archie division are the two most completely at odds in traditions and customs and political splits are most likely to occur along their geographic lines. Among Tecalote people the maam and waaliw sibs predominate, but there are also many of that nondescript sib, the ókari who do not know their moiety and are accused of being no sib at all but a catchall for scattered people whose sib was lost.

### Kokololoti Village Units

Kupk (Closed, referring to a dam)

This and the other villages of the dialect division occupy the broad Quijotoa Valley, known in Spanish accounts as the Llano, or plain. The Papago name for the area is komaki wihtco, (Under the Gray Mountain) which the Spaniards wrote El Comac. Kupk, the parent town, has shrunk and the prominent place is now taken by Pisinimo, whose name is said to come from the fact that a Bison head was once brought there. This would have meant importation from a great distance and the only possible agents are the Apache but the legend is vague.

Pisinimo has as daughters hahri mihïtak (Burnt Squash) and Cheeweeton (Long Pond), and Mulberry Pond or Santa Cruz. The Well for all four is Poso Blanco, while Kupk still uses San Antone.

Another recent offshoot of Kupk is Kavolik or Cowlic. This was originally not a field but a mesquite grove. Some families moved there from kupk and others from its relative, Tecalote. Another group of immigrants came direct from Mexico bringing with them Mexican ideas of government and housing. They wanted a plaza, with houses in regular rows and the Mexicanized Catholic ceremonies so familiar in Sonora. They live together in a group and engineer the Easter ceremony which is unique among the Papagos but otherwise have not converted the village to their views. Kavorik has a daughter, Burro Pond, and a smaller one upat kïhk, Acacia Stands, which uses a Well in the mountains south of Sells.

Tecalote

This village, near the border, is in the same broad north-and-south plain with Pisinimo. The plain extends south into Mexico where many of the wells are. In Spanish accounts it is called the Llano, Plain. In Kino's day all its inhabitants were one community, their main village El Comac, now in Kupk territory. Tecalote and Pisinimo have been separate villages for two centuries. Tecalote was once as large as Pisinimo at present, with farms stretching north as far as Sells and south into the present Mexico. Being nearest to the Altar settlements, it was the first of the Papago villages to have cattle in quantity. Perhaps for this reason it was always a point of attack for the Apache and had a fortress for keeping the stock safe during their raids. During the Mexican war, 1853, its chief took twenty men from Mesquite Root and some from Tecalote and went to Mount Baboquiviri to draw off the Mexican attack. He was defeated and some of his men were taken prisoners.

Many of these people never came back but settled with their families near Baboquiviri and at Kavorik and Wamori, with the result that hamlets of Tecalote dialect are interspersed with the fringes of Archie and Kupk. Tecalote remained a prosperous village till some time after the Mexican war for Emory reports it as thriving and already possessing cattle while the northern part of the reservation was in a much more primitive state. But soon after this the village broke up, perhaps as a aftermath of the war and those families which did not settle elsewhere wandered in Mexico. Here they learned to speak Spanish, took over many Spanish customs and must have undergone considerable racial intermixture. Only one family returned, to find the old field deserted and to establish itself as in a new settlement, with a new pond, and fields a short distance away at a spot called Onion Fields.

Tecalote's well was Cobabi (Badger Well) in Sonora and later Cabota in Sonora where a fortress was built.

The daughter villages are now larger than the almost deserted parental settlement. The most important are Sells, where the government agency now is, Topawa, the Catholic headquarters, San Miguel, Cowlic and Wamori. Since the agency has become the headquarters of more paid work than was ever before available on the reservation, people from all divisions have tended to congregate there. The result has been a breaking down of division boundary lines, and even a slight modification of dialects which is bound to continue.

# VILLAGE GOVERNMENT

## THE ANCIENT FORM

The Papago had no central government. Each village unit was autonomous and when two units occasionally joined, for war or games, the union was temporary. There are traditions of meetings, held in time of crisis by the leaders of several different units, generally involving the divisions of Archie and Kuhatk. At such times, the Archie leader was deferred to, since the Archie people were "the oldest settlers" and the "first up from underground". The deference seems to have been a matter of courtesy, not organization and did not apply to Tecalote which had its affiliations in Mexico. We may conjecture from this that there were perhaps loose federations of village units but such formal organization as there was, concerned the village only. The main outlines of this organization follow roughly those of the Pueblos and may be found, in simpler form, among the Shoshoneans, both of California and the Basin.[1]

### CEREMONIAL HOUSE

Every main village, as a mark of its official status, had a ceremonial house, both at the Fields and at the Wells. The one at the Fields was the largest, since it was in summer or just after harvest that most important ceremonies took place. This house was known as the Big House, or the Rain House, since it was here that the rain-making liquor was brewed. At present it is called the Round House, because it is built on the old round plan, while dwelling houses are square.

The house was large enough to accomodate all the men in the village: perhaps twenty-five feet in diameter. At the building of a new one, a speech was made by a hereditary orator, telling of the magic building of the first house, with the help of earthworms to furnish the timbers; the gopher to heap earth on the roof; the birds to throw down feathers for a floor covering. Then songs calling for rain were sung.

New villages, leaving the parent village, erected a house in this way, bringing the orator from home for the occasion. In the winter camps, the meeting place was often a brush enclosure, since no

---

[1] Strong, 1927.

weather protection was needed at that season. Even at cactus camp, where only a few families could gather, some sort of meeting place was contrived though without ceremony.

No ceremonial property was kept in the house. The regular storage place for Papago sacred objects, whether individual or communal property, is some hiding place in the hills. Sacred things are considered too powerful to keep near human dwellings, besides which constant migration and danger from enemies made them safer elsewhere. The Keeper of the Meeting had his own hiding place for all village property which was brought to the Big House, sometimes with special rites, on the day of a ceremony.

### SACRED OBJECTS

Each of the main villages had its arcana, brought up according to legend from underground or acquired from the supernaturals. These were kept, not in a bundle, but in a basket, made in the old plaited style; a system reminiscent of the southern California Shoshoneans and particularly of the Luiseño who also use a basket, or at least a matting bundle.[1]

The contents of the sacred basket were usually kept secret but since that at Pisinimo has been stolen, I have been given an account of it. The chief items may well have been relics of the Hohokam, although informants did not know how they were obtained. One was a small frog, carved of green stone and another a rude effigy in sandstone, said to represent Elder Brother, the Papago supernatural. The frog and the human effigy were both familiar in Hokoham handicraft. There was also one of the slate palettes previously mentioned and several long pendants of slate or lava. A number of well made arrow points may also have belonged to the former culture since otherwise it is hard to see why they should be included. The last item was three dried animal hearts, probably those of deer, with six eagle tail feathers stuck in each. All these were packed in the basket with eagle down and placed in a mesquite tree at a distance from the village. A delegation went to get the basket on all important occasions and then took it back again, after speaking to it and perhaps renewing the eagle feathers.

At Quitovaca, the basket contains a stone, said to be the diminished remnant of the heart of a monster, killed there by Elder Brother to save the people. It is packed with eagle down and with a stone effigy which was found (in old ruins ?) and believed to have magic power. It is brought from the mountains on ceremonial occasions,

---

[1] Strong, p. 292.

carried under escort to a special shelter and there guarded for twenty-four hours. It is opened only in the Big House by the older men, who clean it and renew the eagle feathers. If, while it is in the mountains, any disaster overtakes the village, they consider that the basket has been disturbed and hasten to visit it.

Arcana of the other villages are of the same general sort. Reports mention:

> a bag of deerskin, containing carved stone turtle (Hohokam relic?) wrapped in hand woven cotton cloth. a stick two feet long carved and painted with representations of melons, squash, corn and clouds. Four sticks ten inches long, painted blue with white spots and with a tuft of beargrass at the tip to represent corn leaves. Turkey feather prayer sticks. Various other objects such as arrow heads, curiously shaped stones, eagle tail feathers.

Even the daughter villages often acquired a fetish, in time, if they found a relic of the Ancient People under propitious circumstances or "saw a stone which some shaman thought would bring rain." The fetish must then be enclosed in a plaited basket of the proper ceremonial sort and placed in charge of a man who knew the hampatak, or Wise Speeches.

### CEREMONIAL ORATIONS

The Wise Speeches, treated at length under the subject of ceremonies, were ancient rituals describing interviews with the rain god and the subsequent blessing of rain. The speaches were handed down from one generation to another in the loosely hereditary manner already described, that is, taught to the son or other relative who seemed most promising. They were the safeguard for handling sacred objects and no fetish could be unwrapped or moved without their recitation. A man who knew the speeches told the writer how he visited another village and was interested to see their fetish. He was told that the basket could not be opened without the speech; so he began to recite the one he knew. He was shown the fetish and, in four hours, there was a heavy rain.

### CEREMONIAL LEADER

The man who knew Wise Speeches was the village ceremonial leader. He was called by a number of names: the Wise Speaker, the One Above, the One Ahead, the One Made Big, the Fire Maker, the Keeper of the Plaited Basket, the Keeper of the Smoke or of the Meeting. The last term will be used here as suggesting more of his official functions. As to the origin of his office, informants say:

"The Keeper and the Sacred House go together. They were decreed in the beginning by Elder Brother" (2). Some thought that in very ancient times this Keeper was the only official. "He went to Elder Brother and got his directions. Then he came back and showed the people what to do" (20). "He went before them like a light. He was their teacher and their father" (40). "He got the Wise Speeches from Elder Brother himself" (4). He was, in fact, a priestly ruler, much like the cacique in the Rio Grande pueblos.

His principal duty was the handling of the fetish which gave the village rain and therefore life. This meant the care of the sacred house where the fetish was lodged on important occasions and, finally, the presiding over all meetings held there. In the earliest times, he lived in the ceremonial house and received the men there for meetings while his family slept. At present, he lives beside it and his wife keeps it clean.

The house was used for meetings both ceremonial and secular and, on such occasions, it was the Keeper's duty to make the fire (hence one of his titles) and then mount to the roof of his shade and summon the men. Sometimes he had younger men to perform both of these functions for him. He called meetings to decide on the dates of ceremonies and whenever the other officials, the war, hunt and game leaders, had communications to make. When the men assembled, he sat at the west of the house, facing the door and opened the meeting with a moral talk bidding them pay attention to what was to be said and use their best judgment.

He acted as priest in all the important local ceremonies held for rain, for growth and for cleansing of crops and must know the appropriate Wise Speeches for each occasion. One informant gave him perquisites which remind one most strongly of the Pueblo cacique. "He must not be bothered with quarrelling. The people used to till his land for him because he worked so hard in the ceremonies." Certainly his land is not tilled for him now, and I have known an old Keeper in actual want because even his young relatives neglected him.

Beside his priestly functions, the Keeper acted as a patriarchal advisor to the village. The importance we give to this duty must depend on whether we consider the secular governor a modern official or an old one. Certainly the reliance on some aged leader as a patriarch and almost a dictator to the village is a pronounced Papago custom. At present that leader is often the secular governor and we need to consider whether he has always had such functions or has taken them over from the priestly leader. In view of the frequent statements that the Keeper was once the only village head,

I am inclined to consider the governor an innovation, gradually usurping the functions of the ancient informal leader and adding to them.

Legends represent the people as applying in all crises to "him who goes before us" and taking his advice as to what to do. At present this ancient leader may still be the chief power in a village, sometimes using the secular governor as a "front" but in one case boldly issuing orders in his own name. However, his power is rapidly declining. The White officials take no cognizance of him and, unless he is a man of powerful personality, he is reduced to a routine ceremonialist who appears only once or twice a year. The list of villages shows an X against those which have a fetish and a Keeper of the Meeting. All the northern villages have both while in some of the southern ones, which have come under intensive Christianizing influence, both have entirely disappeared.

The Keeper generally chose his own successor in office from among the male members of his family best suited to the duties. Accounts of the exact arrangements for succession varied in different localities, some informants stating:

"The Keeper chose his own successor. Nobody could criticise," and also, "When a Keeper died, the Elders would go to his brother or someone and say: 'You knew his ways best. You had better lead us'." The latter would seem to be an occurrence of recent times, when anyone with ceremonial knowledge is hard to find.

I am inclined to give most weight to those accounts which state that the successor, having been chosen by the Keeper, must be approved by the council of elders since this is in accord with general practice in the area. If, according to these accounts, the elders disapproved, they would make their own selection and the Keeper would be obliged to instruct the new candidate.

Since the learning of the rituals was a very long task, the successor was chosen long before the Keeper was ready to quit his office and acted for years as a ceremonial assistant. Such a deputy was never a very young man since the young were not considered competent for ceremonial functions. He might be the Keeper's brother or a classificatory sibling somewhat younger than himself. At Santa Rosa the Keeper, who is somewhere near ninety, has an assistant of seventy who stands with him during rituals and sometimes makes the speech himself; this man is a very distant relative.

But the Keeper had also a young man as messenger, known as his Leg. This man often made the fire for him, called out the announcements if there was no crier and took messages to people at a distance. He was in line for the office and was expected to learn the ritual so that when he himself was middle aged he would be ready for the succession. The man who is Leg at Santa Rosa is father's brother's son's daughter's son to the present Keeper. But in this case the Keeper has other assistants, especially assigned to him by the council because of his great age. They are called his Eyes, his Ears and his Voice, and seem to have been appointed as a special favor because the aged official had trouble in seeing, hearing and in speaking loud.

New villages and villages where the Keeper died suddenly, sometimes appointed a Keeper with few formalities. Standing Rock, founded from Mesquite Root, had no fetish and returned to the home town for ceremonies, but they built a house for meetings and selected one of the older men whom they called Keeper. He performed the routine duties and, when the village wanted a rain ceremony of its own, borrowed the fetish from Mesquite Root and invited the speaker from there. The Keeper at Coyote Village died without a successor and the people insisted that his brother take the office, even without knowing the speeches. They invited any speakers they could find. At present, when Wise speakers are growing scarce, a man who knows any portion of the speeches, even if he has no official position, will be invited to recite them.

### THE CRIER

Papago organization being always of a flexible and informal sort, the office of crier was not a fixed one. "The Keeper, if he had a strong voice, would make his announcements himself" (22), while the Hunt and Game leaders would make theirs. But some villages had the system found in the Pueblos of a regular official to make the announcements and to pass his office on by loose heredity. We may conjecture that this was the official pattern and that it was the smaller and poorer villages who cut down the number of officials.

In most large Field villages, the people were awakened every morning and the men called to meeting every evening. The calls seem to have been standardized for each village or perhaps for each individual crier, since any informant was immediately able to recite the official call, but they were all different.

Dawn Call (Komarik) 19
It is daylight. All around is visible the land.
Come forth and see what is around us.

Dawn Call (Kaworik) 14
Hurry! Awake! That you may do something good.
That for the villagers it may be good!

If any communal activity had been agreed upon at the meeting, the announcement of this followed the call. At sunset the men were summoned to the Big House.

### Call to Meeting  (Vamori) 25

Now thus let us arrange to do: let us hold our meeting! Now here, under the west, let them sit down, the elders! Thus says our leader, that we shall assemble; that we shall sit down. The under-the-greasewood-growing tobacco we call for and we request the under-the-grease-wood-growing tobacco. All our friends, let them assemble and let them speak.

### Evening Call  (Kaworik) 14

Hither come at evening. Then we will surround the fire we have made and we will make ready that which we shall do for our future. And do you bring your tobacco.

### Evening Call  (Komarik) 19

Hither come. Hither bring your cigarette. We will smoke and speak of something.

If an emergency arose during the day, the men might be called from the fields.

### Danger Call  (Komarik) 9

Let us assemble!
A man has come running and tells of danger.
Assemble and listen!

Special calls were also used before all the ceremonies. These were more elaborate.

### Call to Sing while Liquor ferments
### (Archie ) 27

Our fire has burned and the sun has gone down. Our fire has burned and the sun has gone down. You have eaten your meal. Now come together, following our old custom. It will not be long. Two nights we will sing and then go back to work. Come do your part, so that the shaman can divine what will happen' This is our old custom. It is not new. It has continued for long.

#### WAR LE ADER

The war leader was, in ancient times, like the Keeper, a ceremonial official whose first duty was to know the war ritual and to recite it on the proper occasions. He received his office from his predecessor, just as the Keeper did his, and held it to old age. It was he who directed a war party and planned its strategy even if he was too old to do much fighting himself.

But there was often a younger man to head the actual fighting. It was difficult to get data on this field leader since the very oldest people were children at the time of the last fighting. But as in other cases, it would appear that the practice differed in different villages. In San Xavier and Komarik he was a different man each time. In Komarik he was chosen by the elders as the most capable young warrior, in San Xavier, he volunteered and got up a war party in the Plains fashion to take vengeance on the Apache for slain relatives. Archie had a more or less permanent field leader chosen for prowess and known as the Bitter Man, "because he would not give in to the Apache." Kuhatk had also such a leader and it was understood that when Kuhatk and Archie went on the warpath together, Kuhatk should lead "because it had been given them by Elder Brother to be the best fighters."

### HUNT LEADER

The Papagos hunted deer, hare and rabbit, small rodents and birds. Most of this work was done by individuals or small unofficial groups. But deer was hunted officially for the cleansing ceremony in the autumn and there were communal rabbit drives when visitors were to be feasted, especially at the time of the drinking ceremony before the rains. For communal hunts of both kinds, there was a leader who set the day, chose the locality, called the people together at dawn, appointed the beaters and made the required speech. His title was tópetam, rabbiter. He passed his office down, as did the others, by instructing a younger man, usually a kinsman, and finally asking the council to ratify his appointment as the new leader.

### GAME LEADER

The title of this official was tópetam tcíticvi, rabbiter for games. Probably the hunt leader originally had the function, since the communal drive and the athletic contest require similar organization. But in many villages the office of game leader was so important that it was held by a special man. His duty was to make the arrangements for inter-village games, see that the runners were properly trained, take charge of the party on the march to the challenged village, lead the cheering, argue for his side in the matter of fouls, appoint the referees, see that the relay runners got off in the proper order. His ceremonial duty was the recitation of a speech before the contest began.

Like the war leader, this ceremonial official might have a younger assistant to lead the cheering and argue the possible fouls. The women contestants had a woman for this function "since it would not be right for a woman to argue with a man."

### SONG LEADER

A man with a loud voice and a memory for songs was chosen to lead the communal singing, particularly at the liquor fermentation. He usually asked certain good singers to stand next to him and head the line.

### THE COUNCIL

In every village, or even where two or three families were camping together, a nightly men's meeting was held. This was the real governing power of the community. It decided on communal activities: agricultural work, hunts, war, the dates of ceremonies, games with other villages. It approved the installation of a chief or of new residents in the village. "And if there was nothing to discuss, they would come together and talk." (21). Men reported whether they had seen tracks of enemies or of deer. Visitors from other villages were welcomed and questioned.

Attendance was a duty for every man and in the myths a man who absented himself was dealt with by a deputation. There was no point at which a boy became officially eligible but when he seemed old enough to understand and wanted to go, some older relative would take him. Women were not admitted but when something interesting was discussed, they would stand outside and listen. "But we didn't do it much, because our husbands came home and told us." According to two informants, the shaman was excluded as a possible sorcerer (1).

There was a distinction between the men who formed the actual deliberative body and the listeners. The word s'tcu-amitcu't means wise, or able. It was not an official title but was applied to men who had shown themselves fit to take part in the council. In some villages these were selected by the Keeper of the Meeting (15, 11), who would test a promising mature man by having him make ex tempore, one of the usual speeches of admonition and seeing if he remembered all the points (21). "He must have good judgment and a quick understanding of what is said. The old men were always looking out for people like that." In some villages no man was expected to speak unless he were a "ripe man", that is, had been through the purification incident on salt gathering or enemy killing (9). In others enemy killing was the qualification (25). Or the wise man might simply attain his position by the exhibition of good judgment. "If he showed sense, they would listen to him" (8). This is the standard exploit in tales of the orphan boy, who makes a good suggestion in meeting before he is considered old enough to speak. The important factors would seem to have been a man's practical sense and knowledge of traditions.

In the summer village the meeting was held in the Big House: in camp it was in a brush enclosure, or even a cleared space on the ground. The Keeper of the Meeting or the man who was acting as such built a fire in the center of the place to be used, called the people or had them called and sat down facing the east. (In a house or enclosure this would mean opposite the door.)

The wise men, as they arrived, took their places around the fire and the listeners behind them. The crier sat at the right of the Keeper. In villages where there was a speaker to put the leader's proposals the speaker sat at the right and the crier at the left. Some informants thought that each wise man had his allotted place which he occupied during life and which was assigned to a new wise man on his death (14). The same informant thought that the shamans, far from being excluded, had special places, at the north, south, east, and west of the circle, as they do at the drinking ceremony. At present certain prominent men are allowed by custom always to have seats near the Keeper, but there is no other formality.

Some informants thought that the Leg always sat behind the Keeper ready to be sent on errands. Another said that when the meeting was held in a roofless enclosure, the fire was put outside it so as to deceive the Apache. One man then had the duty of running to the fire to bring an ember for lighting the cigarettes. He sat behind the Keeper and was called the peg, that is, the peg with which a hide is fastened down for drying (25).

The proper demeanor in this and all other assemblies was to sit on the heels with arms folded and head bent. The hair should be tied with a thong, so that there would be no disturbing motion of raising the hand to keep it from blowing. It was highly blame-worthy to show signs of drowsiness and the offender would have a lighted cigarette thrust between his toes.

The men arrived in silence and when all were seated, the cere-monial cigarette was passed. This was a six inch tube of cane or cornhusk filled, in the earliest days, with wild tobacco. The Keeper lit this or had it lit by an assistant and puffed ceremonially with an invocation, "Now do I breathe out. It will reach you. You will send a benefit" (14). Or, "May he bless me, give me life and lead me along a good road." The power originally referred to was thought to be the sun, although the word tcioc, God, is sometimes used. An upward breathing without words had the same meaning (1). If there was enough tobacco, three puffs might follow the invocation, making up the ceremonial four. The Keeper then passed the cigarette to the man at his right, calling him by the actual kinship term. The man gave the reciprocal term and puffed in the same ceremonial fashion. This passing of the cigarette with the kinship term is a preliminary to all important procedure.

The cigarette passed all the way around the circle, only one man smoking at a time. It was not passed to the young men. When it reached the Keeper again, he put it out by thrusting it, lighted end downward, into the ground beside him, to be lit again at the next interval between speeches. Usually one six-inch tube lasted the whole evening. In later days, when tobacco was more plentiful, any man who could brought his own. They lit cigarettes at a signal from the Keeper, "Now light the jointed reed!" puffed with invocation and passed to a neighbor with the kinship term just as had been done when there was one cigarette for all. Thus several men might be smoking at one time, but they all stopped at the word from the Keeper, "Place the jointed reed in the ground."

After the smoking the Keeper or sometimes a delegated speaker, addressed the assemblage: "Hail, my relatives!" and made the regular opening speech. Though this was in the speaker's own words, its content was standardized. It was, in fact, the Papago moral code with whose points each wise man was supposed to be familiar. These points were: Be industrious. Be hunger enduring, cold enduring, thirst enduring. Practise running that your young men be swift in time of war and that your women be able to escape. Let every man keep his weapons ready. Have an extra bowstring. Have plenty of arrows. See that your women grind plenty of cornmeal so that you will be strong for fighting. See that your women segregate themselves at the proper time so that you will not lose your strength.

There was a definite technique for the admonition speech which was different from that for the ritual orations. These latter were delivered in a sonorous voice with the accent on the last word of the sentence. The admonition speech had the normal accent but the voice was expressionless and exceedingly low. The same effect was used in admonitions to young people given at home. The monotonous murmur with its constant repetitions was, to the writer, almost hypnotic.

Fragmentary versions of such speeches follow:
"Well then! Will you not be ready? Will you not take care! Already I have said thus to you: that you shall make arrows,

that you shall make bows, that you shall be watchful. When
the enemy will arrive, you do not know. It may be at night
that he will come — at night, or in the morning, or when the sun
stands almost anywhere. Beside you do you place your bow
that you may snatch it up and fight. Early in the morning do
you eat, that you may be able to fight.     Always I say this.
Every evening I say it to you at the meeting, that you shall
keep near you your bow, your hunting arrows, your war
arrows, your quiver." "Your women, very early let them
cook. Let them feed the youths that they may fight the enemy,
wherever the sun stands. Let them fetch water, let them search
for firewood, that they may cook something. Early in the
morning let them practise running, that when the enemy arrives
they may run far down yonder and save themselves."
    "This I recite and this I say to you. Do you listen and let it
enter your ears and enter your head. (26)

### Hunting

"Early in the morning you will rise, you will run far yonder to
the foot of the mountain range. You will chase something, you
will kill it, you will bring it home and therewith feed yourself.
White-tailed deer you will follow, black-tailed deer you will
follow and therewith feed yourself and live. This is our food,
thus said he, whoever he is, who made us. The deer did he
make that you should kill it and eat. Look! thus they shall
live, our young men. The deer shall they follow, they shall
hunt and shall kill. Thus they will be great runners. Thus they
shall do, the people. From long ago has this been done and
therewith it has been well. (21)

### Planting

"Something again I say to all you villagers, that therewith you
may be alert. You will cause the rain to fall and you will plant
something." (21)

At the close of the speech, each man in turn, beginning at the
right of the speaker, called him loudly by the kinship term, while
the speaker responded with the reciprocal. This was the ritual
performance of *imik iimi'k himatcu't*, passing the kinship term,
which constituted applause on any occasion. One village was said to
have had an official, the passer-of-kinship-terms, who always
started this applause and saw that it was properly carried around
the circle (9). An unrelated man would say "friend", but such a
person was rare unless he was a visitor from another village.
    If there was tobacco enough, there might be another ritual
smoking and perhaps a period of silent thought. Then any proposal

which was to come before the meeting would be brought up. This might be a suggestion for communal ditch digging, a request by a deer hunter for volunteers for a deer hunt, etc. The man who wished this proposal made might speak of it himself, or he might communicate it to the Keeper who would either make a speech or have it made by his speaker.

Such a speech was followed by the ritual applause and, if there was tobacco enough, by ritual smoking. Generally each man in the circle of wise men commented upon it, taking turns from right to left. A man who agreed completely made another speech in the same vein so that before the process was complete, a project had been many times confirmed and re-stated. One who disagreed took time for thought and then made his strictures, after which the others commented in regular turn, always beginning at the right of the speaker. If sentiment was divided, the procedure was to discuss until opinion was unanimous. The myths often contain the statement, "They held a meeting but nothing was decided. So they agreed to meet again the next night," and so on for four nights.

According to two informants, there were specially selected wise men who were asked for their opinion after each speech had been made (15, 25). According to another, after every speech the men expressed themselves all around the circle: "It pleases me." "It does not please me." This vote was taken four times in case someone might reconsider (25).

The young men did not vote or smoke. Those who were fast runners might be called on to inform neighbor villages when there was a decision about war or ceremony. If volunteers were wanted for a war party or for communal labor, they might step forward. Otherwise they merely listened.

When the meeting was over, the Keeper directed: "We will smoke once more and then go to sleep." If it were early in the night, the men went home. If it were late, they slept in the Big House. No informants had heard of this being a nightly procedure.

Lengthy and repetitive speeches were an essential part of Papago procedure. The first Spaniards noted the trait when they heard Papago converts preaching to their countrymen:

... "it seems the Lord must have given him words to enable h m to speak so long, for he harangued them for a space of two hours, a thing difficult even for a great preacher. Afterward another took up the thread.... In this manner day dawned upon them and the following night it was the same."[1]

---

[1] Bolton, 1919, 2, 211.

Fray Manuel was seeing the usual nightly gathering turned to the purposes of Christianity.

The repetition which causes the length of these speeches is not for the mere purpose of explanation. The writer once questioned a wise man as to the proceedings of a meeting which had lasted past midnight. He was able to state them very succinctly. "We said that at the festival a horse had disappeared, but it had been found at the house of a man in the next village who didn't know the owner. Then someone said that some spurs had been found, too, but they had been claimed."

"And was that all ?"

"Yes. But everyone said what he thought about it."

The purpose of such repetition would seem to be an emotional one: the attaining of complete unity in the group. After an idea has been re-stated so many times and each man has had his share in sponsoring it, every man's conviction has been solidified and there is little danger of an unsympathetic minority. The long sessions before an agreement is reached have the same purpose. There must be no dissenting minority. Action will be ineffective unless the whole group acts with complete conviction.

This is the ideal of every village group and its method of attaining a strong government without any individual authority. Each man has been conditioned to agreement by the nightly recitations of the moral code which he hears from the age of puberty until death. The result is a "grounding in the faith" which few systems of education could better.

The likeness of the Papago plan of organization to that of the Western Pueblos, is very obvious, though these latter have elaborated a ceremonial organization impossible for the scattered Desert People. We may be seeing here a relic of the Puebloan occupation though we have still no means of telling how far its governmental pattern differed from that of the Papagos' linguistic relatives to the south. Certainly, the title of Bitter or Fierce Man for the war leader has an echo in Mexico.[1] The institution of the secular governor, who supplements the semi-priestly leaders, gives the Papago system an even further resemblance to the present outline of Pueblo organization.

POST-SPANISH GOVERNMENT

The Governor

The picture of council and ritualistic leaders without executive power, does not represent modern Papago government. That

---

[1] Cf. Nahuatl "Our wrathy chieftain" Bandelier, AA October, 1892, p. 319.

6*

government centers around an official whose mention has been delayed till the last because he differs, both in function and attitude from the old priestly leaders, who are completely out of touch with the new conditions. This is the secular leader, called by the Whites the chief, and by the Indians kovenal (governor). His function according to the governor of Archie, is to "keep up the morals of the village, deal with offenders and talk with the Whites." He is definitely an executive and, until the establishment of judges under the Indian service, he had police power. He is at present the most important person in the village, completely overshadowing the ceremonial officers and sometimes achieving dictatorship. Is his office also aboriginal or can it be traced, like those of the Pueblo governors, to a Spanish origin?

The writer has discussed this question with many of the old men, particularly the governors and has been given the statement: "The Mexicans (or Spaniards? Papago makes no distinction.) told us to choose a man to take care of the people. At first we chose the Keeper of the Meeting but it was too much work, so we took another man."

Kino, in his various excursions, was accompanied by a representative of the Spanish crown who distributed to the natives canes of office.[1] That was undoubtedly the origin of the governor's office in the form it has today, for one of the governor's titles is u.sakam (staff bearer) and the staff enters prominently into his installation ceremony. The question is whether Kino delivered his staves to men who already had an office of a similar sort. Certainly he picked leaders of some kind to receive the honor and he generally speaks of them as chiefs.[2] Many seem to be chiefs over several villages, which would confirm the idea that there were, at that time as now, daughter villages subject to the parent.[3] But readers of Spanish accounts know that they must make allowance for the powers attributed to the Indian chiefs by the writers. Some of the Sóba Jípuri chiefs and captains mentioned by Kino (who uses the title indiscriminately) are definitely leaders in war[4] which was never the function of the governor. One conjectures that, with these people who were the bulwark against the Apache, the office of war leader may have grown important with use, as it did with Montezuma. Chief Soba, however, was leading his forty people on a food-gathering expedition,[5] a function quite possible for the

---

[1] Bolton, 1936, pp. 395, 398.
[2] Bolton, 1936, pp. 365, 398.
[3] Bolton, 1936, pp. 365, 367; Mange pp. 248, 249, 254.
[4] Bolton, 1936, p. 361.          [5] Mange, p. 220.

Keeper of the Meeting. To combat Kino's picture of the all powerful chiefs, we have the statement by Velarde whose view was that of a resident rather than that of a traveller:

"They have no government, laws or traditions and, in each village, no authority but the one who talks the most and incites them to fight against the enemy nations or who gives the signal for the time to hunt. There are prominent men who gain a following and whom the Spaniards call chiefs but they have no formal authority."[1]

Other Uto Aztecans, the Mission Indians, the Paiute, and the Hopi were without a secular leader[2] and it seems possible that the Papago office has developed as the need for it grew.

By a decree of Philip III, in 1618, every reduced Indian pueblo was to have an *alcalde* (mayor) and two *regidores* (judges). If it had more than eighty people, the number of officers was doubled.[3] The mayor was to enforce Spanish customs. He could punish the people for drunkenness or for failure to attend mass by one day in prison or by six to eight stripes — a completely un-Indian punishment. But he was to leave to the *"cacique"*, the ancient Indian leader anything outside the *"mita"* or enforced service of the Indians.

As time went on, other Indian officers were provided for and a "reduced" pueblo was set up on the model of a Spanish village. A decree of the Royal Court of Guadalajara, in 1746, provided for governor, *alcalde, topiles* (policemen), war captain and *fiscal*, the church officer who took charge of tithes and marriages.[4] These are the officers of the modern Mexican vilage, so well established in their function that it is impossible to look behind them to any aboriginal organization. The royal representatives seem to have attempted something of this sort with the Pimans, for Kino mentions an assemblage at one of his Mexican missions of "the principal *caciques* and headmen of all this Pimeria and, from the most remote parts of it, "ten captains, twenty governors and twenty-six other justices, *alcaldes, topiles* (policemen), *fiscales mayores* (head church officers) *alguaciles* (sheriffs) and *fiscales ordinarios* (minor church officers)".[5] In the San Pedro valley, he gave many staves of "governors, justices and captains,"[6] and he frequently

---

[1] Velarde, Sec. 2, p. 134.
[2] Appendix II.
[3] Recopilacion de leyes de los reynos de las Indias, Madrid, 1756 II, p. 198.
[4] Rudo Ensayo, pp. 235—6, Doc. Hist. III, vol. 4, 592.
[5] Bolton, 1936, p. 391.
[6] Bolton, 1919, vol. I, p. 171.

was guided on his trips by Indian "justices".[1] Just how universal
the system of appointments was, he does not say, but the complexity of organization probably depended on the size of the town
since the "very great rancheria of Adid" received a governor, chief
*fiscal* and sheriff, while Anegam and Bitter Wells received only one
cane apiece.[2] But if the Piman villages once had a complete outfit
of officials, they lost them in subsequent years and there remained
only the governor whose functions as leader and judge were so like
those of the old Keeper of the Meeting that the people found them
easy to accept. Governor and Keeper existed and still exist, side
by side, but the governor, on account of his connection with the
Whites, continued to grow in importance, while the Keeper subsided.
The governor is now the village dictator and it takes inquiry before
the existence of a Keeper can be established.

The governor had an assistant, sometimes more than one, called
his Leg. He was generally a young relative, chosen by the governor
himself and trained as his successor. He can hardly be thought of
as a lieutenant governor for his duties were the menial ones of
carrying the messages and doing the whipping. Still, he was sometimes inaugurated with the same solemn speeches and warnings as
were given the governor (40).

The governor attained office in various ways. The decree of 1618,
mentioned above, provided that the Indian officials should be
elected every year in the presence of the parish priest. But the
Papago villages (except Bac) had no parish priest and they soon
relapsed into their traditional method of choosing an official by
heredity, subject to the approval of the villagers, and holding office
for life. The different villages, in time, worked out slightly different
methods. At Kaka, "the elders gathered around the fire and talked
until they settled on a man wise, kind-hearted and brave" (41).
At Santa Rosa, the governor selected his successor just as did the
Keeper of the Meeting. He would announce his selection by standing
up in full council meeting and pointing his staff of office at the
candidate. Then the elders must approve and, on the rare occasions
when they did not, another man must be suggested (15). At present,
there is a growing tendency to elect the governor though, in consonance with old custom, the first candidate thought of is generally
a descendant of the former incumbent. Two new settlements, Imikah and Burnt Saddle, had governors appointed for them by the
representative of the Indian Office and the docility with which
these were accepted supports the idea of the governorship as a
foreign institution.

[1] Bolton, 1936, p. 284.　　　　　　[2] Bolton, 1936, p. 398.

The governor had, sometimes, a very formal installation. At Archie, the former governor, if still living, handed him the staff of office, with a formal speech of admonition. Then each of the elders, in turn admonished him: "You will have a hard time. The people will not agree with you. But we have chosen you as one who will do right" (40). Most northern villages seem to have had the same ceremony but in Mesquite Root and Cowlic the badge of office was not a staff but a rawhide whip. A whipping post was set up in front of the governor's house and he was expected to chastise offenders. This is an institution not found in the north nor among the Pima. Out of harmony with the usual Papago practice whose only punishment is public disapproval, it points to a Spanish tradition. Church records mention whipping as the regular punishment for Indian neophytes around a church settlement and the missionaries were sometimes accused by laymen of choosing the most cruel of the Indians as governors in order to maintain discipline.[1]

But, however the governor was installed, his appointment was not ratified until he had journeyed to Hermosillo, the Sonoran capital to "get his power." How ancient this practice is, there is no means of telling, for Papago makes no distinction between Spaniard an Mexican and knows nothing of Mexico's war of independence. Orozco y Berra mentions it in 1848 as a long established practice[2] and the Papago informants confirm it.

In 1854 the Americans came into power and their representative[3] summoned all the existing chiefs to be informed of the change of government. The San Xavier calendar stick has a long record of the occurrence.[4] They met at San Xavier and those present were: Many Skirts, for Archie; the Gambler, for Mesquite Root; Green Mesquite, for Kaka; At-the-Base-of-the-Sunset, for Anegam and Gold Ears, for Tecalote. All these were confirmed in office and Archie was given the hegemony. From this date, the succession of chiefs is known and their authority very much enhanced.

These appointments cover only five main villages whereas there were already eleven. The custodian of the calendar stick says that several of the five considered themselves overlords over two or three villages. Thus the Archie jurisdiction included Santa Rosa, Komarik and Akchin and Kaka included Kupk and Hikiwanyi. There were

---

[1] Cancio, quoted in Bancroft V, 1, 571.
[2] Orozco y Berra, p. 346.
[3] Bancroft, Arizona and New Mexico, Vol. II, p. 544.
[4] Underhill, 1938, p. 25.

small federations existing and indicating, perhaps, that the leading village had been the parent of the others. But the whole of Papagueria was never federated except in theory. The American idea of government demanded that there should be one head chief for all the Papago and Archie claimed the position. "But Gold Ears of Tecalote never had anything to do with the Archie chief.. His village was not related and so he ruled by himself" (40). This indicates how little weight the head chieftainship had with the Papago. After the death of Many Skirts, Con Quien of Mesquite Root wished to be considered the head chief and was so spoken of by some of the White settlers but "the people did not follow him."

With the recent forming of daughter villages, several new governorships have arisen, each subsidiary to the rule of its mother village. Standing Rock was colonized from Mesquite Root and regarded that town as its superior until it was abandoned; the colonists turned to Archie, related to Mesquite Root. Tobacco Mountain in the Archie valley had no chief until one of its leading residents was constituted chief, out of hand, by the representative of the United States government (2), but he also is considered subordinate to Archie. Finally he took two or three other settlements under his wing. One of them, San Isidro, now feels itself large enough to have a chief of its own and has picked a man who will be submitted to Archie for approval. When Imikah, near Hikiwanyi, was settled, the Indian agent again asked one of the residents to act as chief but the chief of Hikiwanyi considers him a subordinate and countermands his orders when he disagrees. The system by which the governor of the main village is the superior of those in the daughter villages must be a firmly entrenched one since it holds good, even against the prestige of American appointments.

The governor can be deposed if he is "not good for the people." According to the governor of San Pedro, the elders meet in his absence and make the decision, then one of them calls on him privately and invites him to "take a rest. Some one else will do the work."

The governor, in spite of a growing importance, is supposedly subject to the will of the council. This fact was used when the famous Hunter claim came before the supreme court in 1910. The governor of Santa Rosa had signed a deed giving half the land of the village to a certain Hunter in payment for legal services. The court ruled on the evidence that no one man was entitled to sign for the whole village and the governor had no such power.

The office of governor, starting perhaps from the informal leadership of "him who talked the most" has come to be the pivot of present day Papago organization. The White authorities who are constantly needing advice in important decisions, cannot summon a whole council nor wait for its deliberations. More and more the governor has come to stand for his village. He must make a decision and report it to his council rather than wait to receive orders from them. The course of events has placed him in the position of dictator rather than mouthpiece.

His authority as a judge has lapsed, since the institution of regular native judges and policemen. But that also grew, under Spanish and church influence until he conducted a form of domestic relations court, to be further described below. We may wonder at the docile acceptance by the Papago of the whipping which was so out of keeping with their own highly democratic organization. They accepted it, apparently, as part of that visitation which also gave them new foods, tools and cattle and it added enormously to the prestige of the governor who practised it. In short, the two centuries and more since Kino's time must have seen a decided shift in Papago government from the informal conduct of an intimate group which was handled like a family, by admonition rather than formal law, to the establishment of an executive power which, in response to the need of the day, is still growing. The old Papago system allowed very little scope to the ambitious man, which gives another reason why the new openings to authority were so eagerly seized upon. Yet there are still individuals who regard themselves simply as the mouthpiece of the council, while others have the attitude of the responsible patriarch and others again are practically dictators.

# ECONOMICS

Poor as the Papago country was, its economics were those of abundance. Papago did not hoard property; they did not quarrel about land boundaries; they were constantly giving, as though from an inexhaustible supply. The answer is that the supply, meagre though it was from the modern point of view, was sufficient, for their simple needs and more.

Food was the principal gift and food will not keep in that hot country except in dehydrated form. Because of the migratory life, it must be left unguarded in storehouses and caches, subject to attack by animals or enemies. Better to dispose of any surplus while it was available and palatable and thus invest in good will! And anything but starvation rations was considered a surplus. The standard meal was corn meal gruel: luxuries much beyond that were donated with lavish hand and never missed.

Giving became the regular Papago investment and the franker individuals say so. It never reached the extravagant proportions demanded in the Plains for all Papago life was in a gentler key. But one who gained the reputation of stinginess had damned his prospects in village and family life while the lavish giver not only achieved honor but had a continual income pouring in. For all gifts were returned, in equal quantity and more. The constant exchange of goods in the form of gifts was the Papago equivalent for trade and merged only occasionally into trade in the stricter sense. Papago economics involves principally the study of groups which had gift relations.

The center of the system was the patriarchal family which, rather than the individual, must be taken as the unit both of property holding and of gift exchange.The family was a business concern, producing and disposing of goods under the direction of its male and female heads, and such production meant a full time occupation. This was not the sort of society where the men, when not hunting or fighting, had the privilege of leisure: the men were day laborers like the women. All rose with the morning star, rested in the heat of noon and did not stop work until dark. It was slow motion labor, for the heat forbids haste. But it was unremitting. Industry was the prime virtue and no one could get a mate or keep one without it.

We have noted the division of labor between male and female: a division so sharp that it kept the two sexes in separate groups during daylight hours. But there was also a division according to season and age. In summer, the older men did the farm work, with help from the young men and women at planting and harvest. The young men did some hunting, travelling, ditch building, house building and practiced for the races on which the old men bet. Women, in summer, gathered wild foods, the older women cooked and made baskets while the young ground corn and fetched wood and water. In winter the old men made rope, tools and weapons while the young men fought and hunted deer: the old women still cooked and the young ones were, as always, the wood and water carriers.

The distinction between young and old approached that in a modern society between laboring and employing classes. Heavy labor, everywhere, was done by the young, under the direction of the old. Young men had no voice in council or even in the planning of a war raid, an occasion when, in some Indian societies, they were so prominent. Young women did not manage their households. Youth was considered unfit for thinking and planning and, both in the household and the village, the commanding positions belonged to the old.

It was also the old who practiced the special crafts whose returns went beyond the scope of gifts and became commercial goods. The constant labor required of youth left little time for the long process of learning pottery, netting, mat plaiting, skin dressing and weaving by the Papago process of imitation and repetition. Men and women did not "sit down" to these crafts until middle age. Coiled basketry was the one exception to the rule, for baskets were a necessity and every girl had to learn enough about them to make one during her puberty seclusion. But the other specialties often were not begun until there were grown sons and daughters-in-law in the home to carry on the day's work.

Among the mens' specialties, deer hunting was the most common and was the only one practiced by young men. It meant a long apprenticeship beginning in boyhood and involving the learning of magic and the clever use of the deerhead disguise. One man in a family was sometimes the hunter while the others attended to the land. The other arts were tool making, weaving and skin dressing. The last two are handed over to women in tribes where all the men are busy with war and hunting. But young Papago women had a full time occupation as mere carriers and neither war nor hunting was a major occupation. The women's arts were the plaiting of sleeping mats and of ceremonial baskets, the netting and dying of the intricately made carrying net, the weaving of bands on the belt loom and the making of pottery.

A specialist exercised his craft as his part of the family work and was excused from other labor. He supplied the family with as much of his product as was needed, for use and gifts and the rest he traded His product might be considered individual property in that no one but he had the right to dispose of it and that payment was made to him personally. But he gave the payment to the family just as the younger members gave their labor and if he gambled his products, he gave the family the winnings. Papago needs were such that the family unit required the full time labor of all its members and few thought of operating independently.

The family owned very little permanent property, the food which was obtained and consumed every year, constitutuing almost its entire capital. Such other goods as they had were managed for the benefit of all by the heads of the two working groups: the patriarch for the men, his wife for the women. The patriarch directed the building of a new house or camp and traded when necessary for house posts or stone for tools. It was he who decided on gifts of agricultural produce or meat though he might consult with his wife. The wife managed the use of household mats, pots and baskets. When more were needed, she either had them made in the household or traded for them with womens' goods. She decided on the distributions of cooked food and the harvest from the womens' food gathering. Relics of this system can still be seen in the careful way in which the modern Papago family often separates "man's money" and "woman's money" the woman paying for household goods with her baskets and the man for his saddle with home made rope.

Since Kino's time, the Papago have begun to own cattle, at first in the lands near Mexico, later in the north. Cattle are in charge of the men, like house building and agriculture and their care is directed by the family head. He usually delegates one of his sons as cowboy, just as in former times, one was the hunter. If there are few cattle, the one cowboy may take charge of the cattle of several related families who in turn give produce to his family but not to him personally unless they are very modern.

Each individual had, as his personal property, the scanty clothes he wore, the tools and weapons used and probably some paint and gambling sticks. The whole equipment could be carried on his back, as a girl's was when she went to her husband's house. But more important was ceremonial property: the shaman's plumes, the animal fetish of the curing singer, the eagle feathers, sea shells or Apache scalp won by the "ripe man". These were the most personal of all property for no one but the owner dared touch them —

some said, look at them. Nevertheless, they brought blessing to the whole household since it was unthinkable that the owner's fate should be separated from that of his family group.

To some extent, this blessing was general good luck but the owner of a fetish also earned food by it. The owners of the purification and the curing fetishes were all empowered to cure certain ailments and, for this work, they received their meals. "Thus you will feed yourself" was the regular encouragement given them at the purification ceremony. But the shaman had the rank of a specialist with a highly paid craft. In fact, it was paid out of proportion to all other services so that he stood alone as the one person whose income was great enough to make him independent of the family. This independence, so contrary to the social scheme, must have contributed to the fear in which the shaman was held.

Songs and ritual were also individual property. The owner of a dreamed song could work magic with it and receive a meal just as he would if he helped harvest a field. But he could not sell it. Such a song, to have magic, must be dreamed by the singer and people resorted to many expedients to convince themselves that they had dreamed a song. But pay was not one of them. Ritual was not dreamed but was handed down in families, the current practitioner choosing his heir from among the eligible males. Reciters of this sort of ritual had the function of priests and were not renumerated.

Much Papago property was destroyed and buried at a death. The house was burned if possible, but the heavy posts being hard to obtain, the thatching was sometimes burned and the posts moved. The clothing, paints and tools of the individual were buried with him, also food and water and as much more equipment as could be spared. A man might have a buckskin and a woman a jar or two. Fetishes and shaman's equipment were not buried but kept by the family.

Arrangements have been changed in recent years since the Papago have owned more property. The house, now of wattle and daub, is never destroyed but those who keep to the old customs at all, often bury large amounts of property with the corpse, buying new saddles, clothes and canned goods for the purpose. A man's horse, which had something the status of a tool that he used, was often killed at the grave, though not now.

Cattle are considered family property and distributed to the children. They should, logically, be mens' goods, since their care belongs entirely to the men but modern life has brought no corresponding womens' goods and, in the instances known to the writer daughters have received cattle as well as sons. But customs, in this case, are still in process of formation. Wagons and farm tools, sewing machine and kitchen range, are family tools, in the same status as, formerly, the stone axe and the rope twister, the pots and baskets. They used to be distributed, by informal arrangement, men's tools to men, womens' tools to women. But the added value of present day tools causes disagreement which must finally lead to some form of testament.

LAND

The essential interest of a family was in the land which had been cleared and ditched by its men and whose use was, therefore, regarded as a perpetual right. An agricultural settlement was known simply as the Fields, the flimsy houses being secondary and these Fields had generally been discovered and settled by a family group. The place chosen was in the flat plain where a wash, rushing down from the mountains, finally lost its momentum, ceased to cut a channel and spread its waters over the level land for a square mile or more. The clay, soaked by the standing water, furnished the planting ground while the houses were placed on some slight elevation away from the flood.

The group of settlers distributed the fields among their households, choosing a leader to oversee the process. If they were only a few, any older man might take charge. A larger group elected a leader who must ultimately be approved by the leader of the home village. Under his direction, the group held a meeting and parcelled out the flood plain into plots of two or three acres. At the beginning, there was usually more than enough for all since the Papago planted very little wheat and all they needed was a garden patch for corn, beans and pumpkins. The writer, on inquiring how all could be accomodated so easily, has often been told: "But you don't know how small our fields were. There was more than enough."

Each family head received a field which would serve for himself and his sons and he marked its corners with large stones or stakes. These were frequently washed away and then there were boundary difficulties but most Papago denied that they resulted in quarreling. "They just talked together and put the marks back." However the writer has seen clowns at the harvest feast, mimicking farm life and surreptitiously moving boundary stones. If there were a dispute it is acknowledged that the parties went to the governor, who generally reconciled them by common sense and moral suasion. If one of them insisted that he needed more land, the governor suggested that he go further out and dig a new field.

This is an example of the economy of abundance. The land was all subject to drought and the fields were tiny but there was enough for every one, either at the wash in question or at another. The peaceable acceptance of this fact is in sharp contrast to the attitude of the neighboring Mohave in the Colorado bottom. There the land was rich but it was limited and boundary disputes were so frequent that a special form of fight was developed to settle them.[1]

With the fields marked out, each family had the duty of clearing the land and perhaps digging a ditch which would bring the water to a point where it would flood the area. This meant labor and when such labor ceased, the governor might allow another family to use the land, but they must relinquish the right, if any of the original family even the most distant relatives, came back and asked for it.

There were certain duties which the family owed to the village, as a form of tax. It must join with the others in digging a reservoir to catch rain water for drinking purposes since the water of the wash was too muddy and intermittent. Also, if the plain was such that the flood water was not distributed well, it might be necessary to build a short main ditch. Both ditch and reservoir must be cleaned every year and sometimes there were subsidiary ditches though never a real irrigating system. The decision as to cleaning was taken up in council and every man was bound to help.

During the father's lifetime his sons worked the land under his direction and after his death they might continue to do so for a while. (I, 1, A, B, C, D, E; I, 6, A, B, C, D; I, 5, A, B, C). Ultimately, as their families grew, they divided the land between them but with very little formality. Sometimes two sons kept their land together (I, 5, A, C) sometimes one was a hunter and got the family meat while his brothers did the farming (I, 8, E). If more land was needed, one of the sons asked permission of the council and broke land at a distance, his brothers helping him in the work (I, 8, B).

Daughters were expected to marry into another village and share their husbands' land. Until they did so, their living was provided in the family group and they were sheltered in the house of any brother who had room. If they returned after divorce or widowhood, they were treated in the same way. There is one instance of an unmarried woman being given land by her brothers but in that case, she was apparently about to marry and the land was given to her husband as a member of the group. (I, 3, C, 2). In another case, a widow with a grown son had land which we may consider as given to the son on the same system (I, 1, A, 3). A woman, in fact, was

[1] Kroeber, 1925, p. 744.

not considered a member of the farm group, since she had other duties and land assigned to her immediate family was really assigned to the man who supported her.

There are a number of cases of matrilineal residence which are explained in the above way. When a married woman brought her husband to live in the family group with her brothers, informants never took it for granted but gave one of four reasons:

1. There were no sons, or not enough and the daughter's husband was needed to work on the land. (I, 2, B, 1; I, 2, F, 1; I, 2, I, 1; I, 7, A, 1).

2. The daughter's husband had no land so came to share that of his wife's family. (I, 6, C, 1). (The husband in this case was obviously a poor match and his labor must have been needed to make the arrangement desirable.)

3. The daughter's husband had land but, his relatives being all dead, he did not wish to stay there. (I, 2, F, 4; I, 2, F, 5; I, 2, F, 6; I, 2, H, 1; I, 3, D, 5).

4. The daughter's family were breaking out new land and her husband joined them as one of the group of settlers, sometimes keeping his home field as well. (1, 3, B, 19; I, 3, B, 1; I, 8, A, 1; I, 3, C, 1; I, 3, D, 1; I, 8, A, 1; I, 8, F, 1).

When the daughter's husband entered the group in this way, he was placed on a par with the sons, one of the indications that affinal relatives were treated like blood relatives when geographic nearness permitted. The land was assigned to the husband, not to the wife, and if she died and he married again, its use went to his descendants This is just what would have happened if the family had called in a distant relative on their own side to make use of their land-right.

Such relatives were, in fact, called in or invited themselves for the same reasons as applied to the daughter's husband. I, 1, F, 1 used the land of his father's younger brother's grandchildren and I, 6, D, 1 that of his younger sister's daughter's husband. On this basis it would have been logical for the family occasionally to turn land over to friends or share-croppers but there is no record that commercial procedure progressed so far. Land was connected with the family and not with trade.

Ultimately, the field became inadequate and the group must get new land. If the settlement were still small, the digging of a ditch further down the wash would make a sufficient plot available. Permission was asked of the Council so as not to interfere with the rights of others and then all the family united in digging and clearing, as compensation to the migrating members for giving up their claims. There is record of one brother who did his own clearing and felt that, thereafter, he need not share the produce of his fields with those who were using the family inheritance (I, 8, B, 1). As the village grew larger, available land was further and further away: those who took it up moved their residence and the family group became segmented. Ultimately some of the segments had to found new villages.

There are a few examples of men who had land but moved to get something better. These did not relinquish the old land but sent a member of the family to cultivate it so that in the end the family possessed plots at two different Fields (I, 1, A, 1; I, 3, B, 1). There was here a chance for aggrandizement and for a higher standard of wealth than the Papago usually had, but few seem to have thought of warding off starvation in this way. The close family group and the Fields which barely gave it a living, were the rule.

Occasionally families died out and then the Council, on request, assigned their land to someone else. After many deaths, the surviving members often deserted the land on the same principle that they pulled down the house, to prevent its being visited by ghosts. The ghosts would not lure away with them any but the family so it was safe for non-relatives to live there. But they must ask the family's permission and if any of them returned after a safe interval, the land must be given back. But no payment in crops was made during its use.

Since almost every one in a village was related it was rare for any one to move in who was not provided for in some family group. But if a stranger did wish to enter, and take up land, abandoned or new, he went to the Council and asked permission. The Council did not look up his references but simply tried him out. If he proved a desirable neighbor, he was allowed to stay.

The Well villages were composed of groups of relatives, smaller than those at the Fields, since the Well could serve only a limited number. But often the personnel at the Well was somewhat different. The group in 1, 1 were living at the Fields of their mother's family since their father was dead but in winter they went to the Well used by the father's group as they had in his lifetime. Through this sort of shift, a family might belong to two economic groups, one functioning in the dry season, one in the wet. But some, like 1, 5, A, 1 formed a new group and did not change.

Beside the shift from Field to Wells, there were briefer migrations to food gathering grounds where families kept permanent camps. In late June and early July, every family went for three or four weeks to the foothills to gather the fruit of the giant cactus whose juice was fermented for the liquor ceremony. As a rule, each

7

village located a good grove in the foothills nearest it and the families chose their camping sites there. In this case there was no consultation with the Council for the cactus groves were very extensive and there was plenty of room. Nearly related families placed their camps together with a picking grove around them a half mile or more square, or such that the women of the combined families could just manage to keep the groves picked clean as the fruit ripened. The next campers settled far enough away so as to give themselves room and not interfere. No one would settle near an established camp unless he was a relative and then only after asking permission and no one, looking for a new camp, would go to the hills already pre-empted by a village not his own.

However, residents of one village often asked their relatives from another village to make cactus camp with them; married daughters came back to camp with their families and people who had formed new Field villages used the old cactus camp. This shifting of personnel furnished almost as much excitement as the journey to a ceremony and formed a relief for relatives living in close contact the rest of the year.

A family thus using the cactus grove of a village not their own felt bound in honor to bring the gathered juice to the ceremony of the host village. Tradition says that, in the old days, all juice was fermented in the council house with none kept for private consumption. That constituted the guests ceremonial laborers for the host village. At present a great deal of the liquor is used for home consumption and people want more of it. Also they are less willing to camp in the waterless groves where water has to be transported a long distance and they are beginning to encroach on the groves of people camped in the more accessible places. "But I would not say anything," said a man who had suffered this. "The cactus is for all. We did not make it and the people who pick it are bringing rain." A woman, less tolerant, followed the trespassers all the way out of the grove, scolding them. But the rest of her family disapproved and would say nothing. The Papago tradition of peaceableness was strong.

The cholla and the prickly pear grew in the same general locations as the giant cactus and when they were in season the women of the family went back to the cactus camp for two or three days, drying or eating the prickly pear and pit-baking the cholla on the spot. For each of the other staples they had a special location: mesquite beans by the washes, yucca on hilltops; roots and greens in low wet places. There were no family camps in these gathering grounds but each was understood to be pre-empted by a village or by several related villages.

The most formal procedure was for one of the older women of the village, frequently the Keeper's wife, to have the gathering party announced by the crier. All the able bodied women of the village would then go out together and pick the spot clean. Each patriarchal family made its own arrangements as to the disposal of the harvest, some putting it in a common storehouse, some dividing it among the various young wives. Women who could not go because of illness or segregation shared the harvest of their families.

The picking lasted three or four days and the women camped in the open, the older ones acting as directors and chaperones. Sometimes an old man or two went with them and, if there were danger of the Apaches, some husbands with bows and arrows. But no man ever worked at food gathering and the guards spent their time hunting rats and rabbits. The women dried or pit-baked their harvest on the spot and made a holiday of it with songs and stories. This was the time when daring youths sneaked to the camp at night and tried to decoy a maiden out into the dark.

Often the women of a village did not go all together but in different family groups at different times. The female head of one patriarchal family would command her youthful subordinates to be ready and might invite the heads of other families. Then they proceeded like the large group. There was little danger of their taking what others might want because no woman could carry more than her one burden basket full, but there was a general feeling that it was wrong to be greedy and not give others a chance. When they returned they made small gifts of their harvest to relatives in the village: gifts which were reciprocated in the usual way.

The mens' deer hunting grounds were determined in a very loose way, like the women's gathering grounds. A mens' hunting party was arranged in the council but not for relatives only, since skilled deer hunters were few. They went to certain mountains rather loosely understood to be pre-empted by their village but no informant could say what would be the consequences if they went elsewhere. "Probably no one would say anything." Then follows another example of the economy of abundance. "There weren't many hunters. There were deer enough." Each hunter's kill had to suffice for the whole of the economic unit to which he belonged, which might mean from two to ten families. He butchered his deer on arrival and then called his children to carry pieces to each household, according to the number of its members. Occasionally "the deer was all gone but the bones before he had finished" and his own family got nothing. But the gifts were, of course, reciprocated and he had done his part toward the support of the unit.

7*

Now that cattle raising has taken the place of hunting, its arrangements are very similar. A village unit uses the neighboring range as it formerly used the hunting grounds but the range has no definite limits and no objection is made if the cattle of other units are found there. A few families have accumulated enough cattle so that their ownership ranks as a business, managed on modern lines. Many, however, sell only two or three head a year to local buyers and butcher about as many for the family as they formerly butchered deer. They distribute gifts of beef just as they once distributed venison.[1]

FOOD GIFTS

Food was the currency of the Papago economic system. Small gifts of it were continually passing within the intimate family group, and penetrating now and then to further connections. We have described under kin behavior the frequent interchange of cooked food within the geographic unit. There was no particular rule as to quantity. One family gave two large wooden spoonfuls to every household at every meal; another, cooked for each meal, a four gallon pot and distributed it all, sometimes leaving nothing for the home household which subsisted on gifts. Other households sent gifts only once or twice a week or when they had something unusual. The ratio of giving was determined by custom with each group as the elaborateness of Christmas gifts might be determined in a White family. But it was kept up regularly, each gift being reciprocated with a like amount.

Gifts made to more distant kin were generally at the time of harvest but there was an exception when kin came to visit. People travelling through a village made the home of any relative their stopping place and then they were not only fed but given cloth, buckskins, beads or anything the family had. It was a sort of insurance which made it safe for the host family to travel in their turn for there was a strong feeling that land outside one's own village unit was dangerous ground.

Besides the gifts which cemented relatives together, the Papago had a system of charity. Although they did not feature generosity as did certain Plains Indians it was a highly appreciated virtue and a man known to practice it had a high status in the community. No one was ever rich and the little extra that any family could accumulate was better invested in good will than kept. Most dependents were cared for by their family groups but in the unusual case that

---

[1] This section was written before the new regulations for cattle raising were instituted by the U. S. government.

someone was hungry while there was food in the village, he had only to sit outside a house where people were eating. It was bad manners to ask for food but equally bad to fail to offer it. One informant objected to having any house too near her own because "they will see us eat and we will have to send them something." If the hungry person owed his trouble to laziness or a stupid wife, he would be talked about and shamed into reform.

Occasionally, disaster overtook a whole family through illness or enemy raids and then it was the responsibility of the village to take care of the sufferers, the most generous man getting the most credit. It is safe to say that no one ever went hungry while there was food in the village for farmers, food gatherers and hunters would all share with him. No definite return was expected except general respect and good will but "if a person got the name of being stingy, he always had a hard time. Even his relatives didn't help him more then they had to" (26).

Papago gift basket.
Quantities are measured by the lines parallel to the basket rim.

In the constant interchange of gifts, certain equivalents had been worked out. The usual container was a basket bowl with a black pattern involving many lines parallel to the rim. A person receiving such a basket would note to what line the corn or beans reached and then fill it to the same point for the return gift. To fill it even higher was an act of virtue but to fill it short of the line was to commit social suicide. The bowls were made in two or three standard sizes so that almost any bowl formed a rough measure. The women's carrying nets were also about the same size with patterns which served for markers. One carrying net was equal to two ordinary basket bowls. There was a rough understanding as to the number of squash or jars of cactus syrup which equaled these measures for corn and beans.

## TRADE

Such measures were always kept in mind in the exchange with non-relatives. It was not trade in the full sense, for there was no bargaining and the merchant looked upon his product somewhat like a ceremonial gift which was being reciprocated. The difference between it and a gift to relatives was that the exchange was supposed to be equal, with no effort of one giver to outdo the other, and that it established no relations for the future.

The most common gift of this sort was venison. Many families included no hunters at all so when a deer was butchered in the village, they would go and proffer a basket of beans or corn. The hunter, when he had distributed what was proper to his relatives, would "give" a piece to the donor of the beans. The latter never specified how much he wanted or from what part but accepted his share like a gift. The same thing is done at present with beef. Usually there was no opportunity for more organized trade for the family needed the whole product. However, I heard of two young men from a family of hunters (I, 1, A. 5, 17) who used occasionally to take their kill to a village where wheat was raised. The villagers had been told it was wheat they wanted and brought baskets of varying sizes, receiving what the hunters thought was their equivalent in venison. In the same way salt, saguaro syrup and melons or other special crops could be "given" to the neighbors. after family demands had been satisfied.

Barter for such luxuries as buckskin and cotton cloth had more of a commercial tinge, for here the purchaser had special needs and could not take any piece offered. Still, there was as little deviation from the gift pattern as possible. The purchaser brought his gift and stated what he wanted. The seller rarely asked for any different pay since the purchaser probably had but the one thing. If it was not enough, the seller reciprocated with poor skins or a small sized mat or blanket. If the gift was entirely too small he might send the buyer home to get something in addition. If it was still to small, he would not complain but would avoid dealing with him in future.

The dresser of deerskin was generally an old hunter who had an equipment of scraping post, tools and dying pots and who traded for his skins with younger men. For a skin, dressed and dyed, he expected corn and beans amounting to two bushels. For the trousers and shirts made later in Papago history, he might receive a horse.

Only a few old men in the whole country understood weaving, for very little cotton grew in Papagueria and since it was bartered from the Pima, the weaving was usually done by them also. But ocassionally a family who had been working for the Pima would take their pay in cotton. If they traded for it, the price for enough to make a blanket was half a sack of salt, a buck skin, a hair rope or two baskets of beans and corn. Most old men knew how to spin cotton on the thigh and the purchaser's family might spin it or call in the neighbors for a working bee, giving them their meals meanwhile. If they brought raw cotton to the weaver, he got it spun in the same way. The chief articles made were large blankets to sleep on and narrower strips for womens' skirts. For the large blankets the price was a horse or its equivalent in produce or buckskin. The skirt the woman bought, herself, with a good willow basket of her own make.

Plaited baskets, plaited mats, netted carrying baskets and pots were made by elderly women, too old for the heavy work of corn grinding and food gathering. They were not such expensive articles as skins and cloth, an olla being worth enough beans or corn to fill two basket bowls while for a mat the measure was a winnowing bowl.

But besides this exchange among themselves, some Papago made a business of trading trips to the Pima, to Mexico and to the Yuma. These were a winter occupation on the same basis as hunting and sometimes combined with it. The Papago were homeless in the winter and many of them, instead of camping at the Well village wandered about trading their goods or their labor for enough to support them until the wet season came again.

Russell gives a list of the goods which the Papago, supposedly so poor, managed to get together for trade with the Pima. It includes giant cactus seeds, cholla fruit, agave fruit in roasted cakes and syrup, Rcat (wild potato), wild gourd seeds, small peppers, acorns from the Bellota oak, prickly pear syrup, baskets of agave leaf, sleeping mats, carrying baskets and fibre to make them, maguey fibre for picket lines, dried meat of deer, mountain sheep and cows tallow .... deer and beef, .... cheese, buckskin, livestock, red and yellow ochre, buff-colored ochre for baskets, salt.[1] What they wanted in return was food, principally wheat, which they themselves raised only in small quantities. But frequently their price was corn and beans enough to keep them alive. The people who used this expedient came from the northern villages, the Archie and Kuhatk groups and Káka, who were the Pimas' nearest neighbors. They often had relatives in the Pima country or at least friends and they pursued their exchange in the same manner they used at home.

The southern villages had their contacts with Mexico where they took principally dressed skins, cooked mescal from the mountains and their labor. They brought back knives and clothing and the knowledge of a more advanced culture than was to be found on the

[1] Russell pp. 93—94.

Gila. The Mexicanization of southern Papagueria can be laid largely to these winter trading trips. However, the people with whom trade was carried on were the Mexican Papago and the method was essentially Indian.

Trade with the Yuma was less frequent but of old standing. In 1698, while Kino was at Kuitatk, an old woman trudged into town from the west, with a pack on her back containing snails and little shells from the sea which she herself had brought from there.[1] She had probably been close to Yuma territory.

### LABOR

Often what the Papago had to exchange was not goods but labor. Within the geographic unit, there was constant need for assistance in planting, harvesting, housebuilding, ditch digging, spinning, arrow making. Any individuals available gave their labor and their household was repaid in labor. goods or, sometimes, goodwill. But if no relatives were available, neighbors would be called on. The pay for such labor was return labor when it was needed and the meals eaten while working. But the meals were a very slight expense for "In old days people never ate much." For what was needed, there was abundance.

Harvest was in a class by itself for, at this time, the workers were often paid in produce. To invite relatives to help at harvest was a favor to them and families invited the distant ones seriatim in different years. Such an invitation meant a close tie and the family sometimes went into council as to who should receive it. The group in App. I, 5, took turns in inviting the wife's relatives and the husband's. As pay, they asked them to help themselves but the amount they took would be regulated by what they thought they could repay. One informant mentioned two sacks of wheat out of ten or "a pile" of unhusked corn or beans about three feet in diameter (21).

With the present scattering of Papago residence, relatives are not always available and neighbors are invited. No bargain is made but they are paid, as in trade, with whatever the giver can afford. "But those who are stingy can't get any one to work for them. I always have lots of help because I give a big pile of melons or a sack of wheat" (2).

It was on this same basis that the Papago worked for other people and, since their most constant employers were the Pima, we may assume that the pay was calculated in the same way. The River

---

[1] Bolton, 1936, p. 399.

People, before their water failed, had such large and constant crops that one who wished could pay in produce to have all his heavy work done and could still have plenty to live on. Many of them had relatives in the neighboring Papago village groups of Archie, Kuhatk and Perigua and, as far back as tradition goes they have called on them to help with the work. But in the middle eighties, Pima agriculture grew to large commercial proportions, when thousands of bushels of wheat were sold to passing American pioneers. The Pima, with their hands full, sent for more and more Papago workers until it became the regular thing for the northern villages to be almost depopulated at wheat cutting time and for the roads to be filled with covered wagons going to Pima country. Each Papago family traveled and worked together and each had its regular employers, whose attitude was that of relatives or feudal protectors.

The trek to the Gila began in May, the time for cutting winter wheat. This was also the end of the dry season when the Papago were almost out of food and it meant, for some families, release from starvation diet. The work lasted about three weeks with a little time more for trade and for cutting basketry willow which did not grow in the desert country. The pay, in wheat, settled down to about two sacks to the acre. The workers came home in July to have their rain ceremony and do their own planting and sometimes they returned before winter to plant for the Pima, to harvest and to pick cotton.

With the failure of the water, after 1774, Pima agriculture lessened and, in some districts, stopped. This had its repercussion on the Papago and helped in turning the northern villages toward cattle raising, which they had left largely to the south. But the habit was very strong and, though cotton raising has ceased and wheat has much lessened, many families still make the yearly journey.

The southern villages turned to the Altar valley much as the northern ones did to the Gila, with the difference that the relationships here were not so close. Apache raids and White influence broke up the Mexican Papago organization so that the employer was usually a stranger and not a relative. Nevertheless families formed permanent relationships and would go every year to camp outside the same town and work for the same people. The work was harvesting and threshing beans, harvesting and drying squash corn and peppers. The pay was a share of the produce. But there were also a few chances for range riding, work with skins and casual day labor for which the pay was money. Sometimes a family would camp outside a Mexican town, getting work when it could, otherwise hunting and making pots and peddling the product. All these contacts of the southern villages made for more flexibility and disorganization than there was in the north.

The Papago had one ceremony which involved large payments between villages. Ostensibly they were for ceremonial services which brought blessing and rain but they performed, as well, two very practical functions. One was that the village making the payments could invest its harvest on a much wider scale than that permitted by family gifts and the other, that gift relationships were cemented with what might be called foreigners: the members of another village and even of another dialect group. The ceremony was the dance of greeting and blessing which preceded intervillage games.

Games were played between two village units or groups of units, the same opponents challenging each other alternately, year after year. The time chosen was autumn, when the crops were in and when there was not only leisure but goods for gifts and gambling. The challenging village always "sang for" its opponent, either a rudimentary operetta, in which costumed dancers performed to singing, or a series of songs which glorified the important residents of the host village. Songs of both kinds brought good luck which, according to Papago ideas of reciprocity, should be paid for.

When a village had been challenged and had paid it was etiquette for it to issue the challenge next year and be paid in turn. After that, either village was at liberty to pick out a new opponent but, as a rule, they continued together over a long period and established definite gift relationships. But occasionally, a village which had had a poor harvest would strike out in a new direction and sing for somebody "rich". Russell[1] mentions the Papago (probably the northern villages) singing regularly for the Pima, and some Papagos from Somerton (Sand Papagos?) came yearly in regalia, marched and danced with rattles for the Yuma.[2] But the wealthy agriculturists were too busy with their own affairs to need this form of exchange and the visits were seldom returned.

The visiting party arrived a day early, camped outside the host village and sent in a costumed messenger with a formal challenge to games. The messenger carried a bundle of sticks, each representing a household head in the visiting party, who would expect a gift. If the household head could not come, some younger male represented him, but gifts were made only to households, not individuals.

---

[1] Russell p. 171.          [2] Gifford, 1933, p. 262.

The sticks were given to the Keeper of the Meeting who then called a council in which each of his households volunteered to take one of the sticks — two if necessary — and provide gifts for "the name". Everyone had been saving for this purpose since to give now meant not only blessing for his village but honor and good luck for himself, and return gifts next year.

In this way, there were gradually formed what might be called gift partnerships. A householder, having once selected a "name' as the recipient of his gifts, continued to take the same one, year after year. He called this vantage point among the strangers *nyi owih* (my opposite) and "felt toward him like a relative". It was an excellent device for securing friendly relationships in foreign territory.

The relation of opposites might continue for generations and very often led to marriage alliances. But it was more flexible than a kin tie and could be broken off if either party failed in his obligations. "If they didn't give much one year, we knew they had a poor harvest and we gave even more when it was our turn. But if they kept on that way, we knew they were stingy and we asked in meeting for another name" (26). But there was a good deal of latitude in choosing the names for new ones were always appearing and old ones dropping out. A householder might try some new name in addition to his regular gift partner, just to see how it worked out and often people threw out small gifts in various directions, as an overture to new relationships.

The visitors had a few payments to make on their side. As they danced, it was the polite thing for members of the host village, generally old women who were beyond shyness, to skip beside some chosen dancer. Then his parents would run out with a basket or ornament taken from the goods they expected to gamble next day. When the dance was over, all the women of the host village joined in serving cooked food to the guests. Then the householders made piles of their donations and each called out to his gift partner: "Come and get your pay over here." Some of the gifts remembered were:

### Santa Rosa to Kuitatk (43)

Gift: One large winnowing basket each of cooked squash, cooked beans and ash bread.

Return: One winnowing basket each of dried beans and dried corn and six fresh pumpkins.

On the last occasion an entire stranger made overtures to the family with a sack of roasted corn and another with a jar of cactus syrup. These were reciprocated within the month with a sack of beans and a sack of wheat but later the same strangers gave presents again and a regular partnership was established.

### Kuitatk to San Xavier (26)

Gift: A saddle (made of a straw-stuffed bag in the Papago manner) with two saddle bags, one filled with beans and one with corn. A coiled basket filled with seeds of the giant cactus (used to make flour).

Return: A horse with a leather Mexican saddle, a serape, a willow basket of chick peas and another of cooked tortillas.

### Pima to Kuitatk (26)

Gift: A cotton sheet full of threshed wheat, a gray woolen blanket, a willow basket bowl filled with cooked squash.

Return: A two year colt, two plaited sleeping mats, a decorated clay pot containing about three gallons of cooked beans, a plaited tray bowl about a foot square filled with tortillas.

The etiquette of distribution was for the giver's wife to hand the goods to the wife of the recipient who would carry them home on her back. But the giver's wife often playfully chased her "opponent", pelting her with tortillas and syrup; a symbol, perhaps, of the enmity between the two villages which was now a joke. The giver placed the stick representing the name of his "opposite," in his corn bin, where it brought increase.

The use of a village name, in auspicious ceremonial circumstances, was always a service to be paid for by village residents. The special songs for rain were sung at the drinking ceremony, given at each main village for its whole unit but all visitors were invited to attend and share the blessing. If such a visitor heard the name of his own locality mentioned in the descriptions of the coming of rain clouds, he must provide a gift, for the mere singing of the name in such a connection would bring rain. Visitors used to come prepared with gifts but a recent one had nothing to hand over but his cowboy hat. The same principle holds in the curing songs, which describe the habits of the animal guardians. Any locality mentioned in the description will have blessing and its residents must show they are not stingy.

The second important occasion for ceremonial payments, was the purification of an Enemy Slayer. This man, during the sixteen days of his retirement, had a ceremonial godfather who called him by the same term used by a senior paternal uncle and who was, afterward, treated like an uncle in the matter of gifts. There were no clan, moiety or kin restrictions on the guardian's appointment. Here was another expedient for establishing relationships of trust with non-relatives.

The sixteen days of retirement were succeeded by a public ceremony when the Enemy Slayer was purified by the singing of men who had been through the same experience. They formed a kind of unorganized priesthood and were not paid. But the Slayer's weapons and, according to some, the scalp also, were purified by a special dance, performed by people of another village. The *kapetua* (leaping dance) was a graphic representation of a man in battle, performed with the warrior's own weapons. Any agile young man familiar with war technique was eligible to do it and groups of them habitually practiced. Women might follow them, carrying weapons and imitating their movements. A victory in war was often followed by intervillage games in celebration but even if it was not the time for this, all neighboring villages were invited to the purification ceremony "because the warriors suffered for all". Among them might be several men prepared to do the leaping dance. Paying the dancers was the duty of the hero's family and particularly those who formed part of his geographic unit and would share his honors and good luck. But a scalp brought into the village gave it rain and any villager who helped in the payment for this would have specially good luck with his crops.

One dance was performed for each Enemy Slayer, sometimes by the same performers, sometimes by different ones. After each dance the two leaders, who bore shield and club, should receive horses or cows (or a bit of manure representing them) while the others had lesser gifts. The hero's father and uncles should give the animals and any of them who could, provided the gift. "He didn't get anything back. Just good luck."

If the family could afford no animals, some one else would volunteer for the honor of the village, and probably be paid back in time by gifts from the family though the statement is that "he did not want anything. He did it for the village." It was at this time that the generous man got his reward "for if the hero's father had not been stingy, then everybody would help him make gifts "but otherwise, the provision would be meagre and the other villages would "talk about him and his son." This was disgrace.

The gifts collected were placed in two piles near the dance ground, one pile for men and one for women, and a man and woman of the hero's family were selected to distribute them. There follows a list from a ceremony at Kuitatk, about 1860. The hero, in this case, was a mature man, with no father to make his gifts and those contributing were:

Enemy Slayer: A horse, and a dressed buckskin
Enemy Slayer's younger brother: a horse, and dressed buckskin
Another younger brother: a willow basket
Another younger brother: a dyed cotton belt and a buckskin
Sister: a plaited mat and a willow basket.
Younger brother's son: a basket of corn and beans
Sister's son: a basket of corn and beans.
Children of the other siblings gave baskets of food. There were a few gifts from villagers not remembered. (26)

After this ceremony and after the intervillage games described above, there was always gambling: the occasion *par excellence* for exchange of goods on a large scale with people who were otherwise strangers. The Papago had no public markets and the people who had opportunity to travel for trade were comparatively few. But, for the intervillage games, several villages might move bodily to one spot taking with them all their worldly possessions to bet on the games. This formed one of the principal occasions for distribution of goods and it was often by this means that Mexican knives and cloth found their way to the northern villages and American goods to the south.

The games played have been described under another heading but the method of exchange may be noted. The Papago used, for matching bets, a word which means literally "to meet" and they matched the stakes article by article. If a buckskin shirt was bet on one side, a shirt of equal value must be found among the stakes on the other and the two tied together. Baskets, pots and skins must be placed two and two. Horses and cattle must be in the same corral but since it was at some distance from the racetracks, pieces of manure were tied together to represent the animals. When the games were over, the winner took both articles. Beside the public games, there was a great deal of private betting constantly going on, between women and men alike. It was no uncommon thing for a person to be stripped of everything he owned and the ceremonial aura which hung about all games thus lent sanction to a movement of goods which might not have taken place otherwise, among people with so little surplus for trade.

### RECENT CHANGES

The above system of economics prevailed in the childhood of present old informants. At that time, two gradual changes were going on. The disturbed condition of Mexico was causing movement among the southern villages, so that the arrangement of family geographic units was broken up. The southerners, who had had cattle since Kino's time, were acquiring more through the abandonment of ranches and as pay for their services with the soldiers. Their members were growing accustomed to labor for the Mexicans, paid in money, and to the use of Mexican goods. The northern villagers were still agriculturists with very few cattle. But the Pimas, who had become commercial wheat growers, were employing them in large numbers and thus wheat and American goods were circulating. The northerners kept their family units intact and kept the ceremonial payments which lapsed in the south.

With United States supervision, which began for San Xavier in 1874 and for the mass of Papagos not until 1917, there was an increase in material goods. Papagos acquired wagons, horses and plows and, in very small amount, furniture and kitchen utensils. This property was handled according to the old family system and in many cases, it is so still. Horses, cattle and farm tools were regarded as mens' property, their use directed by the patriarch, who delegated some of the young men as cowboys, some as farmers, as before they had been farmers and hunters. Womens' property did not increase as had the mens' and in fact lessened. The supply of meat and farm produce increased beyond the subsistence point so that the family could trade for store food and the women need not go out gathering. One of the first results, then, was to upset the balance between mens' and womens' work and to make women dependent.

But the relationship of the individual to the family unit was kept. Men still owed their labor to their families and the writer met one young man, even recently, who could not take paid work because his geographic unit contained distant but helpless relatives whose fields he must till. No individual disposed of his harvest, increased though it was by the new tools, until all his relatives had been asked to help themselves. Even those who went out to work used their money to buy store goods for the whole family.

Such a conditions, in varying stages of change, endured until what was practically the economic revolution of 1933 when Emergency Conservation Work spent 350,000 dollars (to November 1935), in improving the water supply of the reservation. This meant that many localities which, heretofore, had been camps, could be permanent residences. There was no irrigation but there were drinking places for cattle where there had been none before. Also from two to six hundred men were employed in a year and received money wages.

It was not possible to fit the sudden plentitude of money into the family scheme. Young men did, indeed buy what clothes and tools the family needed but they had a surplus for themselves as never before. The use of this surplus is now in process of working out but several results are obvious. One is the change of power from the hands of the old to the young, since it was formerly the old who practiced crafts and brought income to the family. Another is the break up of family units since it is the temptation of the young man to move with his wife and babies where he will be free of supervision. In old times he would have needed such constant help that this would have been impossible but modern improvements make such help unnecessary or payable in money. A third is that the concentration of workers from all over the reservation at the work centers, breaks up the village and even the dialect groups. Men can see the possibility of living outside their home localities. A fourth is the habit of looking to the government for charity. The family and village groups, which once took care of all dependents for the sake of their own comfort and reputation, are in process of breaking up. The responsibility of the Federal government which, to the remote Papago, had been but a vague idea, has been strongly registered. In a word, the Papago are making a very rapid change from a barter to a money economy, from the family unit to the individual, and since their standard of living is rapidly rising, from an economy of abundance to one of scarcity.

# SOCIAL BEHAVIOR AND LAW

A Papago village operated with the minimum of formal authority and, to a great extent, it still does so. Each small and isolated group had very much the attitude of a family who arrange their affairs by mutual consent, showing the general tolerance of offenses which is necessary in those who must continue to live together. With the digging of wells which will allow large villages and the roads which encourage travel, this isolation of the village will cease, but it has been, in the past, a determining factor in social behavior.

The village which was, in any case, a group of relatives, looked up to its leader as to a father. His speeches of admonition in the council house were very like those given by the grandfather in the hut. As the Papago father never punished, so the leader guided in most instances by moral suasion. This would be impossible in a large and heterogeneous group, but the village was a small and constant group with common interests.

When differences arise in such a group, there may be enduring feuds; there may be a system of avoidances which prevents feuds or, finally, a glossing over of disagreements and an effort to maintain an unbroken surface. The Papago practised the last method. With them, an open quarrel was the forbidden thing. "People do that only when they are drunk" and the speeches of admonition at the drinking ceremony expressly warn against it. But they had none of the ceremonial avoidances which smooth family relationships by formality. Instead of avoiding particular individuals, they avoided harsh words or open disagreement with anyone. This well established custom is one of the difficulties in modern self government, since the public argument approved by the Whites is shunned by the Papago and one who disagrees with the majority of the meeting is likely to stay away. "I was afraid they might not like what I said." The corollary to such reticence is a criticism outside the meeting and the Papago expedient is to continue with this until some compromise is reached mild enough for public statement.

Training in peaceableness begins in childhood. School fights are rare and the problem of the bully an unusual one. Various Papagos have explained to the writer the proper behavior as it should be taught to children:

> "When people have done us harm, they should never know from the way we act what we feel about it. We should never

speak of what they did. Only we would keep away from them. After a while they would know." (31)

"If a man took my horse without permission and lamed it, I would not say anything. I would even lend him the horse again. If I should get angry with him, he would have a right to be angry with me." (20)

One woman confessed to the writer that some children who had just come back from the white school were bullying her small children and using indecent language. It was unthinkable that she should speak to the parents of the offenders. She had either to suffer or to move away. If the whipping custom be assumed to be a Spanish importation, the village authorities themselves had no means of enforcing proper behavior. They endured in silence to the point where they asked an undesirable to move. Minor nonconformities passed without a sign.

When the writer was inquiring about certain rigorous ceremonial usages which seemed to demand a good deal of sacrifice with little obvious reward, she asked: "If a man did not do this would he be blamed?" "No." "Would people avoid him?" "No." "Would they think him a coward?" "No. They would just think he was a man who didn't like purification" (9). Tolerance could scarcely go further.

This unwillingness to show offense could hardly operate if it had not its obverse in an extreme sensitiveness. The person blamed realizes his position to the full, sometimes to the point of violent suffering. An old story illustrates this:

"A gambler having gambled away all his own possessions, bet his wife's baskets and lost them. (It is to be understood that he had lost all his own possessions before. It was the loss of the wife's property which was serious.) The wife did not reproach him, openly. But that evening she poured the food into a hole in the ground, saying, "I suppose this is the serving dish you like since you have taken away my basket." The man got up and left without touching the food. He went to a high rock near the village. It was evening and the people were all outside the houses. He shouted until they looked up and then threw himself down." (20)

The writer has seen incidents based upon the same attitude. When she was talking to an old hunter about his own subject, hunting, an old woman in the household wanted attention. She whispered to the writer several times: "He hasn't got it right." The hunter took offense. "I shall talk no more," he said. "I am probably an old man, who knows nothing." Three days of assurance and persuasion were necessary before he would talk again. Yet he was aware that he was an authority and that the interruptor had no status.

The objection to adverse comment, even though only sensed, not heard, is a sufficient motive for good conduct. When a young girl is advised not to interfere with her husband, she is told: "If you keep him at home, he cannot hunt. Then there will be nothing to eat and he will go to the neighbors. They will feed him but *they will speak about you.*"

This fear of being "spoken about" was actually the controlling factor in Papago society. In the intimate group, the affairs of everyone were wide open for inspection and any selfishness, dishonesty, treachery, or sexual looseness became common knowledge. The penalty was unpopularity among the neighbors who were one's only associates. They would slack in their food gifts; they would make excuses when asked to a working bee; they would warn against marriage alliances with the family. It was, in fact, the family that suffered and not the individual offender and therefore, the family would reform him if possible or, at least, make good his lapses. There was little need for the authorities to take action when the family machinery could thus be kept in order by public opinion.

A potent aid to this gossip control was the fear of witchcraft. The methods of sorcery will be taken up in connection with the shaman, but it may be mentioned here that every shaman was considered a potential worker of evil magic and therefore it was highly dangerous to offend him, his family or those who might be paying him. Papago life seems to have been shot through and through with this fear of magic for the Spanish account says:

> The whole country is given over to witchcraft... Many fatal illnesses and sudden deaths are due to witchrcaft. ... Witches even kill each other.[1]

> In all the ranches or villages there have always been one or more sorcerers.[2]

All unexplained ills of life, the accidents and the incurable disease, were imputed to the evil shaman and all felt themselves continually surrounded by this malign power. When we realize how little opportunity there was in Papago life for the violence, theft and physical degeneracy which occur in modern society, we must set against this freedom the constant dread of magic. One can imagine signs of it yet in the fantastic machinations imputed to any stranger and the resistance toward new proposals as mysteriously evil.

---

[1] Apostolicos Afanes, pp. 238, 240.     [2] Rudo Ensayo, p. 171.

8*

Such a fear, together with public opinion, took care of many minor offenses which other societies deal with by law and even of some major ones. For the other major offenses, there were various methods of discipline: admonition by the authorities, banishment; supernatural vengeance, and, finally, whipping. We may trace, in the acts catalogued as misdemeanors and in their punishment, two attitudes, the aboriginal and the acculturated, overlapping and combining in various ways.

From the aboriginal point of view, the major offenses against society were incest (which meant connections with any known relative); the failure of a woman to segregate herself at menstruation or childbirth, and the practise of sorcery. Any of these were thought to bring calamity upon the whole community and if whipping had been a Papago institution, we should expect these to be the first to merit it. However, whipping was rarely mentioned in this connection and the usual punishments were not meted out by man at all but by the supernatural. Families who knew that any of their members were about to commit incest or had done so, dealt with them by moral suasion and, if that failed, took them to the Keeper of the Meeting or the governor. If they still refused to separate, the only punishment was to force them to leave the family group. This was a serious·economic misfortune and might be considered a punishment though it was done only to avoid calamity for the family. The offenders were certain to be struck with illness or misfortune by supernatural means.

The woman who did not segregate herself brought on her community the danger of flood or lightning and therefore her relatives, and particularly her parents saw to it that she did her duty. If she deceived them, calamity could be averted by her confession and then she was not punished for confession removed the evil influence. But if she did not confess, a supernatural doom would overtake her and some or all of her connections.

The sorcerer was treated in an entirely different way: his was the one case where the Papago performed an official execution. It is possible that sorcery was more frequent than other lapses for the Spanish records are full of it, and one Spanish priest is even said to have died of it. But certainly, vengeance in this case was not left to the supernatural though any good shaman was welcome to try and kill the evil one. But when the latter had proved himself a public menace by the number of deaths he was thought to have caused, the council would decree his death and send some young man out with a club to despatch him. Or the villagers all together might lynch him, or several do the work on their own initiative and be thanked by the council. The record of the calendar stick is punctuated with such executions.

Murder, in the Papago view, was not a crime. It took place generally at the drinking feast or in a quarrel over a woman, and the victim's family then had a right to kill the murderer or a member of his family. The Keeper, governor and elders remonstrated with them and begged them not to make the village lose a man, but if they insisted, "no one would interfere." One instance was recited where the murderer had fled the country but his brother was still in the village. The victim's brothers came to the door of his house and told him: "We are going to kill you. Send your wife and children away." He sent them away and then came to meet his executioners. After his death his wife tore down the house, according to the usual custom and all the village united in rebuilding it for her at another place and in helping to support her for life (2).

Murder was considered by the Spaniards a crime for which the offender should be delivered to the provincial authorities, but the Papago ignored the ruling except when soldiers or priests were sent to enforce it. Assault and battery was considered a family affair, like murder and in old times it was left to the people concerned. However, the priests thought it a matter for the whipping post and in some places it came to have that penalty.

There was considerably less scope for sexual offenses than in modern society and a man, particularly, had a great deal of freedom. If he conceived a sudden passion, he could always take the woman as an additional wife, after the proper preliminaries of divorce for a married woman or proposal for a maiden. There were official nights of saturnalia, at the drinking feast and the maiden's dance when he could gratify a briefer desire. Homosexual tendencies were openly acknowledged and sanctioned.

Yet sexual offenses did occur. Rape is never mentioned and an illicit affair with a maiden was not important, but one with a married woman, without the proper divorce, was an infringement of the husband's property right. The husband could destroy or appropriate the lover's property and, if he killed him, would not be interfered with. A woman had less freedom and less consolation. There were no female transvestites and a woman could take advantage of the saturnalian feasts only with her husband's consent. She could have only one husband and, if she preferred another man must be divorced and become a second wife. If her husband was having a love affair, she had no remedy but to scratch the other woman while the village looked on. When too much outraged, she could but return to her family. However, sexual offenses were a point where the native and Christian points of view overlapped. Adultery, in the eyes of the Church, was a cardinal sin, and in villages where missionary influence was felt, both male and female adulterers were punished at the whipping post.

The chief native offenses against property (if we except the stealing of a wife) were theft, the moving of land boundaries, and food hoarding. Theft was a rare occurrence, since all had about the same amount of possessions and since families shared even with their laziest members. In old days, it was dealt with by the Keeper, who asked the offender's family to make restitution. Public opinion forced them to comply or lose their status in the community. The moving of land boundaries was dealt with in the same way. The two landholders concerned were summoned before the Keeper by his Leg and urged to come to an agreement. Sometimes the Keeper would suggest that they should divide the land under dispute and each find an extra plot further off. The hearing usually took place before all the elders and both were ashamed to show themselves quarrelsome; so they accepted the decision. If one were recalcitrant without good cause, the council might ask him to leave the village. Food hoarding was recognized by all as a serious offense, but it was not punished. The offender was simply recognized as a public enemy and avoided to such an extent that he and his family suffered economically from lack of help and socially from loneliness and humiliation.

This seems to sum up the offenses and the discipline of pre-Spanish days. The community and officials acted principally as umpires and used no corporal punishment except in the killing of the shaman which was regarded as an act of self defense. The punishments of admonition and banishment which they did administer, fell, not upon the individual offender but on his whole family. It has been mentioned above that a family, particularly a father and brothers, would not desert a man no matter what his behavior. If they could not reform him, they might, themselves, take him to the authorities for a severe lecture on the fact that he was ruining his family's position. They might share in this lecture for having failed to keep him in order. If he was so impossible that he must be asked to leave the village one or more of the family would have to go with him — since an individual could hardly exist alone, -- or distant relatives must take him in. In any case, there was no thought of the penalty singling out the individual and leaving the family free. With supernatural vengeance, this was particularly true for misfortune might strike any member of the family and not necessarily the culprit.

In Spanish days, however, it was the individual who was punished and usually by whipping. It is hard to be positive that whipping is a foreign institution yet it seems likely since the Papago are chary of physical contact especially in public. This may seem surprising in a society where ten or more people could live and sleep in a one-room house, but one may conjecture that it is an avoidance generated by that very fact. They maneuver without touching one another where Europeans, who have more privacy, are continually doing so. They did not, anciently, slap or whip children. It is to be expected that a people with this attitude would object to corporal punishment, particularly when they have cultivated such a violent sensitiveness and openness to humiliation. The missionaries, on the contrary, whipped their neophytes as they would whip the children they considered them to be. That the Papago should have been willing to adopt this system is the surprising thing. We may lay it to the extreme prestige of these givers of wheat and horses, and also to the fact that the native selected to dispense whipping felt himself raised to the supernatural power of the priests. Certainly the institution of whipping grew, from the eight stripes delivered by the *alcalde* for drunkeness or absence from mass to a standardized penalty for all misdemeanors, sometimes including murder. Those which were mentioned as always whipped fall under the heading of sins in the Christian sense. A list of these offenses and their penalties follow:

Murder: The chief would have the murderer whipped and force him to make restitution in property.

Adultery: Both offenders whipped and the wife sent back to her husband.

Quarrels between spouses: Either a wife or a husband might complain of the other's laziness, cruelty or light conduct and have the offender whipped.

Disobedience of children: Parents might complain of laziness or light conduct, particularly in a daughter, or of her disobedience in not taking a husband. Some cases are reported where the chief felt that the parents had been in the wrong and had them whipped instead of the child.

Slander: All reports of misconduct were investigated and if, they proved untrue, those who had spread the rumor were whipped, whether male or female.

There follows a provision heard from only one informant and showing an interesting combination of the old and the new systems.

If a father failed to have the puberty ceremony for his daughter at the proper time, he should be whipped. If he proved that he had not been told, the mother was punished instead. (26)

Whipping was ordered by the Spanish appointed governor who held his court with some little ceremony. On receiving a complaint, he sent his Leg out to bring in the offender whom he received in front of his house, generally with some elders present as advisors. If the offense was acknowledged, he announced the penalty immediately and the Leg carried it out. But if the plea was not guilty, he sent the Leg for witnesses and asked each of them, "What do you know about this?" He made up his mind after hearing their stories and consulting the elders. However, the Papago are not a people given to formality and the following instances, remembered by the daughter of the governor of Kuitatk reflect a neighborliness not perhaps contemplated by the Laws of the Kingdoms of the Indies.

Once a wife came, very angry, to complain about her husband. "He beats me," she said, "but I love him." My father sent his Leg for the husband. He said to that man: "Do you beat her?" he said. "Yes," said that man. "I beat her because I am jealous. I think she looks at other men. But I want to keep her." "Then," said the woman, "let him pay me with his body. Let him be beaten too." My father thought about that and he said, "Very well. How many stripes?" "Fifty." "Do you want to kill him?" said my father. "Twenty." So the man took off his shirt and knelt down and the Leg beat him.

A man came with his daughter. "She went off into the arroyo with a man at the last girl's puberty dance. I want her beaten." "How many stripes?" "Twenty." "Fifteen," said the chief. "She is young."

Then a husband and wife came with their girl who had just been married. "She will not sleep with the man to whom we gave her." That man was an old man but he was all right. My father (the chief) knew that. He knew the girl was just scared. He said, "Well, we'll beat her and see how she feels." So they tied the girl's hands to the post. She began to cry. She said, "I'll go with him." So she went off with her husband and my father said to the parents," If she doesn't behave, bring her back." (26)

The governor's whipping post lasted on during the early years of American authority in Papagueria, before the reservations were organized. With the latter event came the appointment of Indian judges, Indian policemen paid by the government and a reservation jail. These deal with minor offenses, principal of which is the old one first turned over to the *alcalde*—drunkenness. This neurosis of a transition stage is at present far more frequent than offenses against property or morals. However, the Indians show a tendency to bring to the court their family difficulties as they brought them to the governor under the old regime. Problems of rape and illegitimacy, which did not figure under the system of polygyny, are beginning to appear. These and other major offenses are dealt with by the Federal courts.

Under the Indian Reorganization Act, the Indian courts will have jurisdiction over a definite number of offenses punishable under American law. The transition to a code of morals consonant with that of the individualistic and property conscious society around them should proceed rapidly and the rate and manner of adaptation in the different departments of morals will furnish an illuminating study.

# KNOWLEDGE AND TEACHING

Beside the crafts already mentioned, Papago knowledge included some techniques in counting, measuring and time reckoning. Any individual knew the measurements connected with his craft and those who had older relatives versed in history or star lore might pick up these also. But for a young person to question an older one was considered forward and discourteous so one desiring to learn merely haunted the society of an older relative until information was offered. If he had no relative with the desired knowledge, his chances of learning were small, since prolonged contacts with people outside the family were few.

## COUNTING AND MEASURING

Papago has words for the numbers up to ten; the one for ten definitely meaning "all the fingers". Other numbers are expressed as multiples of ten. For 100, the Spanish word *cien* is used. The Papago, in ancient times, rarely counted as high as this, nor had they a word for it. The expression which indicated counting was "to cut the notches" or "to lay down the sticks". This was done when making an appointment more than the ritual four days ahead. Ten, twelve or sixteen were the usual numbers, indicated by a stick with the proper number of notches or a bundle of small sticks. The recipient marked off a notch every day until the proper time or stood the sticks up in a row and laid one down each day.

In scoring for games, the Papago, according to Culin, used as much as 100 grains of corn[1] but they need not count to 100. Both sides drew from a common pile, uncounted and, when this was exhausted, played until one side had acquired all the corn of the other. In this way, even several hundred grains could be used without the necessity of naming the numbers.

Another occasion for counting was when one village "sang for" another and every householder among the singers had to receive a gift. On the night before the ceremony, the singers sent to their hosts a bundle of sticks representing the household heads in their party who might be as many as thirty or forty. However, they were not necessarily counted. The messenger connected a name with each stick and in the council meeting of the hosts, he held the sticks

---

[1] Culin, p. 354.

up one by one shouting the names and presenting them to the proper gift partners. Each stick recalled to him the name of a particular individual, a difficult form of mnemonics for Whites, but the Papago, trained in memorizing by rote, did not consider it as hard as abstract counting. Something like the same process may be observed today when an Indian, in trading at the store, points to an article, pays for it and gets the change before dealing with the next one.

The Papago word now used for *count* is kwint, obviously from the Spanish *cuentar*. But the writer, in studying a Spanish grammar of the Lower Pima,[1] was puzzled to find a Pima word which was translated count. After much conference with Papagos, it was decided that the word was *ha kiwikitat*, to whip them continually, and seemed to have been derived from the counting of strokes under the Spanish punishment system.

MEASURES

Dry measure was calculated by the basketful. The basket bowl, the winnowing basket and the carrying basket were roughly standard sizes and all had various decorative lines parallel to the rim by which fractions of their content could be measured. In measuring quantities for trade, however, both parties to the bargain used the same basket so they could be sure of equal measure.

For linear measure, parts of the body were used. Women, in making a basket, took as a unit the handbreatdh: the distance between the outstretched thumb and forefinger. Half a handbreadth was the length of the first finger and "less than a handbreadth" the distance between thumb and first finger. For more exactitude, the worker used the distances between various fingertips, with the hand outstretched.

Men measured the length of wood for a bow by the distance from the tip of the second finger to the breast bone, when the arm was stretched forward. The arrow should be as long as the space between the hands when pulling the bow string. Lengths of rope were measured by the distance between the fingertips when the arms were outspread or, for short ropes, the distance from elbow to wrist.

CEREMONIAL NUMBERS AND DIRECTIONS

The Papago ceremonial number is four and four is continually used whenever small amounts are thought of. Possibly, in former

---

[1] Grammar of the Pima or Nevome, a language of Sonora, from a manuscript of the XVIII Century. Edited by Buckingham Smith, 1862.

times, this was as far as they counted without the aid of sticks and notches. Four directions are recognized, with ceremonial colors. East literally "under the sunrise" is always white, and west, "under the sunset", always black, possibly because a disagreable wind comes from there. North is "the direction from which floods come," its color red or blue. South is "the direction where rubbish is piled" (in floods) but also "the direction of the ocean" and "the direction of suffering," since the Gulf of California, the goal of the arduous salt expedition lay that way. The color of the south is red or yellow.

Papagos have no words for left and right and never speak of the hands or of the directions in that way. Neither do they often use the ceremonial terms for the directions but point with the lips or the hand and use an adverb which means yonder far, yonder near yonder up (which always connotes east and the upward movement of the sun) yonder down, (which connotes west). But they are always conscious of the directions and all ceremonial groups are oriented so that a description of them involves a plan drawn in the sand. The circuit in dancing or passing the ceremonial cigarette is always counter clockwise. In at least one ceremony, the orator speaks first at the east, then north, then south and then, making three quarters of a circuit, comes back to the west.

### TIME RECKONING

The Papago year begins in July with the ripening of the giant-cactus, the beginning of rainy season. There are no standard names for the months, but a number of descriptive terms can be used for each period between one "death of the moon" and the next. Since these describe well known natural phenomena, anyone can recognize a month by any of its appellations. The following are terms frequently used:

| July | tcuuki(macaṭ) | rain (moon) |
|------|---------------|-------------|
|      | haacainyi paʼk | giant cactus ripe |
| August | cópori iïcapiʼk | short planting |
|      | kïʼï tcuupiopiʼk | big rain |
| Sept | wácai kákitaʼk | dry grass |
| Oct  | ari tcutcukiopiʼk | little rain |
|      | wiʼkhanyiʼk | frost |
| Nov  | sʼkïïk sʼïhpitciʼk | pleasant cold (time for games and races) |
| Dec  | kïʼï sʼïhpitciʼk | big cold (month for wiikita) |
| Jan  | kíhutaʼkc | animals thin |
| Feb  | uuwarik | smelling (deer mating, strong smell) |
|      | komaki macaṭ | gray moon |

| March | tcïïta'ki macaṭ | green moon (mesquite begins to green) |
| April | úam mácaṭ | yellow moon (greasewood and other yellow flowers) |
| May | u'us wihoktari'k | mesquite buds |
| | ko'o'k macaṭ | painful moon (no food yet) |
| June | kaitc tcukuri'k | seeds black |

For indicating the time of day, Papagos still point to the sky and say: "when the sun stands there" or "there". There are definite words meaning the first gray of dawn; the time when objects are visible, sun-rise, midday, sunset and night. Time at night is designated by the position of the Pleiades.

The Pleiades are called the Travellers and they, rather than the sun, are used for designating seasons. The calculation is made from their position at dawn, as follows:

Pleiades rising in summer, start planting
At the zenith at dawn, too late to plant more.
Past the zenith, time for corn harvest
One quarter down from the zenith, time for deer hunting
Setting, time for the harvest feast.

The winter solstice was noted and the sun was considered to stand still then for four days, beginning with the first day on which the Pleiades had set at dawn. The writer heard of no devices for watching the position of the sun itself, as the Pima watch the gap of the Sierra Estrella. The four day solstice period was, with the Papago, a sacred one on which the origin myth was officially told. The explanation of the moon's regular disappearance was that it died every month and a new moon took its place. Both sun and moon were said to die in an eclipse and to resurrect themselves as did Elder Brother in the origin myth.

Several star groups were named, many of them not coincident with our own. The three stars in Orion's Belt were called Deer, Antelope, and Mountain Sheep, while a bright star as short distance away is Wind Man who has just shot an arrow at the sheep and missed. The arrow is a small star, nearly invisible. The Milky Way is called the second harvest of pitahaya (organ pipe cactus) since this harvest is very abundant. The Dipper is the *kuipaṭ*, cactus stick, a long pole with two transverse sticks for hooking the fruit from the top of the saguaro column. Five stars in a semicircle, with five more stretching down at right angles to them are called Elder Brother's Hand and Arm with which he once held up the sky. They may be part of Scorpio. Others not identified are:

Maiden at Puberty with Instructors: — a semi-circle of stars with one bright one in the middle; the Pestle: — two stars horizontal, two vertical; Flock of quail: — a cluster of small stars; the North Star, called the Unmoving Star: — it is the stopper for the hole in the sky through which Buzzard took refuge in the flood.

Papago youth were taught the tribal traditions by listening to the official narrators who told them as often as asked during the winter months, but always during the "four days" of the winter solstice. Beside this ancient history the record of recent events was kept on a calendar stick similar to that recorded for the Pima.[1]

The first entry is in "the year the world went wrong": 1839 while the facturis of Sonora were at war and the southern Papago settlements were broken up. The man who began it was a boy at the time and was "startled" by the catastrophe; so cut a notch in a stick to remember it. However, the earliest Pima stick known had been begun in 1833 so that he may have had model to suggest the idea. The Papago stick was kept first at Standing Rock, then at San Xavier, and there were, besides, one at Anegam and possibly others. Keeping a stick was entirely a personal venture, undertaken by anyone who had enterprise and memory for the task. The keeper stored it in his own house and passed it down to any male descendant capable of memorizing its record.

The San Xavier calendar stick is a length of cactus rib, six feet long and with notches cut on its flat side about an inch apart. Each notch represents a year and is cut after the liquor ceremony which inaugurates the rainy season and the Papago year. In the space between the notches, the keeper of the stick marks any crude device which occurs to him as a means of memorizing the year's events. The symbols are roughly incised and colored with red and blue, made from red clay and greasewood soot. A few simple signs have been worked out, such as a puncture in the middle of the space, representing the quadrennial harvest ceremony and a scratch at the side, meaning a death. Otherwise the symbols are the personal invention of the maker and his successor must learn them by heart.

The San Xavier stick was, until twenty years ago, at Standing Rock in the keeping of the man who began it. He frequently recited its record and some of the older men learned it. At his death, his widow broke the stick and threw it away as a ceremonial act, but two San Xavier men rescued the pieces and copied them. The present custodian is the son-in-law of one of these two, the son having been unable to memorize the symbols. The custodian, in

---

[1] Russell, pp. 34—38.

reciting the history of the stick, uses the technique of the origin myth: he begins at the beginning and proceeds straight through, without interruption and using as many nights as are necessary. It was by hearing such recitals that he himself learned the record. The writer negotiated with him for pauses at certain points when questions might be asked but he found it very difficult to remember under such circumstances. Papago etiquette requires that the learner shall never interrupt.

### MEMORIZING

Akin to the learning of the calendar record is the learning of rituals. These, as mentioned above, are passed down by their owners to chosen male relatives but when no relative is available, the council itself may ask that a stranger be instructed. The method of instruction is for the teacher to recite the whole ritual through as many times as needed and then for the learner to say it all through. This sounds difficult but there are certain aids to memory in that the directions are always mentioned in order, every episode occurs four times and there are standard poetic phrases always recurring in specific connections. Still, learning a long ritual by this process may take a year.

Understanding the ritual is a separate accomplishment, not possessed by all. The writer found some old men who had spent years in thinking over their memorized material and discussing it with others. But this had been done after the learning was finished: while in the position of pupil, they had no right to ask questions and many of them had never done so. As a result they had learned by rote not only archaic words but misplaced words, and could not understand their own ritual. The habit of learning by heart, with the meaning a secondary consideration and questions forbidden, is to be considered in the teaching of Papagos in modern schools. The doubt and analysis to which White children are conditioned, even before school age, are absent in Papago attitudes and must be taught in school, not taken for granted.

# WAR

War, with the Papagos, was not an occasion for prestige as with the Plains tribes nor of booty as with the Apache. It was a disagreeable necessity. The enemy, generally the Apache, was regarded as a shaman. His person, or anything that had touched him, was taboo. Therefore all booty was burned and the man who had killed an enemy or been wounded by him had to go through a long ordeal of purification.

War was enveloped in a mass of ritual but none of it was in glorification of combat. The ceremonial orations frequently end: "It is that vile wretch (the enemy) not we, who is uttering threats." Men were urged to fight in order to do their duty by their kinsmen and when this duty was done, they had to spend both time and material goods in purification during which they were frequently adjured:

> "Verily who desires this?
> Do not you desire it?
> Then learn to endure hardship."

The reward of victory for the individual was the acquisition of power, not for war, but for curing. For the community as a whole it was that summum bonum of an agricultural people, rain and a good harvest.

Nevertheless, because of the Apache menace, the Papago were forced to train their youths to war; the respected men in the community had to be Enemy Slayers and a man who had no taste for fighting at all was practically forced to declare himself a berdache. Training began when boys were about fourteen.

In leisure periods, like the time after harvest, boys would be gathered daily at the house of the Keeper of the Meeting and he or the war leader would tell them war stories and explain fighting methods (9). Beginning with the age of twelve or so, they were given practice in using the shield, in shooting and dodging arrows. A row of boys holding shields would stand at one end of an open space and at the other a row with bows and blunt, wooden-tipped arrows. They were told to run toward each other and at a given distance the archers were to shoot, aiming at the legs so a wound would not be dangerous.

The business of the shield bearers was not to attack but to learn to dodge the arrows. They were told never to stand with their legs together, since this made a better target. They were to watch the arrows as they left the bow, to squat to avoid the high ones, leap to avoid the low ones, or throw the body from side to side. Boys practised in this way alone whenever they had a chance. They also practised shooting, by throwing a bundle of rags in the air and trying to shoot it before it fell. Before a war party all the fighters practised in this way under the direction of the war leader or the retired warriors.

The Apache were the enemies of whom the Papago went in constant fear. Although the Spanish writers speak of Yuman captives taken by the "Pimas" and of wars among the Pimas themselves, these differences must have ceased with the growing of the Apache menace. The word *ohp*, enemy, is always translated Apache, for which there is no other term. No distinction is made between the divisions of the Apache or between Apache and Navajo, and the term might possibly include other nomadic tribes, such as the Comanche.

The Apache raided storehouses and carried off young women as captives, but their principal objective was horses, which they wanted not to ride but to eat. "They were always hungry." Apprehension because of an attack was a constant factor in Papago life. "You never knew when an Apache would jump yelling off the roof of your house when you went out at dawn" (27). The men were urged nightly in the council to be on their guard. A typical speech of admonition given by a father to his sons is the following:

"At dawn you must rise. Listen all about you for something. Look all about you for something. All kinds of things there may be for you to find. Apache tracks may be visible. If you find them, you will tell of it and you will follow. Even if you do not overtake them, you will follow far before you drop the trail. You will learn that certainly they passed that way. Perhaps you will learn that there are many of them, camping somewhere, expecting to come down and attack us." (22)

But the principal time for raids was in winter, after the harvest was in. The short rainy season in midwinter was the best opportunity. "The Apaches are shamans. They control the mist and rain and always travel under cover of it." The usual attack was made before dawn, when some horses were run off and a few women and children killed. In one case, there is record of a whole village being exterminated.

"One night my mother told my father she was sure something was going to happen, so they left the village. That night the Apache came. Some of the women were out in the menstruation house, which was a quarter mile from the village. There were severeal women there together, one with a child. They saw three men walking about. Then they heard sounds. The woman with the child went near her own home, where her husband was with some men and called to him that there were men walking about the village He said, "No, it can't be." The woman still heard those men who were really Apache scouts and again she called to her husband. He said, "It is only cows. Go to sleep." The woman did not dare to go near any of the other houses to warn them, because she was unclean after childbirth.

The Apache scouts went back and reported and next morning the enemy came. There was a clear space around the village and the Papagos could see the enemy as they approached. But the Apache had a shaman who prevented the Papagos knowing who it was. The Apaches sang as they approached and the Papagos thought it was another village coming to sing for them. When the enemy came near enough to be recognized, they ran for their weapons and rushed out to attack. They killed many Apache but the Apache in the end killed all of them.

One old man had gathered all the women and children and placed them in the ceremonial house. He used the bottom of a granary basket for a door and he stood by it to keep them in. The Apache, when they had killed all the men, attacked the ceremonial house. They killed the old man and all the older women and the younger women they took away as prisoners." (26)

More often some horses would be missed, or word would be brought by a runner of moccasin tracks in the neighborhood. In that case, the news was shouted through the village immediately, but the men waited till night to make their plans. During the day the Enemy Slayers met in the house of one of them to discuss a plan of campaign to present at the meeting.

The meeting proceeded with its usual formality. The Keeper in the customary low voice made a speech urging all men to do their duty and not desert their kinsmen. Many older men would repeat these sentiments, until the meeting was in the proper frame of mind. Then volunteers were called for. Here the young men, who were not permitted to speak, had a chance to step forward. No man would volunteer if he had not a full war equipment, since the articles were too hard to procure. Also he would not go if his wife were pregnant or menstruating, since this would take away his strength.

After volunteering, the young men left the meeting to repair their war equipment and to get some sleep. The older men remained to discuss the plan of campaign. If there were a permanent war leader, he stayed with them. If not, they decided on a man, who would later be notified.

They might also decide to invite several partner villages to join them and messengers would be sent out, running. The plan was always to fix a rendezvous somewhere near the boundaries of Papago country. This was generally at the base of the mountains to the east. "The Apaches never came down from the mountains except to raid. The mountains were their country. When they were escaping, they always ran straight up hill." (19) If the need were immediate, the meeting might be fixed for the next night. Otherwise the conventional interval was ten days. The messengers were given ten sticks to deliver. The Keeper at the partner village was to stand these up in the floor of the Big House and to lay one down each day. When they were all down, his war party started. The ritual speech made before the start has the title "Sticks Laid Down".

In the ten day interval the warriors exercised and prepared their equipment. They carried shield and club or bow and arrows as they chose. Specialization in one or the other form of fighting was a permanent arrangement, only a few of the bravest using shield and club, which meant close-in fighting. Archers put a new string on the bow and carried another string in the quiver. They carried three hundred arrows, stone-tipped if possible, but a few wooden ones might be used to fill out the number. Every man took two pairs of sandals. Many wore headdresses in any form that suited them and these were repaired and made by the warrior himself.

When equipped, the warrior had his quiver slung over the right shoulder, so that it hung with the opening at the left, just at the waist. His bow he carried in his left hand and while fighting he would have several arrows in this hand also. His other baggage hung from the thong around his waist that held the breechclout. Even if he were not a club fighter, he might carry a club to finish the enemy. This was hung directly at the back. At the right he had a pouch, containing cornmeal which, mixed with water, would be his only food. In the same pouch might be a smaller one for tobacco and cornhusks or reed tubes for cigarettes. Another small pouch contained black and white paints. A half gourd, to serve as mixing bowl and drinking cup was slung from his belt by a thong. Some warriors distributed these various possessions in several pouches, elaborately made of fox or other animal skin with the fur on.

The warrior's hair was clubbed in a knot at the back of his neck. He wore one of several sorts of headdress or possibly none at all. His face according to some informants, was painted black from the start (9), and after killing an enemy, the lower part was white. According to others, it was not painted at all until he had killed

9*

an enemy and then all black (19, 26). Black paint was considered
symbolic of dizziness and drunkenness and therefore of war. One
of the chants says:

> "My desire was the black madness of war.
> I ground it to powder and therewith I painted my face.
> My desire was the black dizziness of war.
> I tore it to shreds and therewith tied my hair in a war knot."

When the war parties started out, each had a leader, either permanent or appointed temporarily by the council. The oldest and
most experienced of these leaders would take charge of the
combined expedition. There would be at least one crier who could
make the announcements in camp, or one would be appointed by
the leader.

Each village if possible brought a shaman to "see" the enemy
and to recite spells to disable him. These shamans were of a
particular class, the "owl meeters", who had owls for their guardian
spirits. The dead are supposed to fly back from the east, where they
live, in the form of owls. Dead Papago warriors, in owl form, haunted
the enemy country where they died and with these the shaman
communed.

The parties from the partner villages met at night at the rendezvous and went through a series of ceremonies. During these, it was
the duty of the shaman to retire and to practise divination which
would tell where the enemy might be encountered. If there were
several shamans, they all worked together.

"Once the men from several villages met for a war party at Basket
Cap mountain. At night they sat and sang the war songs, facing
the country of the enemy. All that time the shaman sat apart, on a
little knoll. When the singing was over, the leader asked the
shaman, "Can you give us news?"

The shaman said, "I think there is one here who will help me."
Then he went back to the knoll and the men heard the hoot of an
owl. Soon the shaman came back to them. He said, "Has anyone
here some of the old tobacco we used to use?"

One man had, so he gave it to the shaman. The shaman went
away and the men watching could see that he lit two cigarettes.
They could see their red tips moving as you see cigarettes that are
held by two people. Then they saw one of them thrown away. The
shaman came back, holding the other. He said, "The enemy are
at Smooth Ground. We'll come up with them at noon tomorrow."

So they did and they killed many Apaches. If it had not been
true, perhaps they would have killed the shaman." (19)

The war leader also sent out scouts and continued to do so as
they advanced into the enemy country. They travelled by night and

hid by day until they encountered a troupe of the enemy or a village. The villages rarely contained anyone but women and children since the men were constantly away raiding. One attack on a village was described as follows:

"The men all separated and each one waited outside one Apache wickiup, till the signal to attack. My father was outside a wickiup where there were several women roasting something and he listened to their strange voices and wondered if they were saying, "The Desert People are here." Finally the signal came: the call of a roadrunner. Our men attacked, whooping. The women ran out of the houses and the men stood at the doors waiting to club them. My father took hold of an old woman but she was strong and wrestled with him. He called to the others, "Help! The old enemy woman is killing me!" So others came and they broke in the old woman's skull. A few other men killed but the rest of the women got away. Our men burned the houses and the booty and went home." (26)

If it was possible to locate a band of male enemies, they tried to "make a house for the Apache", that is, surround the band or trap it in a canyon. Various accounts tell how the shaman divined where the enemy would be and how this strategem was carried out. The archers shot first from ambush, then the men with clubs rushed in for close fighting. There were never very many of these and they were only the bravest men. They always advanced leaping and when leaping backward to retreat they held the shield behind them to break a fall. There was no mass formation and no commands from the war leader except the signal to begin. The affair was a series of duels where each warrior got his man, if possible, and then retired from the combat.

"My father and one Apache were separated from the others shooting arrows at each other. There was a giant cactus between them and each kept dodging behind it, till the cactus was full of arrows. They both knew a little Mexican and the Apache called out in that language, "I am a *man*!" My father shouted, "I, too, am a *man*!" Then they wrestled. My father was down and he shouted for help. His brother came and between them they clubbed the Apache. Then they were both Enemy Slayers."

Even if there was no Apache attack, a punitive expedition generally took place each winter to avenge some former raid. For this there was plenty of time and the villages of one or even two related groups might join. The Papago calendar stick which chronicles the events of the last eighty-five years provides a number of typical examples.

1867-68. Some Apaches came to Worm Pond, while the people were singing for rain. They stole some horses and made off.

Later a band of deer hunters, coming through Flat Wells, found Apache tracks. They sent to warn the people at Worm Pond but the messenger waited until after eating before he gave the news. The chief rebuked him and said, "Why didn't you tell us sooner?" Then all went for their horses and one man, approaching his, saw an Apache in the act of untying the hobbles. The Apache escaped. The Papagos followed the Apache tracks all night by moonlight. They would have caught up with them, but there was an evil shaman among the Papagos who advised his people to turn around and go home. So they did, although they were very near the Apache who were tired and expected death.

The next year Apache stole some Papago cattle and drove the animals through a Papago settlement to announce the fact. The Papagos rode after them and got into a canyon. The Apache were on a mountain top above them. There was an unequal fight. The Papagos captured a horse with some meat and rawhide tied on the saddle. The Apache wounded two Papagos.

Next year some people from Kuhatk went on the warpath. They came to a hill where the Apache had left their water bottles and spare moccasins. They thought the Apaches must be near and sent out two scouts who saw them gathered around a fire. The scouts returned and told the other Papagos who rushed in and clubbed all the Apache. Only one Apache shaman had felt evil in the wind and had made his escape with a friend.

Later that year, a man named Blisters led out another war party. At Buzzard Claw mountain one man had to leave and turn back. On his way some Apache spied him from a mountain top, came down, hid in the bushes where he would pass and shot him. The Papagos chased the Apache and found some cattle they had killed but could not catch up with the Apache themselves. The Apache were on a mountain top, which was always their place of refuge. They would come down a little way and then, if they saw the Papagos were still circling about, would go back again. Finally they made a dash down the mountain and got away. The Papagos saw a smoke signal ahead of them and then, as they followed, another and another, so they knew there was no use going on: more Apache were being summoned.

They went home, found the horse of the man who had been killed from ambush and finally followed the trail back to the man himself. The man had been dead some days. They burned the body as was always done with an Apache victim.

The next year two Mexicans were killed by the Apaches near San Xavier and the Mexicans asked the help of the San Savier Papagos in avenging them. San Xavier sent word to their relatives at Coyote Village and told them to come without stopping for supplies: the San Xavier women would be grinding corn for them. The Coyote men came instantly and they all started that night. They travelled

all the next day and then camped close to the Apache village.
Before dawn they attacked it and killed all the people who were
asleep. Those who were awake escaped. The Papagos brought some
children back as prisoners and kept them as their own. When they
were grown and able to work, they sold them in Sonora for $ 100
each.

### COMPARISON WITH PIMA

These narratives bear out the statement of the Papagos that they
fought only in self-defense. They resemble the narrative of Pima
battles,[1] except where the Pimas joined with their more organized
neighbors, the Maricopas. They are decidedly at variance, however,
with the accounts given of the "Pimas" by the early Spaniards.
Kino reports in the Santa Cruz valley fortified towns and a chief
who could command five hundred men.[2] Their battle in the open
with agreements and challenges is entirely different from the Papago
style of warfare, and resembles that reported for Yumas and
Maricopas.[3]

"... the news reached the neighboring rancheria of Quiburi
.... and immediately its captain, el Coro, came to the rescue with
his brave people, together with other Pimas who had come from the
west to barter for maize and who contributed to the fortunate
outcome of the event, for they were supplied with the arms which
we had bidden them to provide to go on the expedition with the
soldiers of the presidio. The captain of the enemy, called el Capotcari, proposed — for with Captain Coro came many Pimas — that
they should fight, ten on one side and ten on the other. Captain
Coro accepted the proposal and selected ten Pimas, while Captain
Capotcari selected ten others, the most valiant of all he had. Five
were Apaches as was also one of the other five.
They began shooting their arrows, and, as the Pimas are very
dextrous in shooting and also in parrying the arrows of their
adversaries and as the Apaches, although dextrous in shooting
arrows and with the lance, are not dextrous in parrying the arrows,
five Pimas soon wounded the five Apaches who were their antagon-
ists, as did four other Pimas their adversaries, who were the
Hocomes and Xanos. Captain Capotcari was very skilful in catching
the arrows but his opponent, a valiant Pima, grappled with him
and, struggling, threw him to the ground and beat his head with
stones. Thereupon, all the rest of the enemy began to flee and the
Pimas followed them .... killing and wounding more than three
hundred, of whom fifty odd remained dead and stretched out

---

[1] Russell, pp. 38—52.    [2] Allegre III, pp. 100—101.
[3] Russell, pp. 40,41.

nearby, and the rest, as they were wounded with the poisonous herb, died along the trails.[1]

The "Pimas" here spoken of were the Sóba Jípuris who later became amalgamated with the people of San Xavier. There was probably a good deal of cultural difference between these agricultural eastern people and the western nomads whose unwillingness to fight was noted even by the Spaniards.[2]

### PURIFICATION

The Spaniards, although they mention the scalp dance, say nothing of the arduous process of purification which constituted a killer an Enemy Slayer. The central idea of this seems to be that the enemy and all his possessions were dangerous. Contact with them, even though it was victorious, put a man in touch with supernatural power which could destroy him unless he fasted and dreamed in order to learn to handle it.

Therefore a man who had killed an enemy left the fight immediately. He blackened his face, fasted and used a scratching stick and kept away from the others until he was ritually purified. According to one informant, it was possible to avoid the ritual of becoming an Enemy Slayer, if one were willing to take the risk and waive the privileges it involved. Some men "like to fight but didn't dream much." These might ignore the killing of an enemy or turn the prerogatives of a Slayer over to another man. The idea of contamination attached also to a Papago wounded by the enemy. He must be segregated and go through the same purification as a Slayer. This was true even of a wounded woman.

"Once the Apache stabbed a woman at Field Pond. The Papagos had had the drinking ceremony and this woman's husband had stabbed her while drunk. The woman ran away to where the Water Whirls Around but her husband followed her on a mare and got her to come back with him.

West of the Place of the Dead Dog they passed a mesquite tree and some Apaches leaped out. The horse shied, the woman fell off and the Apaches stabbed her. However, they did not kill her.

She was then taboo just like a wounded warrior or an Enemy Slayer. She could not be taken into the village, but the Papagos built a fire and an old woman, the wife of an Enemy Slayer, came out to take care of her. Then they built a shelter and the old woman stayed with her for sixteen days." (19)

Dead comrades and all their possessions must be burned, not buried as was the usual custom. Dead enemies must not be touched

---

[1] Bolton, 1919, 1, p. 179.          [2] Doc. Hist. III, v. 4, p. 892.

except by one who had been through the purification of an Enemy Slayer or who was about to go through it. But as many as liked might gather around and make comments on the dead enemy's appearance. Whatever they shouted would be used later as their own nicknames and such names were much prized. One man had the nickname Gold Breasts, because he had used this expression about a dead Apache girl. Another was called Big Ribs because of his comment on a man.

No booty could be taken. All enemy possessions must be burned by Enemy Slayers, qualified to touch it. There were two exceptions. Enemy women and children were sometimes captured, not to be adopted, but to be sold as slaves in one of the markets. They could bring nothing with them, however. All their clothes and possessions must be burned.

Also, each killer took a trophy from his victim. This was originally the scalp and so it appears in the tales of Elder Brother's campaign. Later it was only a lock of hair or four hairs from' each temple. These were subsequently tied up with beads and ornaments or made into an effigy of the enemy himself with Apache dress and weapons. After the warrior's purification this served him as a fetish which must be tended and which would, in turn, give him power. Some men did not take scalps at all but brought one article of clothing, such as a moccasin or belt. This object was purely ceremonial. It was not to be used but to be kept in a basket like the effigy.

The formalities after a fight have been given in detail in another place. They involved the segregation of the Slayers for sixteen days, during which they were tended and instructed by ceremonial godfathers who, ever afterward, were regarded as relatives and so adopted into the gift giving circle. The wives of the godfathers tended the warriors' wives who were also secluded and made the new clay bowl and the olla for bathing water which was supplied to them each every four days. Meantime the warrior's relatives collected goods to pay the performers of the leaping dance which would purify his weapons on the final night of purification.

During the warrior's seclusion, the whole village danced around the scalp every night. It was finally purified on the last night by a leaping dance, performed by people of another village bearing the warrior's weapons and paid by his family. If the warrior were one of those particularly daring ones who fought with club and shield, a new shield was sometimes made for him on this occasion but this seems to have been optional. He sat through the purification of his weapons and finally was, himself, purified by the singing of other scalpers who, as mentioned before, had something the status of an informal priesthood. Finally he was given the scalp, enclosed in a special ceremonial basket, like those which held the village arcana.

It was for this final reward that men really went to war. The safety of the village and the fact that a scalp brought it rain were stressed in speeches and were certainly the motive for a war party being ordered. But the individual had a definite emolument when he procured this trophy which would bring him luck ever afterward and which was a definite source of material income. The presence of the scalp and the songs learned during purification cured the scalp sickness which meant any nervous disorder or sexual excitement. Such things were thought to be akin to the madness of war and the warrior who had power over such madness could cure them and thus "feed himself."

His scalp trophy, as the saying was: "worked for him like a relative." The interpretation of his relationship with it was that he had taken it into his family. He now had to "feed" it with tobacco and eagle down, and, according to some, talk frequently to it, telling it his plans. It would reciprocate, as relatives did with that which it had to give, *i. e.* power in war and general good luck. But if he neglected it, the gift would not be made: the scalp would cease to be a relative and would do him harm just as it did to the uninitiated.

# GAMES AND BETTING

Legend says that, when the Underground People were considering their emergence, they sent Gopher up to spy on the earth and he reported favorably in these words: "There are many people there playing all sorts of games." This gives some indication of the extreme importance of games in the Papago system. Men and women played whenever they were at leisure and each village had its famous athletes and its experts in games of chance. These had attained their eminence through supernatural experiences and were not only an honor to the village but a source of income. For all games involved gambling. It is a question whether the subject of games should not head a chapter on economics for there was probably more large scale exchange of goods in the betting on games than in any other situation of Papago life, not excepting marriage. Although bitter hardship kept Papagos frugal most of the time, they abandoned caution in their wagers. This intimate connection of betting with all sport has proved a problem for Whites who wish to revive the excellent old games. To the Papago mind, those games do not exist without the accompanying bets.

All games for adults had probably some ceremonial connected with them though little remains of it at present. They could be played informally by any group of men or women who had leisure, for the two sexes never played or bet together. But they appeared in their most elaborate form at the intervillage meets which took place after harvest when a formal ceremonial of challenge was observed, magic songs were sung and all the surplus harvest was wagered on the outcome. These games may be divided for descriptive purposes into two classes: the sedentary games which were almost all pure games of chance, and the athletic contests, involving chance and prowess.

### GAMES OF CHANCE
### Hidden Ball (wópitah, laid down).

Four sections of hollow reed are filled with sand and in one of them is hidden a wild scarlet bean, Erithitheria flabelliformis. One group of players hides the bean while the other guesses its whereabouts. The sections of reed are about four inches long, cut so there is a joint closing one end while the other is open. The reeds are marked with notches colored with soot and each has a name, and, to the Papago mind, a personality.

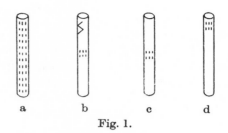

Fig. 1.

a) Old: Man three vertical rows of notches.
b) Old: Woman a zigzag line near the top said to represent the tatoo mark on a woman's chin. Sometimes the Old Woman is unmarked.
c) Black belly: black dots in two rows around the middle.
d) Hair-tied-up: black dots in two rows near the open end.

The number of dots in the rows seems not to be constant since several different numbers were met with, while Russell for the Pima, gives another number still.[1] Apparently the requirement is that the "Old Man" should be covered with dots, that Black Belly should have them near the middle and Head Tied Up near the end, while the Old Woman has none at all or a zigzag line. The four are thought of in sets of two, Old Man and Old Woman being partners and also the two "young people". This elaborate personification of the reeds, however, has nothing to do with the game which could quite well be played with unmarked sticks.

Two men play on each side, one to hide and one to guess, but any number more may bet, sing and assist the leaders with suggestions. The four who are to play squat in pairs opposite each other. A blanket is laid across their knees and two or four men stand ready to hold it over the side hiding the bean until the operation is concluded. Sometimes the men are hidden, heads and all.

To decide which side shall hide first, each takes one pair of "partner" sticks, hides the bean in one of the two and tosses the pair to the opponents. Their guesser is supposed to pick up the tube holding the bean and the side guessing right does the hiding first. If there is a tie, both sides guessing right or both wrong, they continue until one side wins.

The side winning this preliminary takes all four sticks, is covered with the blanket and hides the bean in one of the four. There is

[1] Russell, p. 176.

much science in this for, the bean being lighter than sand, the opponents are supposed to tell by the balance of the tube whether it contains all sand or part bean. The hider, therefore, inserts sand in varying quantities each time. The hiding being done, he throws all four tubes down before his opponents, open ends toward them. The hider's side sing furiously to distract the guessing. The guesser makes up his mind by the apparent weight of the reed and by the expression of the hider's face as the guesser lets his hand hover first over one reed and then another. A good hider will achieve a poker face by keeping his eyes down so the guesser can catch no glint in them.

The guesser does not speak but, having made up his mind, arranges the reeds in position. First he eliminates two in which he does not consider the bean to be by laying them crosswise, one over the other. Next he lays down the one he thinks contains the bean and then the fourth one. They should lie as in fig. 2 or occasionally the two eliminated tubes lie parallel (fig. 3) with *a* furthest away from the chosen tube.[1]

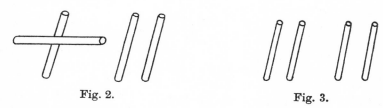

Fig. 2.     Fig. 3.

He picks up first the third tube, where he thinks the bean is and empties out the sand. If the bean is there, he does not score but has the privilege of hiding the bean again. If the bean is not there he next empties the fourth tube, (d) and if the bean is there he loses 4. Then he takes b, the upper one of the crossed tubes and if the bean is there he loses 6. If it is in (a) the lower one of the crossed tubes he loses 10.[2]

---

[1] Although Spier, Havasupai Ethnography, p. 352, states that the Papago expect to find the bean in the fourth tube, contrary to the usual Southwest custom, my informants said definitely that it should be in the third.

[2] This corresponds in amounts with Maricopa scoring, Spier, 1933, p. 341. Spier, however, states that the Pima and Papago expected to find the bean in the fourth tube while my informants said that it was in the third as is usual in the Southwest. There are, doubtless, many variations in scoring.

One informant thought that the guesser simply picked up one tube and if it proved the wrong one he lost "the value of the tube". Values were: Old Man, 4: Old Woman, 10: Black Belly, 0: Head Tied, 6. This is similar to one form of Maricopa scoring, and gives a reason for the differentiating of the sticks.

Scoring is done with grains of corn a pile of which is placed on the ground between the two sides. When one side loses by a wrong guess, the opponents take the proper number of grains from the central pile. When the central pile is exhausted the winners take from the losers' pile. They play until one side has all the corn.

Culin states that the original pile should contain a hundred grains[1] but the writer as previously explained, doubts if the Papago counted so high.

A game of hidden ball usually lasted from sunrise to sunset. It could be played informally by a few men who had leisure time on their hands but all important games were formal occasions. Each village had a few men who were famous gamblers, known for unmoved faces and trickiness in hiding the bean. Such men had usually had a supernatural experience which gave them the requisite power. One informant, after killing an eagle, had been visited by the dead bird who promised him success and told him always to fling down the tubes with their openings toward the east. He never lost.

Two famous gamblers in a village might challenge each other. Then they would ask for a meeting in the council house, announce their intention and each would ask for volunteers on his side. His relatives and those who believed in his luck would join him and spend the intervening time collecting goods to wager. Their leader generally did the guessing and had an assistant as hider. All the others offered suggestions and sang to confuse the opponents. If they thought the leader's luck was failing they would put forward another guesser. A young man who had had a vision might suddenly offer himself in this capacity and win great fame.

If the game was between villages, a challenge might be issued in the spring for a meet after harvest. Each village held a meeting and selected its principal guesser and assistants. Almost all the male population assisted with suggestions.

The songs for hidden ball were, like other magic-working songs, the high points of a myth recounting a legendary occurrence. A young wife was pregnant when her husband's older brother, who had wanted her for himself, killed her husband. The murderer fled and became a famous gambler. The child, growing up, continually asked his mother as to his uncle's whereabouts and how he could take vengence. He decided to gamble with his uncle and to bet his life, and for the purpose, invented the game of hidden ball.

His mother told him where to find the reeds and he marked them as they are now. He made Hair-Tied first and that reed was always

---

[1] Culin, p. 354.

the most powerful. When he practiced the game, he put the bean first in Old Man but that reed is not powerful and his opponents guessed it. Next he tried Old Woman which also they guessed. Then he put it in Hair-Tied-Up which they did not guess. The superstition still is that the first bean of the game will be in that reed. He played with his uncle, won all his goods and finally his life.

Only one of the songs was transcribed:

> Hair Tied Up, that is my pet!
> Before my adversaries I drop it.

Another form of hidden ball was *tciwit wɔpitah*, (laid down in the earth) where the bean was hidden, not in a reed but in one of four piles of sand. The two lines of players sat with one long heap of sand between them. The blanket was held over the hiding side and over the heap of sand while the hider, holding the bean, ran his hand along the sand and dropped the bean into it. He then separated the sand into four mounds; the blanket was removed and the opponents guessed which mound held the bean. Their procedure was to go direct to the mound selected and pull it apart. If the bean was there, they obtained the privilege of hiding it. If the bean was not there, their opponents scored one. Scoring in this case, was done by making marks on the sand and ten marks won the game. There were songs for this game also but none was recorded.

The hand game was called *i nonhai ap-i-wɔpitah* (in their hands laid). Four men played on a side, each having a stick one to two inches long tied to his middle finger by a loop of string or cotton cloth, which must be of the old, handwoven sort. Some thought that the sticks should be of four different woods: mesquite, ocatillo, palo verde and acacia. To decide which side should play first, a man of one side hides one stick while a man of the other guesses. A clap of the guesser's hands indicates that he has made his decision and that the hand to which he points must be opened. The guesser goes through the same sort of feints used in the modern game of Up Jenkins to make the hider open his hands before the clap. If the hider does so, the guesser's side gets the sticks to hide. Also if he guesses correctly they get the sticks but if incorrectly the hider's side gets them.

After this preliminary, the hiding side put their hands behind them, while attaching the sticks to the middle finger of either the right or left hand. The guesser may guess all the hiders at once or individually, thus: "In the outside hands, the inside hands" (the terms right and left are not used) "In those two outside, those two inside." Or he may point to players individually, always feinting first. Those who have been guessed correctly, leave the game, those guessed incorrectly, remain and hide their sticks again, while, for each wrong guess, the guessers lose one point. When all the hiders have finally guessed correctly, the guessers take the sticks.

Only one handgame song was transcribed, evidently part of a long story:

> The fly woman, the slim woman sits,
> The pumpkin in the pot (before her).

*kinyskut.* This dice game, like parchesi on a large outdoor scale, is played also by the Pimas[1] and by the Tarahumares.[2] The latter calling by the Spanish name *quince.* Since kut is a Papago nominalizing suffix, the word *kinyskut* might seem to have the same origin.

For kinyskut a space is cleared on the ground about eight to ten feet square. Each corner is marked with a hole one half inch deep and with four other holes extending along the sides of the square in each direction. These holes have names, the furthest from the corner being called the end, the next, end-top, then middle, corner-bottom and corner. At the upper right hand corner there is a semicircle of five holes outside the square. The game consists in moving stones, as counters, around the square beginning with this upper right hand corner, each move being made according to the shake of the dice.

The dice are four smooth sticks of ironwood, about ten inches long by one and one half inch wide, flat on one side, rounded on the other. On the flat side they are marked in red and black as shown below.

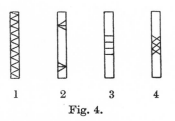

Fig. 4.

Stick no. 1 counts 15,   no. 2 counts 6,   no. 3 counts 4,   no. 4 counts 14.

The player holds all four sticks upright in his right hand and taps them on a flat stone which he holds in his left. Then he gives a slight jerk to the stone and the sticks fall apart on the ground. The count is as follows:

---

[1] RBAE 26, p. 176.        [2] Bennett.

stick no. 1 face up, others down 15
stick no. 2 face up, others down  6
stick no. 3 face up, others down  4
stick no. 4 face up, others down 14
all sticks face up           5
all sticks face down      10
two face up and two face down  2
one face down and three face up  3

The players are two or four men, never women nor children. They move the counters the number of places indicated by the throw, beginning with the semi-circle outside the upper right hand corner. East and West play together, moving clockwise around the circle, while North and South move counter clockwise. A player may move his partner's counter if it is advantageous. If his move brings him to a hole occupied by a counter of his opponents, that counter is "killed" and must go back to the beginning.

Only one *kiniyskut* song was remembered and that was to be sung at home, before playing:

> Down I shall throw!
> The smooth stone I shall move
> Move it to the corner. (26)

### GAMES OF CHANCE
#### (for women)

*ko'omai* (stick dice). The dice were four split sticks, their rounded outer sides with the bark on, or blackened with charcoal, the inner side left white or painted red. Each woman kept her own set of sticks. They sat in a circle and each one staked something which was placed inside the circle. Then each one in turn tapped her sticks on a flat stone and let them fall, as in kinskut. The scoring was:

| | |
|---|---|
| all black | 2 |
| all white | 1 |
| mixed colors | 0 |

Each girl threw once with her own set of sticks, then if she scored anything, once with her opponent's. If she scored O, she lost her second throw. Four points won the game and the winner took all the stakes.

Girls habitually played this on winter afternoons when they were at leisure. They would be surrounded by a ring of both men and women, betting on the result, while the girls themselves might bet any of their clothes or of their own manufactures.

*taawo* (bone dice) was played with four small bones, two inches long, from a cow's foot. They were thrown by each player in turn while all bet as to whether they would fall down or stand upright.

*mikitowua*, (similar to American "jackstones".) The game was to move small pebbles in various ways during the time that a thrown ball was in the air. The ball was a smooth round pebble, about two inches in diameter which each girl found for herself and called her *coika*, pet. The pebbles were four smaller ones of equal size. The girl playing threw up the pet and meantime made successively the following moves with the pebbles:

  1  Pick up pebbles one at a time, in right hand, each during one throw.

  2. Pick up two at a time.

  3. Pick up three at a time, then one.

  4. Hold left hand with finger tips touching ground, fingers apart. Push one pebble into each interstice.

  5. Hold one pebble in the hand with the pet and throw both up ten times, then place pebble as in no. 4.

  6. Lay left hand on ground, throw pebbles across it.

This game is played by children for pleasure as well as by women for gambling. Four girls would play at it all day.

### ATHLETIC CONTESTS
#### (for men)

*wuitcu'ţ* (kickball.) This was the typical Papago sport at which all young men were expected to show prowess. They practised constantly and a man going a long distance across the desert would kick his ball in front of him rather than run without it. The stimulus made running easier.

The ball was four inches in diameter, made of a small stone covered with mesquite gum or of mesquite wood hewn to spherical shape and polished with a stone. The men ran barefoot and kicked the ball ahead of them by pushing the big toe under it. The toenail in time, grew down over the toe and those of old men who have played all their lives are horny shells at least an eighth of an inch thick. Shoving the ball with the outside of the foot was also allowable.

The track was some particularly flat portion of the desert where there was little vegetation. The length was decided on for each contest and marked by a man standing at each end, an average length being twenty miles. Generally, two men played on each side, but more were possible. One man from each side started with the ball and his partner was stationed about 150 feet along the track. As the ball came down the track this second man rushed out and kicked it and took it along until the starter caught up and took his turn again. Any number of men might play if the sides agreed, each one kicking as he got a chance. When they approached the marker at the far end of the course, they left the ball, ran around the marker, and came back to kick the ball toward home.

Watchers accompanied the runners to cheer and to see fair play. After horses became common, the watchers were always on horseback.

Long distance racing without the kickball was almost equally popular. It is hard to calculate the territory covered without actually going over it but informants point out areas which should mean twenty-five or thirty miles. The race lasted from sunrise to sunset and was generally between only two men. They started from one village, raced to a distant village and returned, choosing their course over the desert as best they could. At frequent intervals men from both sides were stationed to watch their progress. Later there were horsemen who followed them all the way. *i-wopoitcu'ṭ* (making them run for themselves — footrace).

Every summer village had a racetrack near it, about a mile and a half long and eight feet wide. From this space every bush had been cleared away and it was swept daily with greasewood branches that thorns and pebbles might not injure the runners' bare feet. The youth of the village, boys and girls, practised running here and there were frequent contests between them on which all the villagers bet.

The rival runners started, not side by side but from either end of the track. If the race was between two individuals, they simply ran the length of the track or some lesser distance agreed on. The runner who first reached his rival's starting point had won.

An old woman told of this sort of racing in her girlhood. "I beat a woman at *ko'omai* and won a shawl and a necklace. Then she said, 'I will race you,' and she brought out everything she had, to bet: a sleeping mat, a basket and a big pot. We went to the racetrack and all our relatives came with us. They were all betting. We chose two umpires, one of her male relatives and one of mine. Then they laid hair ropes down at each end of the track and the two men started us. All the people yelled. But pretty soon her relatives stopped yelling; she was not winning. I came in first and the people brought the things she had bet up to my house. I heard her crying that night out in the desert, because she had lost everything." (26)

When several ran on each side, they ran in relays. The sides were divided and a number of runners from each stood at each end of the track. Each side had six officials, three at each end. One had charge of the runners and decided when they should take their turns. In cases where the whole village ran, he had to grade the men according to their capacity. If his side was short of runners, he decided which ones should run twice or three times. The second man pushed the runner off when it was his turn, using a stick of cactus rib, which he held horizontally in both hands. The third took charge of the incoming runner and saw that he passed the outgoing one before the latter started. Failure to do this constituted a foul and his side lost the race. The same penalty held if one side started off a runner from the opposite side instead of one of its own. If a runner was disabled during the first lap, the race started over again: if during subsequent laps, the victory went to the opposite side.

The race was won when one side got a lap ahead. To measure this, two markers stood in the middle of the track, each holding a stake, which was to mark the point where the two runners passed each other. For the first lap this would be in the middle of the track. As one side gained, they would pass on alternate laps, first nearer to one end, then nearer to the other. A stake was placed at each of these points. It was called the moving line. As one side gained, these stakes would move further and further apart until they measured a gain of half a lap, when they would begin to move together again. When they met, the race was over.

Runners were barefoot. Men wore only a breechclout, girls tied the ends of front and back aprons together so that they formed a very short skirt above the knee. Men tied their hair in a knot as for war and also bound it with a thong; girls matted it over the crown of the head and tied the whole mass with thongs. For big races the upper part of the runner's body was painted with some large, distinguishing mark in white clay which would identify him to his side. This was done by the man in charge of the runners, who called their turns. The marks remembered were horizontal stripes for one side, vertical for the other, or large crosses, large spots. They were decided on by the markers from each side and had no symbolism.

### ATHLETIC CONTESTS
#### (for women)

Women ran relay races just as men did, but over a shorter course. They did not try long distance racing or kickball but they played double ball.

*tohka* (double ball.) The "ball" was usually two bits of cactus rib, three inches long and an inch and a half in diameter, tied together with maguey cord so that they were about three inches apart. A short length of maguey cord with heavy knots at both ends was also used. The stick was made of catclaw (Acacia greggii) cut to the height of the player and with the end bent at the angle of a ladle.

The playing ground was a cleared space about "one hundred steps" long. If there were no trees at either end to mark it, sticks of cactus rib would be set up. The players all gathered in the middle and threw up the ball. It was picked up and thrown with the sticks, the aim being to carry it past the opponents' goal; The myths tell of women travelling from village to village to play this game, so enthusiastically that they left their babies uncared for. Spanish missionary nuns, as late as two generations ago, confiscated the sticks and burned them in order to get the womens' attention for household tasks.

The children's games can be played without betting though small wagers are not uncommon.

The ring and pin game is played with a stick of hard wood to which is attached a buckskin thong or a string of yucca fibre about eighteen inches long. The cord is strung with five rings made by slicing through a small squash when it is fresh. The pulp dries out and the circular strips of rind shrink until they resemble flat leather rings, from four to two inches in diameter and with an opening at least an inch across. The largest is placed nearest the tip of the stick and the smallest at the end, where it is kept from falling off by a solid tab of squash rind. The game is to swing the cord and then impale as many rings as possible on the stick.

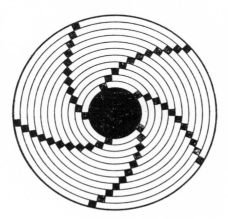

Fig. 5.

Papago Basket Designs used for Game Scoring.

For each ring caught, the player scores a point but if he catches all five, he scores ten. Scoring is done by moving pebbles from mark to mark along a helix, counter clockwise. In old times, the bottom of a basket was used for the purpose, and, if the "coyote track" design were used, the squares of the pattern formed the stopping places for the counters. Even now, when children mark the design on a piece of cardboard, they always make, at the central starting point, the plaited square with which a Papago coiled basket begins. The game was long or short according to the size of the basket, the final mark being called "menstrual hut" since these were always built away from the village, while the central starting point was Big House, or council house, which was the village center.

A variant of this was to toss a bone into the air and catch it on the end of a split stick. The bone was tossed high and two children, their sticks split into two or three openings, fought to catch it.

Boys tossed up a bundle of leaves or rags and shot arrows at it, the boy who hit it taking the arrows of those who missed.

Women and children played cat's cradle, of which some thirty versions were mentioned.

Even very young children used the racetrack, cheered and sometimes gambled on by their older relatives. "I ran every day," said an old woman, "until I was old enough to grind the corn." (fifteen years). "When I was not nearly as high as my father's shoulder said a man (2), my uncles used to bet on me. They said I would grow up to be a racer."

### INTERVILLAGE GAMES

In the good old days to which informants look back, there was an intervillage contest every year at kickball, long distance racing or relay racing. The same intervillage contests are reported for the Tarahumare,[1] Opata,[2] and for the Acaxee, another Piman-Sonoran group[3] The Papago games took place in November, when the harvest was in, but all the residents were still at the summer village However, the challenge had usually been issued in spring or even in the previous autumn. The contestants might be two villages in the same group, two groups, or one or more groups against the Pima. If villages from two separate groups had runners who wished to race, they never thought of doing so without the support of their partners. Thus for years the whole Archie group backed one runner who was at Mesquite Root and who ran successively against the Koloti and the Pimas.

---

[1] Culin, p. 672.        [2] Ibid. 666.        [3] Beals 1933, pp. 11—33.

Choosing runners was an elaborate matter since their backers risked all their small amount of property on them. It was the aim of every village to have fleet runners among its young men as the speeches show. A village which felt it came up to the mark might challenge another village or might invite its partners to witness the boys' speed and decide whether they would join in betting on them. Or a defeated side might select its most likely youths and have them trained. In any case, long and rigorous training was necessary. The runners practised daily, running as much as twenty-five miles. They ate no meat, honey or cactus syrup and in the morning before starting took nothing but water.

Some of the older men backing them must know the cycle of running songs and sing them daily. If this were done for him, the runner himself need not have a supernatural guardian but many of the most famous runners did have. Thus one man had been visited by a hawk who caused feathers to grow at his elbows and wrists. Another carried a piece of the rainbow, which made him unreachable, as the rainbow is.

The calendar stick gives several descriptions of challenges and the training of runners:

"A man invited his friend from Comobabi to the drinking ceremony at the Place of the Burnt Dog. The friend got drunk. Some people came from Plow-Land, southwest from the place of the Burnt Dog. They called the visitor by name, Garment-Falling-Down, and said, 'We know you can't beat us. Do you want to race again? Our horse is fast but even at kickball you can't beat us. We have good runners.' They kept taunting. Garment-Falling-Down sat still with his head down. The visitors, who were on horseback, rode at him. His host drove them off. He then invited Garment-Falling-Down back to his house to drink, where they got to talking. When the cactus liquor was all gone, Garment-Falling-Down went home. He kept thinking and from down in his heart he decided to race with the people from the Tecaloti region. That evening he said to his sons:

'I am now going to tell you what I have on my mind. From the beginning it says that if you have a son, as I have, make him get up in the morning and run, from the time the sun rises until it has been shining for two hours. Teach yourselves to run — you'll get strength that way. As Elder Brother said, that's the way strength began from the very beginning. Do this always from now on, and in the afternoon get your kickball and run. Early in the morning go out with your guns and look for the deer on the mountain. From them you will get strength. And I'll be watching to see when you have got enough speed.'

Thus he talked every evening and every morning. At dawn he

would wake up and sing the same songs that Elder Brother sang to get strength. When through singing them, he would say to the boys, 'It's morning, get up and go.'

After a long time he thought they had enough speed, so he called the other towns, his partners, and told them his plan. He set the date for the meeting at which to plan the games. At the meeting they agreed on the date on which Garment-Falling-Down should bring the boys and show their speed. He brought them to Carrying-Basket Mountain, and all assembled. A man from Mesquite, who had once been a very good runner, was to take charge of the boys and train them. He sent word ahead to have the track laid out. It was to be five miles long. He would go out and run with the boys, but he would only go a quarter of the way because he was now old. However, he would be there to urge them on. When they got there, he saw that the track was longer than he had said it was to be, but since the boys did not get tired he did not change it. When it was finished, the track was twenty-five miles long with the return. When the trainer felt sure they could run, they would place another runner about two hundred feet along the track. The boys would run and would pass the one with a handicap. They kept lengthening the track and increasing the handicap. Every night the trainer sang the old running songs, given by Elder Brother's trainer, Pure-Cactus-Seeds.

Then the boys' father went to Tecaloti and proposed to play. He said, 'I have found out what game to play, — kickball.' Garment-Falling-Down told them to invite all their partners. He said he would be back at a certain time to hear their answer. At that time the partners accepted. Garment-Falling-Down went to town to propose his plan. In the meantime their runners were training. Then the date was set."

The giving of the challenge included many formalities. A man from the challenging village rode to the challenged in the autumn or spring before the contest. In the case quoted he was the father of the runners, but the Keeper of the Meeting or any appointed envoy might go. In order to find his opponents at home he made his proposal at night in the council meeting. He was seated at the right of the Keeper and after the preliminary speeches he allowed a proper silence. Then he produced his own cigarette, handed it to the Keeper with the salutation, "Friend." The Keeper smoked, then the visitor, then the Keeper again. Then he made his proposal, "Let us see how fast runners our boys are."

Very often a race had as preliminary a dancing pageant, which might be called the Visiting Dance. (See Ceremonies. In Press.). The race might be followed by the Naming Ceremony, in which the visitors sang songs containing the names of the hosts. In both cases the visitors were "paid for their entertainment" in goods. If they planned either of these elaborations, it would be proposed at the time of the challenge, the challenger saying, "We want to sing for you." This singing rarely took place without the subsequent race, so that "we want to sing for you" actually meant a challenge to a race.

The whole performance was not only a way of exhibiting prowess but definitely a means of getting material goods. The Papagos have been accused of exploiting their agricultural relatives, the Pimas, in this way.[1] They did the same for the Yuma at Somerton,[2] always making their visit at harvest season. Their skill at running and singing was made a weapon with which to fight hunger.

The challenge accepted, both sides trained their runners. Soon after harvest the challenger again visited the council of the challenged, again proffered the cigarette, and went over the proposition: "I have said that we would train our runners. We are now ready. I have come as I promised." He was answered: "It is well. You have come as you promised. We also have trained our runners."

Then the date was set: usually the conventional ten days ahead, the contest to take place on the eleventh. During this time both sides collected all the goods they were to bet and made the journey to the village of the challenged. "We filled the roads going along on our horses. Everybody was leading extra horses to bet and we had baskets and pots and buckskins tied on their backs. "We bet everything. Women would take off their dresses, men their shirts. Sometimes when people went home again, they had not a single pot or basket in the house. They would dig holes in the ground to serve food." (26)

All the stakes were placed in a pile which was guarded all night by shamans from both sides. The shamans "raced for us with their tricks all night". They performed feats of swallowing fire or sticks and of causing articles to come to them out of the air. Meantime in each camp singers, who knew the running or kickball songs, went through the whole cycle to make the opponents weak and blind.

"There was a shaman at Archie, called Something-Laid-There-Loose, who could shoot at a rainbow, cut off a piece and put it on top of a runner's head. Then that runner remained always the same distance ahead of the others, like the rainbow. He had done this for the best Archie runner, who was known everywhere as the champion. Mesquite Root wanted to challenge Archie, but their shaman advised them not to. "I can do nothing," he said, "against the Archie shaman. His knowledge comes from the morning star, but mine only comes from Elder Brother."

---

[1] Russell, p. 171.    [2] Gifford, 1933, p. 262.

The shaman received no compensation for his services to the runners. "He bet like the others and if they won, he won" (21).

When the race began, no one was allowed within a hundred feet of the starting point because an evil shaman's power "could not fly that far", and thus the runners would be safe. As an extra precaution they were kept behind the crowd and no one knew when he was to run until the last minute. For one famous race they were brought from half a mile away on horseback, each sitting behind a horseman and leaping off just in time to start running (21).

In long distance races many men followed the runners part way and waited for them to return. The race was considered over at sunset, no matter where they were, though one "moonlight race" is recorded.

While the people waited for long distance racers to return, various smaller games might go on. Older people played the gambling games, always men against men and women against women. Young people raced, played kickball and double ball. When the runners returned, the people cheered. Men made a shrill sound and slapped the hand rhythmically over the mouth. Women ululated: "ki-yi-yi!" The whole pile of stakes was then handed over to the winning village or group and each individual retrieved his own stake with the duplicate tied to it.

There follow two accounts of races from the calendar stick:

"The Tecaloti people kept on training runners. In the middle of the summer they notified the former victors, "You've beaten us now we are ready to play again.. Tell your partners to start training your boys. We'll train ours."

All started training. Every once in a while the Koloti chief would come to see how the training was coming on. When the date was near, he came and said, "The time is nearly up." The two chiefs were conferring, the boys were training. The next month he came again and the date was set. Two days before the race all gathered at Carrying-Basket Mountain.

The next morning the Koloti arrived. The corrals were full of cattle, which they had brought to bet. The runners did not start until afternoon. There were only two, the eldest son of Garment-Falling-Down and a Koloti. The race started at four o'clock in the afternoon and was from Carrying-Basket Mountain to Aktcin, (a distance of twenty-five miles.) At six o'clock the runners were just at the other end of the track. Before they got to Where-Water-Whirls-Round it was sundown. The son of Garment-Falling-Down was two miles ahead. The horseman, following the best man, picked him up, rode forward, and said to Garment-Falling-Down, "Your son has won. I put him on my horse and brought him home."

"The Coyote people sang at Comobabi. The women wanted it. The old women went to a man named Having-No-Pet and asked him to sing. They said that afterward the women would race the women. He agreed and started to practise singing. The old woman leader saddled up a horse, got dressed in her husband's pants, shirt, boots, spurs, and Mexican straw hat, and mounted. She also got a bag of silver fox skin, within which she had a bamboo cigarette. Then she went to Comobabi to the home of the rival she wanted to race. The women of Comobabi expected her and were all there. She dismounted, tied up her horse, and came over to them and sat down. A leading woman of Comobabi got up and took a fire brand which she placed in the center of the circle, in front of the visitor. The visitor took the cigarette out of her bag. They smoked. Then the visitor spoke, telling them that she had announced her visit and had now set time for the games. She said, "We will sing and afterward see how fast runners our girls are." The other woman made a speech of acceptance. She said, "What you said is true. You have come as anounced. Make ready your girls and I will get mine. How many days are to be set aside?" The visitor said, "We will have relay races," and the other agreed. Her companions then gave a woman's cheer.

They kept track of the days. The girls trained; they could eat nothing sweet, no meat and no syrup. They could eat only gruel and salt. In the morning they took only water; in the afternoon they ran.

When the days were up, they went up and camped close to Comobabi, where the singing was going on. The Comobabi women made up their bets. Their leader, carrying a bundle on her head, came dancing. The Coyote Village woman took it, and danced off with it. Then the Comobabi women furnished food and the Coyote women assembled their bets.

When all were ready, the girls lined up. The best runner for Comobabi and a young girl from Coyote were the starters. The Comobabi woman put her hair up over her head with a band and then let it fall back. The track was about half a mile long. The Comobabi woman won the start over the Coyote woman, and Comobabi won the whole race. The woman had bet their shawls, — they even took their dresses off.

A few days later the Comobabi leader wanted a sing and a race against Coyote. She wore men's clothes for her visit as her rival had done. She got a singer of eagle songs who lived at Comobabi. The races were like the others had been, but this time there was a foul. The Coyote people started a runner for a Comobabi relay instead of waiting for their own. The Coyote people lost."

# YOUTH

A pregnant woman, in former times, did not make fun of a deformed person or stare at him, lest her baby have the same defect. She should give offerings to every such person in the neighborhood. She must not let a dog breathe on her or the baby would have fever with hot breath like a dog. She was herself dangerous and must not stand around to look at a war party lest she injure their strength. She must not visit any sick person, even her own mother, for she would cause the invalid's death.

Her husband must not go on a war party for he would have no strength. If he did by chance go, he must not kill or look on a dead enemy or the baby would die a violent death. He must not kill a rabbit, or if he happened to, he must not touch it. The penalty was croup for the baby. If he killed a rattlesnake, the penalty was convulsions.

When labor began, the mother retired to the segregation hut, where any female relative might go with her. The relative dug a pit in the floor of the hut and lined it with something soft to receive the baby. She suspended a rope from the roof of the hut and the mother knelt and pulled on it with arms raised until the baby dropped in the pit. If the family was travelling, she sought a secluded place and found an overhanging branch to pull on.

If labor was difficult, the helper might kneel behind her and push down over the abdomen. Sometimes another woman squatted in front of her and helped. At present, when birth sometimes takes place in the house instead of the segregation hut, the husband may be one of the helpers. "Some husbands will kneel behind a wife all day and hold her up" (26). Ordinarily, however, men fear everything connected with birth. If there was much delay, the cause was thought to be a hair from an Apache trophy or from a dead man which had become twisted around the foetus. The shaman was then sent for and, after smoking and singing to find the position of the hair, he sucked it out.

When the baby was born, the umbilical cord was snipped about four inches from the body with a sharp fingernail. The rest of the cord was thrown away or buried. There was no special significance attached to it. The afterbirth was buried by a man, "because a woman could not dig a deep enough hole". Men, however, were exceedingly afraid of it and the woman helper wrapped it so that they would not see it. Then they picked it up with sticks and dropped it into the hole.

After the birth, mother and child remained in the segregation hut for a month. The mother must eat no salt until the end of the umbilical cord fell off, or the child's navel would get sore. The best food for her was gruel of cactus seeds or mesquite beans, which was thought to make her strong. She must not wash for the whole month or she would have rheumatism. According to one informant, her husband at this time used separate dishes which at other times were kept outside the house (26). The wife in the segregation hut used the same dishes she had at menstruation.

"When the moon had come back to the same place", she and the husband and child went through a purification ceremony. They went at dawn to a shaman who made a specialty of this ceremony and of child naming. He drew a circle on the ground and placed the mother in it with her back to the east. She held the child. The father, according to some informants, sat in the circle with her (26), according to others, on a cross marked to the south of the circle (1), or simply on the ground outside.

The shaman kept a special kind of yellow clay found mostly in Sonora. He scraped a little from the dried ball in which it was kept; mixed it with water and pounded owl's feathers and stirred it with an owl's feather. He "cleansed" the parents by dusting them off with his shaman's plumes. Then, carrying the bowl of clay and singing, he walked back and forth four times, from west to east, toward the mother and the rising sun (26), or around the circle (1). Then he had both parents and child drink from the bowl, the order varying, according to different informants. If the baby would not drink, the shaman drank a little and spat it into the baby's mouth. Then he gave the child a name which had no connection with the parents or their families, but referred to something he had dreamed. Such names were often poetic, as Boiling Wind, Hawk over Water, Dawn Singing.

The woman was now considered cleansed and might go back to the family home with the baby. The shaman was paid a basket or some food.

The omission of the ceremony would make both parents and child sick. An unmarried mother must hold it, but without the father. A divorced woman went through it with the baby, while her husband went through it separately. If a woman went through it with her husband, when he was not the baby's father, the husband might die.

If the baby died and the woman wanted another, she buried it near the surface. If she wanted no more, she buried it deep. Women professed to know nothing about means of abortion saying that there was little need for them, since an unmarried mother suffered no stigma. Deformed babies and those born by "light women" who did not want the burden were dropped in an arroyo to die of exposure. It was considered that a woman who had a husband and did not bear children would soon die herself of the unnatural condition.

Twins were considered to be born shamans. People regarded both them and their parents with some awe, since whatever they said would come true. Thus, if they said a certain person would die, he would: if they called him ugly, swollen, lame, he would become so. Therefore everybody made offerings to twins (the word used is the same as that for offerings made at a shrine). Their parents did the same. Anyone who rebuked a twin suffered. One informant slapped the cheek of a twin who annoyed her while gambling and immediately her arm swelled. She went to the twin for relief, bringing a gift. The child wet her fingertips in her mouth and touched the arm which immediately healed.

This power of twins did not persist beyond childhood unless they had dreams and became shamans in the regular way. However, they usually did so and were much more likely to dream than the average person. If one twin died, the other died also.

### CHILDHOOD

Babies were nursed until they were two and three years old. One informant said, "My babies died. It was because they came too fast. When there was a new one coming, there was not milk for the old one" (26). The cause of most infant complaints was supposed to be the fact that the fontanelle did not close properly. A shaman or an old women who had dream power inserted a finger in the child's mouth and pushed on the palate. This was thought to push up the whole top of the head and close the fontanelle. Diarrhoea was treated with the vapor of canyon ragweed. The leaves were wet and a hot cloth laid over them, then the infant was set on the cloth in the vapor. Children's fevers were thought to be due to the hot breath of a dog. They and other diseases were treated in the regular way by the shaman.

The child was carried on the cradleboard until it was able to walk. Mothers, on their long expeditions to fetch food and water, placed the cradleboard on top of the other contents of the carrying basket and while they worked, stood it against a tree. When the child was able to walk, it was carried on the mother's hip. When the mother went foot gathering, children of an active age were left at home with the grandmother.

Children went naked until the age of eight or ten. After this, the boys wore breechclouts and the girls a double apron, like their elders. Until this age, which was also that of taking up a few adult duties, both sexes played together making dolls of twigs tied together with corn husk.

"We went to a sunny place and played husbands and wives with our dolls. We girls would make our dolls grind corn. The boys would take their dolls and say, 'We go hunting.' 'Well, go,' said the wives. Then the boys would hunt all around the village and find a deer bone. 'Here is a deer for you.' Once we played a doll was dead and we were crying, but my mother stopped us. 'You mustn't talk about the dead.'"

Children hunted about the camp, generally roasting the small animals they killed on the spot. Boys might dig rats out of their holes. After the rains all children chased the birds while their feathers were too wet to fly and caught them in their hands.

Girls played "jackstones", (p. 147) and practised double ball but did not gamble until they were older. Boys practised kickball and shooting at a mark. Both girls and boys practised daily on the race track, while the adult relatives arranged children's races, umpired them and bet on them.

During this early period before the age of ten or so a good deal of consideration was shown children. Girls were not allowed to pick cactus; "they are too young, thorns would hurt them". They need not go through the privations which their parents endured during a purification. "Children cannot suffer." The whole family showed them a great deal of affection. If a small child in a Papago house is not actively playing, it is generally in the arms of someone, male or female. The children run freely among their elders without rebuke. The writer has seen a child interfere constantly with the work of a potter without receiving more than a smile.

When taking texts, the writer was seriously inconvenienced by two boys romping through the small room and drowning out the informant's low voice. She asked the interpreter if it would be possible to stop the boys and he replied, "I don't think so. They are his (the informant's) grandchildren." Therefore, the text taking stopped occasionally, while the grandfather smilingly waited for the noise to lessen (4).

Children habitually run among the dancers in a ceremony and talk and shout during the singing. One informant, telling of an

important rite to stop an epidemic, mentioned how a group of
children followed the shaman and clutched at his paraphernalia.
"We don't mind those things. We know the children don't understand." At the dance around the enemy trophy where, if ever,
fierceness is to be expected, several of the songs are concerned with
Elder Brother's directions.to mothers for lulling the babies who are
tired with the dancing.

At present, when there is no hiding from the enemy, there is
little in Papago daily life which demands the subduing of children.
Nothing in the hut is breakable. There are two or three pots in the
outdoor kitchen and some tools hanging from the roof out of reach.
Otherwise, the child may feel quite as free in his surroundings as
the adult. Since noise from the child does not shame the adult in
public, as it would in our culture, there is little occasion for rebuke.

Children made a very matter-of-course entry into adult duties.
There was so much to do that as soon as a child was able to do
anything whatever, he was allowed to do it. The writer saw an
interesting example of training in this respect. A family and its
guests were gathered in a hut on a cold night and the door was open.
The person nearest the door and unoccupied was a three year old
child. One of the men guests, a very distant relative, said to the
child, "Close the door." The door was heavy and the sill high. The
child made an attempt and then stopped. The man repeated
smiling, "Close the door." The child moved it a few inches and
started to cry. No one sympathized with him. The quiet direction,
"Close the door," continued until he had moved it a few inches at
a time and finally finished the task. There was no clamor of
approval and petting. The child had done his part of the evening's
work and came back to the fire with the rest.

Children were graduated from this sort of task to that of running
errands and especially carrying gifts of food, often for long distances.
As soon as they could manage the distance, girls followed their
mothers on food gathering expeditions and boys followed their
fathers hunting. When a girl was ten years old, she might be
grinding all the corn for the family and a boy might be shooting the
jackrabbits for their food. At fourteen a girl should be a fully
qualified housekeeper, since she was nearly ready for marriage.
A boy should be a swift runner and attending the council whence he
might be sent out as messenger, though not on important occasions.
He would be only beginning his training as a warrior and a hunter.
Though he married later than the girl, this training might continue
some time after marriage.

In spite of their freedom as children, young people were expected, as they grew up, to be extremely modest and retiring. Girls, after the age of ten, hardly spoke to a man unless he were a relative and then only to offer him food. If a stranger approached the house, they ran out and hid. Since the women did most of their work in large groups, a girl was always completely surrounded and protected.

Boys also were expected to be retiring. As has been mentioned, they did not speak in the meeting until they were mature men: their part was to do the work in silence. No young man ever interrupted an elder. The following typical conversation took place with a young interpreter who had been asked to question an old informant: "Did you ask him (the informant) thus and so ?" "I tried to, but he wanted to talk about something else." In such a situation the young man, though paid to ask questions, was powerless.

The writer has several times been told by Papagos, apropos of working for the Whites: "But our young men cannot go out and approach people as yours do. They are taught to be bashful."

Young people were ceaselessly trained in the moral code (see p. 80), whose principal tenets were industry, fortitude and swiftness of foot. Industry was a woman's virtue, without which no girl could hope to be kept as a wife. Fortitude was a virtue of both sexes and Papago life, which was so frequently on the verge of starvation, brought it to the foreground. The augury on all auspicious occasions was: "You will be hunger-enduring, thirst-enduring, cold-enduring." A man undergoing purification for any reason, voluntarily endured these three hardships and boys were urged to practise them regularly on the Spartan principle that one who was slightly hungry and thirsty all the time would not feel the privation in a crisis. There seems no doubt that the Papago were brave in battle, but aggressive courage is never praised in their poetry. All the emotion is called forth on the theme of enduring hardship.

Speed in running might almost be called the root of all virtue. The life of these nomads in flat, open desert country was based on covering long distances. Women were taught to run with the carrying basket, men ran on the hunt and on the warpath. A young man who could not run was nearly useless. Therefore, running came to mean in Papago parlance the mark of an admirable man and the thing which drew to him the attention of the supernaturals. The following admonition by a father to his sons is on this theme:

"Listen well to this talk. To all of it listen! Look well at my mouth. Keep looking and you will learn. Thus I say to you, that this night, while darkness covers us, you are not to sleep early in the evening. You are to listen to me.

11

Perhaps some time in the night, something will arrive. Then if you are a good runner, you will jump up, you will run (after it). Early in the morning you will get up. Far over there (down to the west) you will sit and will listen for something. You will run over there and something which is good-luck-bringing will meet you: a coyote, an eagle, a hawk. Then you will be a fast runner. You will be a good hunter.

You should run constantly, no matter how much hardship it means; even if you are thirsty, hungry, tired. Then truly this will happen to you. You will throw yourself down repeatedly (worn out). Then there will come a hawk, an eagle, a mountain lion, a jaguar, a bear, and will tell you how to follow something alive (game) and to kill it.

Then when you come back after much running, they will put before you the clay dish. Then you will merely sit and look at it. Even perchance it will speak thus to you, "Go to! Eat me!" Do not eat it until a scum has formed on it. If you eat it before a scum has formed, you will have wrinkles. If you eat but a little, you will be a lean man. You will be light. You will be a fast runner. If you eat much, you will be fat. You will be much wrinkled; you will not be a runner." (1)

This short sermon, delivered by a parent, was a regular pattern with the Papagos and recalls the admonitions delivered by the Aztecs to their children, as reported in Sahagun.[1]

There was no rigid form of words for such talks but, as in the speech at the men's meeting, the moral code must be gone over and over until, in modern phraseology, the youth's reactions were fully conditioned. The father was generally the speaker, though the mother might take her turn, especially with the girls. The time chosen was when the family were all lying in the dark on their sleeping mats, sometimes at night, more often in the hour before dawn. There was a special method of speaking: a low, insistent monotone. As one informant said, "You thought you were still asleep. You thought you were hearing that voice in your dreams" (26). As the writer has heard these speeches recited, they have an effect which is almost hypnotic.

"Open your ears, for I am telling you a good thing. Wake and listen. Open your ears. Let my words enter them. Wake up and listen.

You boys, you should go out and run. So you will be swift in time of war. You girls, you should grind the corn. So you will feed the men that they may fight the enemy. You should practise running. So in time of war you may save your lives. Wake up. Do not be idle." (26)

---

[1] Sahagun, F p. 384—390.

"I can never forget what my father told me," various informants
have stated. "I heard it every morning, even before I was old
enough to understand." "I was little," said one (26), "and I would
go to sleep. Then my father would pinch my ear. 'Wake up and
listen. Let my words enter your ears and your head'."

This constant, though unaggressive, repetition of the principles
of living must have had, as did the speeches at the council meeting
the effect of producing a unity of sentiment in the community
as profound as it was unconscious.

### GIRLS' PUBERTY AND MENSTRUATION

The puberty of boys was not signalized. For girls, the puberty
ceremony centered on obviating the malignant effects of menstruation and, secondarily, on making the girl industrious for the
rest of her life.

Menstruation was regarded with horror. The touch of a menstruating woman could weaken a man and take all power from his
weapons. The taint of it would cause the deer to avoid a hunter,
cause a shaman's crystals to rot and tobacco plants to shrivel up.
Therefore, for a menstruating women not to segregate herself
was a crime against the community. Men were urged nightly in the
council meeting to see that their women obeyed the rule. The
punishment for disobedience was usually a supernatural one:
lightning or flood would destroy the family of the offender or,
possibly, her whole village.

First menstruation was particularly malignant. For announcing
it, for having the girl ritually cleansed, and for instructing her as
to her future responsibility in the matter, the father and mother
were held responsible. In old days a father could be whipped for
laxity in this respect, or the mother, if the father could prove
ignorance. Mothers watched their girls very closely and at the
appearance of first menstruation, the girl was sent to the regular
segregation hut. Here she stayed four days. She was given a new
pottery bowl and a drinking cup, into which women poured the
food which they brought her from the house; she was allowed
no meat or salt; she was given a scratching stick and must not
touch her hair on pain of losing it.

Generally an older woman relative was appointed as the girl's
instructress, though if the family were away camping, the mother
would serve. The idea was that if the girl practised industry and
alertness at this time, she would have those virtues for the rest of
her life. She was waked very early in the morning and taken to
fetch water and wood, a Papago woman's chief duties. She might

11*

leave her burden outside her father's house, but she must not go in.
In the rest of her time she practised making basketry. Her instructress told her:

"Work hard. Practise running every day; you will need to run
when the Apache come. When you go to sleep, tired, the *kots* (a
magic serpent) will come and show you designs for basketry. If you
are industrious, some day you will meet an old man (circumlocution
for "some day you will marry a young man"; the informant said this
expression was considered more modest). When you are married, do
not interfere with your husband. Never object when he goes away.
If you do not let him go he cannot hunt and you will have nothing
to eat. You will have to go to your neighbors. They will feed you,
but they will talk about you behind your back." (1)

The instructress continually urged the girl not to sleep at this
time, or she would be sleepy all her life; not to be idle, or she would
be so always. During her four days, other young girls might visit
her at the hut, whether or not they had menstruated. Non-men-
struating women might come but menstruants must not. That
would be too "strong". None of the visitors must touch her.

After four days the girl was given a bath in water as cold as
possible and for this purpose, a new porous jar was made, as it was
for the warrior during his retreat. At dawn the girl knelt, facing
the east, while the mother or instructress poured the water over her
head, saying:

"Hail!
I shall pour this over you.
You will be one who endures cold.
You will think nothing of it."

Her extreme seclusion was now over. According to some, she
might now go back to her father's house, though she must still
refrain from salt and use the scratching stick. According to others,
she remained at the menstruation hut for another four days. In
either case, at the end of four days she had another bath.

Meantime the puberty dance had begun. In some villages it
lasted for a month, in others for four days. The period also depended
on whether the family was in camp where they had little to feed
the dancers, or in the summer village where there was plenty.

The father announced the girl's maturity and the whole village
came to the house at sunset. They formed in two lines facing each
other, composed of men and women alternately, their arms over
each others' shoulders. Where they wore cotton blankets obtained
from the Pimas, these were held in a line across the backs. At the

end of one line danced the song leader,, any man who knew the puberty cycle. He held a rattle in his right hand while his left arm was across the shoulders of the girl. His wife danced opposite.

The lines went with a running motion toward each other and then back wheeling a little so that they finally covered a complete circle. There was no fire: "We got warm dancing." They danced through the night and at midnight were given a meal of succotash by the girl's family. The girl was expected to dance all of every night, though the other dancers came and went. In the course of a month or even of a night, there might be several singers, as one man got tired and another took his place. At the end of the month the girl made presents to all her girl friends who had danced often and "gone without sleep" with her. One informant said that when her dance was over, she had nothing left. She had given her deerskin dress, all her beads, her pots, sleeping mat and baskets (27).

"I got so thin, so thin! We girls are all like that at our puberty time. Running all day with the carrying basket and no rest. Before dawn that woman who taught me would come and say, 'Get up. Get water, get wood. Do you want to be lazy all your life?' So then we would go running, running over the mountains. When we got home, I slept a little. It seemed I had hardly shut my eyes before they were telling me, 'The dancers are here. Go out and dance.' I did not want to dance. I used to, when I was a little girl and watched them. But now I only wanted to sleep. But my father would say, 'Here comes the singer. Better go out or he'll drag you out. He's mean.'"[1]

The puberty ceremony, according to the oldest informants, was a time for promiscuity, (26, 27) which apparently had the connotation of fertility magic. It is one of the practises connected, in the myths, with the first inhabitants of the land and the reason why Elder Brother, the creator, offended these first inhabitants, was that he, an accomplished singer for the ceremony, used his privileges with girls beyond all bounds.[2]

At the end of the dancing period, the girl was given another bath at dawn and then she went to the shaman for cleansing. The rite was similar to the cleansing after childbirth. The shaman drew a circle on the ground, within which the girl sat, at the east with her back to the rising sun. The shaman stood facing east and walked

---

[1] In this dancing ceremony there is no suggestion of the "baking" which occurs in nearby California. However, tcuuwa, to reach puberty, and tcuuwam, girl at puberty, come from the same root as tcuwa, to bake.

[2] Cf. the Yuman reason for killing the creator: that he had raped his daughter. Kroeber, 1925, p. 790.

four times up to her and back, each time blowing on the top of her head and brushing her off with his eagle plumes. He then mixed yellow clay in a basket bowl, stirring it with a feather and gave it to her to drink. After this he marked her with the feather dipped in clay, on heart, forehead, right arm, left arm. Some shamans then gave her a new name which was, like the name for a baby, anything he had dreamed. It would seem, since this name came at the end of the purification period that it should have been used, not during that period, but permanently. But informants said that they were usually called by their old birth names. One woman who had been named at puberty cha-wila (untranslatable) had never used the name at all.

The shaman was paid with some small gift like a basket and the girl was free to mingle with people again. At her following menstruation period she must again use the scratching stick, but after that, it was not required. She must always go to the menstruation hut for four days and must use the dishes kept there, not touching those of the family. One informant said that, when a woman was married, her husband must also use separate dishes during her period. These were kept outside the house and only brought in when necessary (26).

The same informant, who had not menstruated for a year after her puberty dance, suddenly menstruated again after marriage. It was thought necessary that both she and her young husband should be "danced" and then purified. They danced for a month but since the husband also was concerned, she did not go to the menstruation hut. Both remained in the family house and observed continence.

In the life of a woman after puberty, conscientious segregation once a month ranked as the chief virtue. Chastity was scarcely stressed at all in comparison and even industry took second place. Since knowledge of her state rested entirely with the woman, she had opportunity to conceal it and personal narratives abound in tales of the dire consequences of such an act.

"There was a girl in our village who became dangerous and she did not tell. One day all the village was planting in her father's field and he had given them a meal of succotash. They were eating out in the field; her mother was cooking over a campfire. It began to rain. This girl and her sisters ran home to take in the bedding because we sleep out-of-doors in summer and it was on the ground. There was a crash of thunder. All the eating people stood still and then from the house of that girl they heard a long sigh. They ran there. All the sisters were lying stunned on the floor, one was blind and this girl was dead. The men dragged them out into the rain and the house began to burn. Her relatives buried that girl all alone and no one would go near." (26)

"Then there was a girl who was going to build a fire and it seemed that it reached out and took her and burned her up." (26)

"And there was another whose mother was struck by lightning. Because when a woman commits this fault, anyone in her family may be punished. That is why, when the lightning strikes a village, they send for the shaman to see what woman was dangerous. He summons all the girls and looks at his crystals to see whose fault it was. They don't punish that girl. She knows that she has killed her relatives and that is enough." (26)

Women admit that an intrepid woman, if she were particularly busy, might conceal her state for a day or two. "But not more. She would be too much afraid." She might also practise the reverse procedure and keep her husband from going to war by telling him falsely that she was menstruating. An injury like this would be far less likely to be forgiven by a husband than would unfaithfulness,

As a rule, the women found the four days segregation no burden. Rather it was a pleasant chance to sit still and give up the household responsibility. They took their basketry to the hut where all women, except first menstruants, might visit them. The groups gambled, sang and told stories. No man might shout to the menstruant or even look at her from a distance. A tale recounts that once a woman in the segregation hut saw an approaching party of Apaches. She shouted to some men in the fields but they would not turn round nor watch her signals and she dared not approach, so the Apaches attacked the village. Another local tale says that a woman who frequently quarrelled with her husband would on each occasion retire to the hut whence he was powerless to get her back. He had to move the family before she would come out.

The segregation custom is still in use, though not so widely as formerly.

### DREAM POWER AND CHOICE OF CAREER

The puberty of the youth was not signalized. Even though he married, he continued in his father's house without much change in status until he achieved some noteworthy deed which stamped him an adult. There was no ceremony or definite crisis. He began to take part in men's affairs; ultimately would be consulted and would speak in the council.

Papago life admitted of a number of specializations. A man could be a leader or a ceremonial officiant, a planter, hunter, trader, runner, gambler, shaman or lay curer. For two of these activities, that of the shaman and the lay curer, dream power was essential. For several it was out of the picture. These were the hereditary offices of Keeper of the Meeting and ceremonial officiants where the emphasis was on learning a task from a predecessor. In contrast to the Yuman attitude, proficiency was enough without dream confirmation. Planting, the task of everyone, was outside the need for dream power and was taken care of by standardized magic practices ordained for the whole community. Trading, although it might seem the place where initiative and energy (that is, power) would be called for, is never mentioned.

There remain the activities where chance plays a large part: hunting, racing, gambling and war. Here there were magic group rituals but also the individual could gain much with the aid of a Visitant. The aid was not essential: a crack deer hunter has told me that he never had a dream in his life (22). Certainly the youth who failed to dream did not feel agonized and frustrated. But I relate this fact, not to a lack of desire to dream, but to the fact that the Papago is not avid for power. He has some of the Pueblo abhorrence for the idea of prominence and he feels quite content to be an undistinguished member of "the kin".

The subject of dreaming should receive its detailed treatment in connection with the supernatural but no discussion of social or economic life can omit some reference to it. Mention has already been made of the way in which a boy was urged from infancy to invite a supernatural Visitant by the practice of the standard virtues, of which fleetness of foot was the chief. Constant frugality was enjoined but he did not definitely fast and he never implored. The Visitant came unasked. The visitation occurred in natural sleep or during the state of exhaustion after running.

When a boy reached young manhood, there were other avenues of approach to the supernatural. The retreat of the Enemy Slayer after killing has been mentioned, with the fact that this gave power not so much for war as for curing. There were two other activities which were thought to bring their participants into almost as close a connection with dangerous power as enemy slaying. These were the ceremonial fetching of salt from the Gulf of California and the killing of an eagle.

After each of these the neophyte went into a retreat similar to that of the Enemy Slayer, though not quite so rigorous and he was called by the same term, possibly meaning Powerful. During this time he had the dreams that ensured future prowess. A Visitant often sang to him and took him on a journey which might have the Yuman form of visiting mountains but might be to the sea or beyond it. Or the Visitant might simply instruct the dreamer.

It would seem that an unimaginative young man, faced with the necessity to "dream" dramatically before he could have the inspiration to success, might be frustrated. The series of speeches delivered to the neophytes before their retreat both in war and on the salt expedition fills this need for they are narratives of the vision experienced by some primeval dreamer. These, recited night after night, under impressive circumstances, might easily dispose a young mind to a nearly similar experience. In one of the war rituals, the guardian recites the experience as though it had actually happened to the neophyte:

> "At the east there lives
> A great yellow buzzard, a great shaman....
> He picked you up, and far he threw you,
> You fell half dead, you awoke, you came to yourself."

Sixteen days of fasting, following this recital, might go far toward producing the experience.

In the salt ritual there is a description of the state of mind which precedes such dreams. It gives a picture of one definitely working himself up to a state of tension.

> "Food she cooked for me
> I did not eat.
> Water she fetched for me
> I did not drink.
> Then thus to me she said:
> What is it?
> You did not eat the food which I have cooked,
> The water which I fetched, you did not drink.
> Then thus I said:
> It is a thing I feel.
>
> I rose and across the bare spaces did go walking
> Did peep through the openings in the scrub.
> Looking about me,
> Seeking something....
> I rose. I reached the shade before my house,
> There did I try to sit. Not like itself it seemed....
> On my bed I tried to lie.
> Not like itself it seemed....
> To the center of the house did I go crawling
> And the center post
> Seemed a white prayer stick
> So like it was...."

The primeval dreamer then recites his vision which the youth may well duplicate in all its particulars.

The dreaming neophyte made no attempt to call his Visitant and had no prescience of what power would be conferred. Young men went on the salt expedition or killed an eagle in order to find out their vocation. It might be shamanism or lay curing in which case they would continue to dream. Or it might be a profession for which a single conferring of power was enough.

There were certain standard Visitants, with loosely defined powers. The hawk and the cranes (always in a flock) gave speed in running. Coyote, turtle, spider and many others gave curing powers. The crow gave cunning as a scout, the puma, wildcat and deer gave hunting prowess. Luck in gambling came from a number of small birds, in one case, from the eagle. The vision of a youth who had killed an eagle follows:

"The eagle I had killed came and sat beside me. Then it told me to sit on its back, hold to its wings and never look back as we flew. It flew up into the sky as far as where people say Heaven is, (informant was a nominal Christian), but there was only darkness. Then the eagle said, "Well' go down. You look at the earth. Maybe there will be something you can use."

We came down, but the earth was not as I remembered. In one place, where there should be desert, there was a river. The eagle said, "Sit beside this river and anything you see, take it." I saw a reed floating with the roots pulled up.

I woke up. My heart was here (throat). I looked for the reed. It was not there. The next night the man — he was really the eagle — came again. He said, "Don't feel bad at losing what you found last night. I took it. I'll give it back to you. On the third night I will give it." On the third night he came but he did not give it. He said, "I will give it on the fourth night."

On the fourth night he said, "Go anywhere. Find a reed. Cut it in four pieces at the joints." . . . . (16)

There follows a description for making the tubes used in hidden ball, with a little extra painting and the direction to hold the openings to the east while filling the tubes with sand. The dreamer followed directions, always played hidden ball with the magic tubes so made and always won.

Many traditions relate to the dreams by which runners procured their powers.

"A champion runner used to go early to a place where he always ran. A long narrow clearing was the race track . When starting, he heard the sound of something falling and he saw a man standing there who wanted to run with him. This was an eagle in human form. They ran to the end of the track, returned and the stranger walked away. This happened four times and on the last one he appeared as an eagle. He told the runner to follow his advice and be like him, a killer and runner. The eagle took some of his feathers and thrust them into the runner's arms on the inside above the wrist pointing up, under the skin toward the hands. After a while the feathers began to grow on his arms almost like wings and he continued a fast runner. He was instructed not to tell of the eagle nor to boast. People would find out his power." (21)

"There was a very fast runner at Mesquite Root. Once, after an Apache attack, this man was escaping. He came to the other side of narrow Mountain, where there was a shelter for the cactus gatherers. He got there at evening. It was cold and he had no blanket, only a shirt and breechclout. He lay down, expecting to freeze, but he was tired and slept. While he was asleep the white birds (cranes) came and took his heart out. They carried it to the ocean where they live and flew around with it. All night they flew around with it, while his body slept. They showed him how to run and gave him kickball power, because they had pity on him.

When the sun rose, they brought his heart back. He woke up warm instead of cold. Immediately he thought of those who had been killed the day before. So he went back to Mesquite Root and helped burn the bodies.

After that, he had dreams. The white birds would take his heart. One night they took him and told him to run from Mesquite Root to the Hollow Place (about fifty miles). They said he could arrive by noon and should then start back. He would get home by sundown. He wanted to test the dream and he did so. He ran the whole distance, through Hackberry Well and Coyote Sitting and got back just as they said.

The same birds told him in a dream he would have a game of kickball against four relays. He had never tried this. But they said he would win. Then they said he would run against one man and win. All this came true. Then he dreamed of a race track as long as from the Black Hill to the Hollow Place with one man running on it, far ahead of the others. In his dream someone asked him to get in and help the losing side, handing him the breechclout which the runners wore. He accepted the breechclout, saw his relay coming in and his rival out of sight. Just as he was going to run, he woke up. He was old now and he decided to go to the Hollow Place and die there, for this would be the last dream he would have. (Since he had not run in the dream, he probably would not run in life.) He died before he could go." (21)

Women might dream but they did not do so as frequently as men and they never went into retreat, except as the wives of Enemy Slayers. The prerequisite was their standard virtue, industry.

"Work hard," they were told, "and the magic serpent will come and show you designs for baskets." An informant had this experience, though she did not see the serpent.

"When I am making baskets, I hear a voice speaking to me. 'Put a cactus here. Put a turtle there. There, put a Gila monster.'" (26)

Women might acquire curing and, in the old days, rain-making powers after the menopause.

Some light is thrown on the psychological function of the dream by the experience of a woman informant which would seem to be typical. She had all her life observed a practice of midwives: pushing up the baby's palate to produce closure of the fontanelle (see p. 89). This appears to be an old Aztec practice.[1] Although the action was perfectly simple, the informant had never attempted it but in old age she took to dreaming. In one dream the Virgin Mary "and another lady" came and took her through a typically Papago visit to four pools, each guarded by a turquoise and each with a baby's head in it. The Visitants showed her how to spit on a shaman's crystal and touch the fontanelle, which then closed. When she awoke, she knew she could cure the baby's disease. She had no crystal but she did not trouble about it nor about the rest of the ritual. She proceeded to cure babies by pushing up the palate as she had seen others do. All she needed was the dream validation (26).

The Papago dream experience takes its place as a local version of the Guardian Spirit idea which is, in essence, a proclamation of the ability of the individual to attain eminence, regardless of his hereditary status. Such an idea is held both to east and west of the Papago, in varying forms.

The River Yumans, to the west, believed that power-bringing visions came by chance, in natural sleep, and, though an individual's whole success in life depended upon his dreams, he was powerless to induce them. Stated in modern terms, this reflects a belief in the innate superiority, perhaps also superior luck, of certain individuals. The subject of the dream was not an animal, as with the Papago, but a mountain or a supernatural being; sometimes merely a prophetic experience.[2]

On the Plains to the east, the vision was induced by efforts of the recipient, demanding a will power would see him through repeated

---

[1] Sahagun, Seler, pt. 9, sec. 8, p. 366.
[2] Kroeber, 1925, p. 754; Spier, 1933, p. 236; Gifford, 1933, pp. 303—4; Forde, 1931, pp. 182, 183, 189, 190.

vigil and torture. Such visions occurred in a waking trance, not in sleep, and they took the standard form of visitation from an animal.[1] But, again, the vision was a democratic expedient which gave a man access both to individual achievement and the holding of office.

Gradations of these ideas are to be found in other areas near the Papago, such as the Shoshoneans of southern California,[2] the Basin and Plateau[3] with sporadic appearances in the Sonoran and Pueblo areas. We have mentioned the two versions which are in strongest contrast, in order better to define the elements of the Papago vision but without conclusions as to the contacts which gave them currency.

The Papago dream experience occurred in sleep, like that of the Yumans, but the spirits involved were the animal guardians of the Plains. And the vision was induced. The purposeful motivating of a certain dream is at odds with the modern attitude of scrutinizing dreams as valuable messengers from the subconscious, to be humbly awaited and studied, rather than commanded. But the Papago commanded their dreams — or at least those they remembered. Inquiry has convinced the writer that there were many symbolic expressions of unrecognized desires, like those so much studied today and sometimes spoken of as typical of all dreams. But these, say the Papago, "did not mean anything. We forgot them." Other dreams however, were motivated by constant thought and desire directed toward one end — say a visit from Coyote — until it must have reflection in dreams. Such a desire was by no means suppressed: these dreams acted as messengers, not from the sub-conscious to the conscious but in the reverse direction. When a man's subconscious could produce, in sleep, a reflection of the very image toward which his conscious desires and those of his society were bent, he had attained supernatural power.

The inviting of this power took no such drastic form as it did in the Plains for both violent ambition and torture were contrary to Papago attitudes. Boys were urged to run and to be frugal in their diet but the purpose was not self mortification. Rather it was training them in those physical characteristics which were needed in useful members of society. Even the purification of the Enemy Slayer had its principal use in proving his fortitude for dealing with daily life. The animal Visitants were pleased with the heroes, not because they had made a sacrifice but because they had shown themselves to be swift and enduring like good Papagos.

[1] Benedict, 1923.
[2] Boscana, 1846, p. 17; Hooper, 1920, p. 335.
[3] Steward, 1933, p. 311; Park. 1934, p. 99; Lowie, 1924, p. 154; Gifford, 1932, pp. 15—65.

In one respect, the Papago vision differs both from that of the Yumans and that of the Plains. In these areas, the experience is essentially democratic, opening to him who achieves it, every avenue of advance. But the Papago dream brought success only in racing, gambling, war and curing. Planting was taken care of by communal ritual and office, both ceremonial and secular, descended by heredity, without benefit of vision. It seems possible to relate this importance of the hierarchy to Pueblo influence. We have mentioned that the group of officiers in a Papago village is a simplified version of that found in the western Pueblos where, also, office derives from family status. Wheter this group was imposed on a society which already had the vision formula or whether that formula found them already established, they would serve as a barrier to the principle that all avenues were open to the dreamer.

### NAMES

An experience of adult life which, from the Papago point of view, must be placed among the crucial ones was the receiving of a nickname. This was actually the appellation by which a man was called while his shaman-given name passed into disuse. Women did not receive nicknames but instead were often the givers.

A distinguishing characteristic of Papago names is that they usually have more reference to the giver than to the person named. This is the case with shaman-given names which describe something the shaman has seen in a dream. The dream has no connection with the child to be named except that, as is apparent from the examples, dreams referring to flowers and plants are used for women. There may have been other distinctions of the same sort. Some shaman-given names follow:

| Men | Women |
|---|---|
| Circling Light | Rushing Light Beams |
| Daylight Comes | Rustling Leaves |
| Wind Rainbow | Wind Leaves |
| Cloud Rainbow | Blossom Tips |
| Rainbow Shaman | Feather Leaves |
| Having a Rainbow as a Bow | Singing Dawn |
| Shining Beetle | Sifting |
| Hawk Flying Over Water Holes | Flowers Trembling |
| Chief of Jackrabbits | Leaves Flying |
| Crooked Shining | Water Drops on Leaves |
| Thundering Wings | Leaf Blossoms |
| Short Wings | Foamy Water |
| Shining Evening | |

In view of the affinity of the Papago system of male sib titles with the Yuman system of female sib names,[1] it would seem possible that some of the men's names might bear sib suggestions. No connection could de traced of Wind, Rainbow and the other natural phenomena which characterize the shaman's dreams with sib or moiety.

The rules for the use of the given name are now obscured, since all Papagos have Spanish or English names and some families have had them for generations. However, all older men and women have shaman-given names and most men have nicknames. They make no objection to telling their given names, though some will not tell that of another. Many people are habitually called by given names. Nevertheless, many signs point to a name taboo and to the use instead of either a kin term or a nickname.

A person is habitually addressed and spoken of by the kinship term, prefixed with the possessive pronoun: my younger sister's child, your father's older brother. All ceremonial greetings made use of the kin term only, even the final salute to the dead, which was a form of exorcism. When unrelated men had, to each other, the relationship of guardian and protégé, special kin terms were coined to meet the case: my made-father, my nephew.

Even with supernaturals there was the same situation. In many of the rituals for the salt expedition, there is mention of a powerful supernatural who is alluded to by no other term than my made-father, or guardian. Since the name is nowhere mentioned, informants, who had learned the ritual by rote, could not tell who was meant. The same is true in the ritual for the rain ceremony. Elder Brother himself had the given name Iitoi, but instead is always called by the kinship term he acquired. Coyote is called "our partner" or the "gray comrade." This usage may de interpreted from the point of view of the importance of the kin term but also from that of the objection to the use of the name. In some rain rituals there is no kin term but a mention of one who sat on the rain house, and in a war ritual one who was underground (presumably earth magician). The smoker's invocation to the sun says simply: "You stand there," without giving a name.

The place where a supernatural power is habitually mentioned by name is in the curing songs. These are descriptions of animals who have by their power brought the disease and can also take it away. There is no myth of relationship with any of these animals as with Coyote. The song often begins with a mention of the animal's name as a sort of invocation and then proceeds with a description.

---

[1] Spier, 1933, p. 196.

It is badger shaman!
In the night he runs.
Venison he brings.

Little blue fly!
It hangs on my horn.
It will bother me.

Red ants!
Toward me they flung darkness

The idea here seems to be not to flatter or implore the animal but to mention and describe him, as though that naming in itself negated his power to bring disease.

With the Papagos, when a man's name had to be mentioned, it was usually a nickname. Even with ceremonial announcements this was the case. When a war party returned, they sent a herald ahead to shout the names of the slayers, so that their families might be secluded and nicknames, not given names, were used. When naming songs were sung in connection with intervillage races, the singing side sent to inquire the names of their hosts, which they put in their songs and again the names were nicknames. The hosts in turn inquired the names of their guests so that they might call each one to come and receive a gift. "But we only gave them silly names. Not our real ones." (26) This would point to a lifelong prohibition from the use of the given name, though Russell says that among the Pimas such a prohibition lasted only from the age of ten to marriage.[1]

Papago nicknames are of three sorts: descriptive names, referring to some peculiarity of the person named; sexual names, referring to a peculiarity of the namers and "enemy" names, referring to a peculiarity of a dead enemy, mentioned by the person named. The last two have the Papago trait of referring more to another person than to the one named. These were names obtained by a man's own exploits, highly valued and traded. The first, the descriptive name, was apparently a mere makeshift, used in daily life, until a man could get something else.

1. Descriptive names. These are always slightly derogatory and may easily be distinguished from the shaman-given names which have a lofty poetic tone.
   Grasshopper ate his arrow (from an incident on a hunting trip)

---

[1] Russell, p. 188.

One-on-top-of-another (a man bought two shawls and wore them home thus)

Begging for yucca fruit (from an incident at camp)

Self-explanatory names are:

| | |
|---|---|
| Looking Back | Gambler |
| Having No Pet | One Who Never Plants |
| Back to the Fire | Girl Follower |
| Many Garments | One Who Lies Down Curled Up |
| Garment Falling Off | Dizzy One |
| Blisters | Bed Wetter |
| Fish Smell Mouth | Girl Beckoner |
| Ridge Face | Rat Ear |
| Neck Tendons | Yellow Legs |
| Gourd Head | |

2. Sexual names. These were given in obscene jest by a woman or by the berdache and referred to the sexual parts, not of the person named but of the speaker. A divorced wife, on parting from a man, often labelled him with such a name. It was also given by one with whom he had had a sex relationship, often also in jeering invitation. The name was made public by the giver, who shouted it after the man when others could hear. The recipient of the name, far from feeling embarrassment, regarded it as a proof of prowess. He accepted it and was regularly called by it, even by his wife and family.

Some names are: Vulva-with-hair-growing-downward, Big Vulva, Skirt String, Long Anus.

3. Enemy names. It was customary, when a dead enemy was left on the field or near the village after a raid, for all who could to gather round the body and shout comments, without touching it. Such comments constituted nicknames for the shouters.

Some names mentioned are: Wild Cat's Back (because an Apache's back was spotted [with paint?]), Long Bones, Full of Dirt, Yellow Face, Gold Breasts (the last of a girl).

This would seem an excellent opportunity to acquire a striking name but in at least one instance the calendar stick reports that a party of men heard there were some dead Apaches nearby but did not go there "because they were afraid of what the people would call them".

The use of a man's descriptive nickname persisted along with his sexual or enemy name so that an individual often had several appellations. Though the derogatory descriptive names were accepted and answered to without objection, many tried to get them changed to something which suited their personal taste. No man

12

invented a nickname and asked to be called by it. But if he had no sexual or enemy name, he might buy a nickname belonging to someone else, or might exchange his old one for it. Thus Devil-Old Man exchanged names with Contrary. Looking-For-Girls-at-a-Dance changed with Big Crazy, but had to give him four pints of whiskey in addition, because of the desirability of the name. Vincenzo, who had only a Spanish name, bought the name of Two Bits from Joe, who in turn was left with a Spanish name. The exchanges were not always operative and a man, even after he had traded for a desirable name, sometimes found that people would not call him by it.

# MARRIAGE AND SEX BEHAVIOR

Polygynous marriage was approved but not practised by every one. Old men, particularly the shaman and the Keeper of the Meeting, often had four wives but most had two. Very young men had only one.

The sororate was in full force. If a man had married one daughter in a family, it was expected as a matter of course, that he would take all the others as they matured, even while the first wife was living. The junior levirate is a vague tradition. It was "a good thing" if a man's younger brother married his widow but it was not required. Some informants had not even heard of the tradition.

Marriage was arranged by the bride's parents. They saw that their daughter's breasts were large and they said, "They should be used for something." This might be immediately after puberty. It was felt that marriage should synchronize with the awakening of sex interest and some informants even quote twelve as a marriage-able age for a girl. (1) The husband, if this were his first marriage, might be sixteen or seventeen. He and his young bride were by no means considered adults but lived with the groom's parents in a state of tutelage until they had several children.

The choosing of a mate for the first daughter in the family was subject to certain rules. There were no clan or moiety restrictions, but the youth should not be a relative, that is, a lineal descendant of any one of the bride's great grandparents. Also he should be from another village. This latter was a social rule but not enforced by supernatural punishments as was exogamy among relatives. If the girl's father had been wounded by an Apache, she should marry the son of a man so wounded, since it produced a form of family taint that must not be spread.

Having decided on a mate, the girl's parents consulted the adult relatives of the father's lineage and of the mother's. All gave their opinion as to whether the youth was industrious and a good runner and if they decided that he was eligible, the girl's parents called on his parents with the proposal: "We have an industrious daughter. We offer her to your son."

The boy's parents, if they objected to the girl, would take care not to be at home for to refuse would be an insult. But if the boy were already affianced, it was proper to say: "He has already been given a girl." Otherwise they replied: "We think as you do." A slight interchange of gifts usually took place, rather as a courteous gesture than an economic procedure. The only other formality was for the youth to sleep at the house of the girl for the first four nights while the marriage was consummated. After that they went to live with his family.

But before the marriage took place, the parents allowed about a month to elapse while they trained their children for the new status. The training took the same form of nightly admonition which had been given during childhood. Both young people were instructed to be industrious and to show consideration to each other. The girl, whose home would now be with her husband's family, was told that she must take over the work for her mother-in-law. A sample of such admonition by a girl's father follows:

"We want you to behave yourself as we have always taught you to do. Stay there in the right way. Don't wait for your mother-in-law to tell you what to do. Get up early, find wheat, grind flour. If you can't make tortillas, have flour ready for her to make them. You stay right there and make your home there. It has been here, but now you belong there. Stay home, don't run around. Do your work, carry the wood, cook something. Any work you see, you do it.

Don't go off to peoples' houses and walk around and gossip. Gossip may spoil a good home. That husband of yours, listen to him. Don't talk when he's talking, for he is like a chief to you. Don't beg him to take you with him here and there, but if he wants you to go, go, whether you want to or not. Don't one day get mad at your new family and think you can run home: a day will come when your husband will want to visit us and will bring you. Now that's your home and if you are lucky, you will grow old and die there. That is the way it is." (26)

Both young people were also given sex instruction. Up to this time, girls and boys had been kept rigidly separate. Girls were rarely out of sight of their mothers, in the house or on food gathering expeditions. They were expected never to speak to a man unless he were a relative, when they should offer him food and then leave him. If a strange man approached the house, they should run out and hide.

This inhibition had now to be broken down in favor of a particular man. The girl's mother said to her:

"You will now have a husband as all women do. If you did not, you would be unnatural. You must not be afraid of him. Try to do as he wishes without restraint. That is what women are for. Do not object or run away. We are bringing this man to you because it is best." ( 7)

The boy's father also instructed him:

"Your wife has not known men. Do not frighten her. If she runs away from you, do not follow her. Wait for her mother to deal with her. Be patient."

When the parents felt the instruction was sufficient, they would confer again. The girl's parents might say: "Our daughter is ready now. We have taught her all we can. Watch her behavior and if she does not do right, instruct her." The boy's parents replied: "You do the same for us. Our boy should know his duty but if he does not, you should complain."

The boy was then sent to spend his first four nights with his bride. He did not come in the daytime, "because he would be ashamed". He entered the hut after dark and left before morning. The pattern evidently demanded that a well-brought up girl should show fright at such a time for the admonitions and accounts of marriage always mention a terrified bride. One informant said she ran around the house until her mother caught her. Another hid in the large granary basket and had to de dragged out (27). This was done by her family, not by the bridegroom.

On the fifth day, the bridegroom having left before dawn, the bride's mother escorted her to her new home. The bride took nothing with her because it would not be good manners to do so until she was established, but her mother brought the groom's mother a small gift. The groom's family, if they were well-to-do people, gave the bride a buckskin dress and might also make a gift to her mother. It was not obligatory, merely out of good will, "when we had something". An informant thus described the formalities:

"He (the bridegroom) left our house in the morning and my mother and I went in the afternoon. My mother had her carrying basket on her back with a jar of cactus syrup as a present.... We stood out behind their house and waited to be invited in.... My mother-in-law came out, took the syrup from my mother's basket and put it away. Then she came out with some beans and corn and filled the carrying basket. She said to me, 'I have put the mat for you.' So I went into the house and my mother went home. My mother-in-law came to the mat she had placed and laid on it a waist and skirt and some beads." (26)

The young people lived in the house with the groom's parents until they had one or more children. They were still practically under tutelage; the boy working and hunting with his brothers under his father's direction, the girl doing the heavy housework for her mother-in-law, often with several sisters-in-law to help her.

As a privilege of the married state, the girl might now be seen at ceremonies and dances, particularly the puberty dance which sometimes turned into a lascivious occasion. She and her husband, as a sign of intimacy, ate out of the same dish and deloused one another's hair.

The system of having the groom spend four nights at the bride's house was only for first marriages and if either party had been married before, it was omitted. When the groom was already the husband of the bride's older sister, there were no formalities. The bride's parents simply announced that their daughter was old enough, received his acquiescence and brought her to him. But parents often decided to offer a daughter to a man who had a wife not her sister or who was widowed or divorced. In that case they delayed to consult their relatives and instruct the girl but then took her to him without the preliminary four nights. If the man were still very young, the negotiations might be made with his family, otherwise with the man himself. Adult women also sometimes made their own arrangements but as a rule a widow or a divorced woman who returned to her family was disposed of by them like a young girl.

"We gave my son a wife when he was seventeen. Some people came to us and said, 'We have a daughter. She was married to a man but that man went away to the White school and when he came back, he did not take her. She is older than your son but she is industrious. She may be some help to him.' We said, 'It is true that she is older but we have seen her work. She may be a help.' So we told our son and he said nothing." (26)

A divorced woman thus recounted her experience after she had come back to her mother's house.

"A few days' later my uncle found out. He said, 'We cannot have this woman here with no one to care for her. We must find a husband.' So he went to an old man and proposed for me. I didn't say anything. No woman has a right to speak against the men of her family." (26)

### MARITAL RELATIONS

All a man's wives lived in the same house. If they were sisters, it was said they always got along together; otherwise there might be quarrelling and he might build a separate house for one of them. The local tales abound in situations where a man had to divide his attention between two wives.

The pattern of female seclusion and modesty was entirely altered after marriage. Women might now go to the drinking ceremonies and to the girl's puberty dance which was the outstanding occasion for sex liberties. For couples to disappear into the darkness at these times was an accepted part of the performance. Women joked freely and obscenely with married men and the words they used in semi-joking invitation were used by the men as nicknames. Very few adult men are called, in daily life, by the name given them by the shaman, but rather by one of these terms. Such temporary liberties did not constitute grounds for complaint on the part of a spouse. It was only when husband or wife left home with a lover that there was serious difficulty.

There was a class of women who assumed a married woman's privileges of free language and contacts with men, without any of her duties. This same class, which closely resembles that of the prostitute, is found among the Pimas and called by a name which means "playful" or light woman. If it has been adopted under European influence, it has at least become thoroughly assimilated to the Papago and Pima pattern, for it lacks both the obloquy and the element of pay present in the European institution. The Papago tradition is that the playful women were called out long ago by a youth who played the flute and drove them mad.

The playful women were always in festal array. Their clothing was the double apron or a strip of cotton cloth wound around as a skirt. They painted their bodies, legs and feet, by smearing them with red or white clay and then making patterns with the wet finger tip. They made lines under their eyes with the black specular iron which the men used in war and called "dizziness". On their cheeks they might have vertical marks of red clay. Their hair was well combed and they wore a fillet of hair around the forehead with a bit of eagle down stuck upright.[1]

So arrayed, the light women would go all together to the girl's puberty dances or to the big drinking ceremonies, where married women appeared only with their husbands and young girls not at all. The playful woman would form a temporary union with some man with whom she would visit several drinking ceremonies or dance through the whole month of puberty dances. At such festivities, food was supplied to everyone and her mate need not necessarily support her. She might follow him on a trading expedition, when he would care for her or occasionally she would go home with him and become one of his wives. In that case the other wives would not object, unless she were too lazy. But she generally left him again to attend a new festivity.

Between affairs she would go back to her father's house. Parents made no attempt to control a daughter, if she seemed inclined to

---

[1] That this type of woman was not a Spanish importation is indicated by two mentions of "prostitutes" in Sahagun: Seler, Neunter Abschnitt, b, 7, p. 366 and Jourdanet et Simon, Livre X, chap. XV, p. 616.

this way of life but simply gave up and allowed her to have her way. If she had children, they would take care of them, since no stigma attached to a fatherless child. The only penalty was that they could not find her a husband, because she was not industrious. But when she was ready to settle down, she frequently found one for herself.

The mother of one informant is reported to have been such a woman. She had wandered to the Altar valley, where she met the young chief (American appointed) of a desert village. "Will you take me to your home ?" she proposed. "Would you pick cactus fruit for me, grind my corn and fetch my water ?" "Yes. I will pick cactus, grind corn and fetch water." She settled down and spent her life as an industrious wife.

Such incidents were not infrequent. In taking family histories, I several times heard the statement, "He married a light woman", without any other comment than a smile. "The light woman can't help it," informants explain. "Her heart bubbles over" (20). "When you talk to her, she doesn't know what you say. Her heart is outside her, running ahead, to the next dance" (31). Some of the most poetic of Papago songs deal with "the wandering heart" of the light woman.

Men who were flirtatious and had many sex affairs were also alluded to as playful but they did not form a distinct class like the women. Both men and women might be made ill by dreaming about the playful people. The symptoms were dizziness and lassitude. The cure was to make clay dolls in the form of man and woman and to have someone sing the girl's puberty songs. Lovesick visions were a common ailment and were attributed to several causes. An unidentified root, called tcïnaca't,[1] was used by men to attract both deer and girls. This root could assume the form of a man, enter a woman's house and cohabit with her after which she would pine. Also the scalps or the Apache effigy in an Enemy Slayer's basket could take the form of a handsome man, and torment women with yearning.

If anyone, man or woman, thought too much of a person of the opposite sex, even though that person were a spouse, a snake would come and cohabit with the dreamer in the place of the loved one. Many tales are told of people who supposed themselves happily married, while others knew that they were going daily to the arroyo to lie with a snake. The same fate will overtake one who is not yet married and who thinks too much about love. Young people who look dreamy are reprimanded: "What are you mooning about ? You must be married to a snake."

---

[1] cf. Zuni tenatsali.

### DIVORCE

A couple who could not get along together, generally brought their case to the Keeper of the Meeting or, later, the governor. He tried to reconcile them until the affair recurred so often that he sanctioned their separation. Where the whipping post was in use, the person whom the Keeper considered responsible for the difference was whipped, the other party naming the number of strokes.

The woman went back to her family taking the small children (1), or the daughters (26). She left her baskets and everything she had made, though it was proper to take one basket of provisions. If the husband decided he wanted her back, he must again get the Keeper of the Meeting as mediator and might have to stand a whipping before she would return. The woman might change her mind and go back to her husband by the same means. Both immediately married again, unless the husband already had wives enough. The wife might look around and find a man for herself, but if she did not, the family would soon dispose of her, since an adult unmarried woman in a house was an abnormality.

The most usual cause for divorce was bad temper and next was the fact that the spouse had gone off with someone else. Laziness was not so often fatal. A man would bring in another wife: a woman would complain to her family and the Keeper, but would not leave her husband except for further cause.

A few accounts of marriages follow:

"Angelita's husband was a shaman who married four sisters. He was old when he took the youngest, but being a shaman, he knew how to make her love him." (26)

"A man had two wives, each of whom slept in a separate enclosure. One night he came out of the enclosure of the second wife and went to that of the first. She threw dirt at him and berated him for going to the other woman. The other ran out and began to scold. This mother-in-law said to the man, 'Don't put a hand on them. It's your own fault. You wanted them.' So the women pulled each other's hair and knocked each other down. But they kept on with the man. They never left. They were not sisters." (26)

"A woman I know married several different men but each one had a wife already. She was always fighting with these co-wives and each of the husbands finally left her. She never had the sense to take a single man." (26)

"Crooked Lightning left his wife. She was lazy and mean, but he never scolded her. He simply left. Crooked Lightning's sister was married to one of his friends so when that friend heard he was free, he gave him his niece to make them closer." (26)

"A playful woman had married three or four men but had left them all. She was at a drinking ceremony and danced all night with a chief who was tall and liked to dance, but he was old. She could not see that at night. In the morning he put her on the horse with him to go home. She said, "Where do you live?' 'At the place of the Dead Dog.' 'Oh, that's too far.' So she jumped off the horse and left him. She had seen by the rising sun that he was old." (26)

"The chief of our village is so old that he is blind and deaf. He has lived all his life with one wife. They never quarrel. That is true of many of our people." (26)

### THE BERDACHE

The male transvestite was a common figure. It is comprehensible that a man who balked at the rigors of war and hunting should accept woman's clothing as an alternative entirely without opprobrium. But the berdache was said to have been discovered in early childhood. If the parents found that a boy liked female pursuits they tested him. The regular pattern, mentioned by many informants, was to build a small enclosure and place in it bow and arrows and basketry materials. Thechild was told to go in and play and then the parents set fire to the enclosure. They watched what he took with him as he ran out and if it was the basketry materials, they reconciled themselves to his being a berdache.

The berdache performed women's work. He made one of the group of women on food gathering expeditions and was treated as one of themselves. He was often a clever potter and basket maker and an asset on food gathering expeditions, because he "didn't get tired as we did". He also played an important role in the village.

When the Apache trophy was hung up, if there was a berdache in the village, he might dance around it with a bow taunting it: "See what you are reduced to! The men will not look at you, but I, even I, can shoot you" (27).

The berdache might marry, but often, since he was entirely able to work and support himself, he lived alone and was visited by the men. To each visitor he gave an obscene nickname and the men were very proud of these, since they were often bolder than those bestowed by women. No scorn was felt for the berdache. He was respected and liked by the women and his sex life with the men was a community institution.

One informant thus described her berdache brother-in-law:

"We girls used to spend all day with that man-woman, Shining Evening. She went off with us to gather plants and she could carry more than any of us and dig longer. She ground corn with us, all taking turns at my mother-in-law's grinding slab. Our husbands used to tease us girls. 'How do we know these children running around the house belong to us ? We are away in the mountains all the time and in the fields. It is Shining Evening who is with the women.' Then they would laugh and say to the babies, 'Run along. Over there is your daddy.....'.

When we learned from the Whites to make skirts with drawstrings, Shining Evening was the first to have one. A man pulled the string and said, 'What's that ?' and she said squealing, 'Skirt string!' So after that the man was always called skirt string."

"There was a berdache in the next village and that one had a husband. She came with him to the drinking ceremony and I saw her cooking for him on the fireplace of some of her relatives. They seemed happy." (26)

When informants were asked about female transvestites, they burst into laughter at the possibility.

# DEATH

If it seemed certain that a person was going to die, he was removed from the house so it would not have to be destroyed. There was no avoidance of the dying: rather all the relatives, particularly women, gathered and might begin to wail even before death had occurred. Immediately after death, ritual wailing began and lasted until the body had been interred. Women wailed the most constantly, but men also joined them. The wail consisted in repeating the kinship term in regular rhythm and on a high note so "it sounded like singing" (32).

In deaths other than those from enemy wounds the corpse was interred. In the foothills, where digging was difficult, it was placed in a cave or a cleft in the rocks, any openings being filled up with stones. Where no cave was available, a rudimentary cliff dwelling was made, one side of the hill being used as a wall while a complementary wall was built up out of dry masonry, so that the whole formed a circle four feet or so in diameter. The corpse, with his effects was seated inside it and the whole roofed over with boughs and brush, weighted down with stones. The work was done by all the men of the geographic unit, the younger ones fetching poles for the roof, sometimes from a great distance, the older ones building up the stone work. This was the only stonework ever used by the Papago except in occasional mountain storehouses.

They made such a grave if it was at all possible, even carrying the corpse a long distance to rocky country, on a rough litter made of cactus ribs. But if rocky country was too far, they dug a pit, six or seven feet deep, with a niche at one side (1, 20). In this the corpse was seated but the grave was not filled with earth. Instead it was roofed over like the house or the rock grave.

The body was placed in the sitting position used in life: a man had his hands around his knees; a woman had her knees to the right. The dead wore his best regalia and paint. A warrior had his headdress and was painted for war; Enemy Slayers had the top part of the face black and the lower part white as they did during purification; ceremonial officiants wore the appropriate paint, but their costumes were generally hereditary and were not buried with them.

Property was laid in the grave, according to some; just outside it, according to others. A man had his weapons, a woman her pots and baskets. In later days, a man's riding horse was killed by the grave. Food was placed outside, generally in miniature dishes[1] (29). There was no prescription as to the kind of food but pinole and, water, the standard diet, were always included.

Ceremonial property was inherited by a successor and not buried. It was in any case kept outside the house so that it had not been contaminated by the death and the deceased had generally appointed one of his descendants or relatives to be the future custodian. A shaman's rattle and plumes were not inherited, but it was thought that they should not be placed in the grave, because that would ruin their power. "The power should be left loose in the world for someone to find."

All the members of the geographic unit came to the grave, wailing. There was no time for others to be summoned and, in that hot country, corpses were disposed of immediately. After the corpse had been seated in place and the property placed around him, one of the oldest and nearest (a father, mother or spouse) spoke to him, im words which were impromptu, but always in the same general terms. He began, as on all ceremonial occasions, with the salute by the kin term.

> "My daughter's child! You were dear to me. Now you are gone. I shall not see you again. Go now, my daughter's child, I beg of you and do not come back to frighten your relatives." (33)
> "My father! We are giving you all your possessions. We give you your horse, so you can enjoy yourself with your kinsmen. Don't wish for us or wish to come back; you have left us. Neither will we wish for you back." (20)
> "My child! Go! Do not come back. Your place is not here any longer. Your place is with the dead. Do not trouble us." (9)

Each relative in turn then saluted the dead, using the kin term for the last time and adjuring him: "Go! Do not come back." Then one of the women, properly the oldest of the household, set food and water by the grave. For four days after the funeral, the relatives took food to the grave or, according to some, they took it on the fourth day (11). "But with children, we took it twice a day, because they need help" (11).

At the end of this time some older relative or friend advised the mourners: "Now it is finished. You know this comes to everyone, but now you must try to forget your sorrow, for if you think too much about it you might get sick. We are all sorry for the dead, but let it be. You know the penalty of thinking about death" (1).

Still, those who were not afraid went occasionally to the grave, sometimes taking food. Bodies tended to mummify in the dry air and could be seen through the chinks in the masonry looking as in life. One Mexicanized woman told of going for years to look at her dead husband with his red sash and his violin. Another married a second husband and, when she still kept dreaming of the first, the second went to the grave and threatened him: "Leave her alone or else I will dig you up and burn your bones!"

There is a yearly festival of feeding the dead, which is now thoroughly amalgamated with the Christian feast of All Souls, but which has some likeness to the Aztec custom of sending property to the dead by burning once a year for four years.[1]

The feeding and gifts for the dead applied only to those who had been buried. Those who had died on the warpath or at home, from enemy wounds, were cremated, without ceremony. Only purified Enemy Slayers were competent to touch the corpse or his effects, because "it would make them sick". The officiants followed no ritual. They placed the weapons with the body, piled what wood they could find over and under it and burned it as quickly as possible. The kindred wailed but not at the cremation site, "because they were afraid."

Cremation was definitely for the purpose of destroying enemy magic, for it did not take place after accidental shooting at the hunt, nor after murder by a fellow Papago. Only enemy wounds made it necessary. That the enemy need not always be the Apache, is shown by a Spanish account which relates how, when a Jesuit priest was killed by revolting "Pimas" his friendly parishioners burned his body; "this burning is the manner in which the Pimas treat their dead whom they most esteem".[2] It was not the heroism but the enemy magic which necessitated the burning.

The Hohokam, or ancient inhabitants of Papagueria, habitually burned their dead and kept the ashes in jars. If the Papago, as Gladwin[3] suggests are degenerate remains of this ancient culture, their habit of cremation in this one respect, might be a survival of the former practice. But it might equally well be related to the custom of the Aztecs, who disposed of their dead by cremation or burial, according to the manner of death.[4]

Immediately after a death of any kind, the family pulled down the house to prevent its being visited by ghosts. The house was a

---

[1] Sahagun, Seler p. 297.
[2] Velarde section 3, p. 145.
[3] Gladwin 1929.
[4] Sahagun, Seler, pp. 300, 301, 298, 299.

flimsy affair and this destruction was probably an aid to sanitation. But the four mesquite posts of the frame work were hard to come by so they were generally moved and a new house built around them. There are traditions of bereaved families who threw away all their property or burned it, after the Mohave fashion, but most people denied this. "We couldn't have lived. We were too poor" (11). But if there had been many deaths in succession, the family left everything but what they could carry on their backs and went to seek asylum with distant relatives. It was thought better to leave the fields to others while they were so ghost ridden.

Women, in mourning, cut their hair to the neck, men to the shoulders. Hair should be buried at a distance, out of reach of animals but since it was such valuable property, there were some who ventured to use it for hair ropes. Used in a carrying basket, one old woman stated, it even brought luck. Those who had not lost a spouse wailed for the ritual four days and then went about their occupations but widows and widowers must mourn longer. A widow, in the very ancient times, wore nothing but a breechclout and went unpainted for a year, after which she might marry again. A widower went unpainted and his period of mourning was thought by most to be a year but one man said he could marry after four days. "A woman could work and take care of herself for a year, but a man needed some one to work for him" (1).

If the husband had died, the wife might marry one of his younger siblings but otherwise she went back to her family group. Very young children who needed her care, she would take with her, but older ones would be left to be brought up in her husband's group, probably by his mother. An elderly widow often remained in the adopted group, with her sons to support her. But there is one example of such a woman who returned, with all her grown sons, because her home field was better (I. 1. A 3). At the end of the mourning period, if she were of marriageable age, her family found her another husband. Children of her first husband were likely to be sent back to his family group, but if that was inconvenient, they stayed with her parents. She rarely took them into the new home.

If the wife died, the children remained in the husband's group, cared for by his mother or one of his brothers' wives. If he had been satisfactory, he might be given one of the wife's classificatory younger sisters. Otherwise he took a new wife and the children of the former one remained with his mother.

The souls of the dead went to the east, escorted by their ancestors, who came for the dying man in the shape of owls. This was true whether they had died of illness or of enemy wounds. The soul on its journey must pass through a gap, which was very dangerous.[1] His owl companions went through it easily but the newly dead had trouble. Some turned back at this point and found themselves alive again. Beyond the gap is the town where the dead live, just as people on earth do. If the newly dead mingles with them and speaks to them, he cannot come back. If he does not speak, he may still regain life. In the town he will find his ancestors who "bring him up like a child," teaching him all their ways. The life is like the life on earth, except that there is plenty of rain, for this is in the east, whence the rain comes.

The dead can leave this land at any time and fly back in a moment in the form of owls and they come thus to call the relatives whom they wish to have as companions. Warriors killed in the Apache country meet war parties and guide them through the enemy's land. Shamans come back and instruct living shamans.

If a person is being called by the dead, he may dream of them or he may fall unconscious, his soul gone. He then applies to the shaman, but the shaman does not send his own soul on a search. He sharpens four sticks, paints them and puts them outside the grave to "shut the door." Or he smokes a ceremonial cigarette and asks the dead to come out. An owl may appear and then the shaman urges him to go away and leave the living alone. Meanwhile a group of helpers, some distance off, sings the song cycle which removes an evil charm.

The California objection to naming the dead appears among the Papagos in a modified form. In the northern part of the area, the names are freely used; (26, 19, 1) in the southern part they are not (9). The mention of the name would evoke the dead who would bring sickness on his kin. Therefore, the kin themselves would not do it, and if a mysterious sickness appeared among them, they would suspect that someone else had done it and be angry. A subsidiary reason given is that the name "makes them feel too bad" (9).

But it is only the relatives who would suffer. An informant once was prevented from singing me a song, where a specific name should be mentioned, because all the people whose names he had heard used in such songs were dead and if he used them, their relatives would be angry. Nor would he use the names of his own relatives. But the interpreter, who had abandoned the old customs, gave permission for the names of his ancestors to be used and then the informant had no fear.

If the name is not used, the dead is referred to by the kinship

---

[1] Compare, Aztecs, Sahagun, Seler, pt. 6, sec. 4, p. 303.

term but either is followed by the suffix — paṭ (deceased). Most names contain adjectives and nouns in common use, but the relatives do not avoid these words in daily speech. The shaman, who names children from his dreams, would not give the name of a dead person to a new child in the family.

A form of tears greeting is practised after there has been a death in a family. When relatives meet, who have not seen each other since the death, they approach weeping and spend some time wailing together. This is now done only by the women, but in the old days men wept too. When a village holds a ceremony to which people will come from a distance, the women of bereaved families stand in front of their houses weeping as visitors approach. Visiting female relatives join them and all wail, using the kin term of the deceased.[1]

---

[1] Cf. Eskimo, Thalbitzer, pp. 78—89, and Navajo, personal information, Dr. Reichard.

# MORES

The habits of the Papago proclaim a peaceful and settled people. Their habitat might have urged them to migrate to the mountains for hunting and raiding and, indeed, they were driven to hunting every winter. But not to raiding. Though the Apache found a predatory life necessary in such a country, the Papago returned doggedly every summer to the unremitting toil of dry farming. War has never fitted the rhythm of an agricultural people, and the Papago found it particularly abhorrent. They gave it such a place in their ceremonial system that no material profit could be derived from it. Everything taken from the enemy was burned; and the emotion of the returning warrior was that of the farmer relieved from an unpleasant task:

> Then came I back to that my land.
> I stood upon it and stood firm.
> I sat upon it and sat still.

Communities with such a peaceful tradition had no bent for developing feuds among themselves. Though each village was self-supporting, neither the villages nor the village units developed an attitude of aggressive independence. Instead, they made a habit of intermarrying so that they were tied together by affinal relationships, and they even developed a ceremony for propitiating non-relatives. In the open desert country communication and gifts were constant. Without any central authority, the Desert People cultivated a mutual dependence and maintained their society by peaceableness.

These ideals held as firmly between individuals as between villages. The Papago had no rules of avoidance which would prevent tense situations between any groups. Instead, they had what might be termed a universal avoidance of quarrelling or even the mildest expression of blame. The social ideal demanded the concealment of all feelings of hostility, so that the opponent himself should no more than guess at them. Those who voiced such feelings at all did so in a low voice "so that no one at a distance would know it was a quarrel." Open fighting and murder were so rare that many said they never occurred. The one outlet for disapproval allowed by public opinion was ridicule and dislike was habitually turned into this channel.

Papago society was completely democratic if we except the class division into old and young which made every one, in the course of his life, first an inferior, then a superior. Within an age group, all had equal rights and even the officials did not dictate. It was their aim to come to a decision which should have the complete emotional support of all and they were willing to take endless time in achieving this. The result was an extremely stable society, moving slowly and not subject to tyrannous changes.

Unity was not a difficult ideal, for all had the same surroundings and experiences, and all had been conditioned from childhood to the same code of behavior. It was this relentless conditioning which made organized government superfluous. People were already prepared for the necessary duties and, unless circumstances changed, would perform them almost automatically.

Unity being the ideal, no one was expected to take authority or to "make himself big". Common sense and industry were what gained respect and any attempt at prestige would arouse suspicion. A man who had been through the various purifications and thus achieved all that individual prowess could, was warned when he became a "ripe man": "Now you must always stay behind the others. When food is passed, you must be the last to take it." This was the accepted demeanor for the great.

The unity of the group was constantly emphasized in words. "We love our relatives. Our pleasure in life is to be with our relatives." The Papago, so restrained in most directions, seem, from the White point of view, over-expressive on this one point, but it is the emphasizing of a principle: a constant reminder of the proper group attitude.

The individual derives his sense of importance from his feeling of unity with the group. There need be no struggle for position for he has position which only the most outrageous conduct can forfeit. As there is no special honor for the officials, so there is no lack of respect for the humdrum group members. The frantic hunger for success which plagues a White society was entirely unknown to the old time Papago.

A good man in the Papago sense, was a useful member of the group. He must be peaceable and loyal. He must be industrious, so that others would not have to support him, and he must be generous with gifts. He must have common sense so that he would be an asset in the group councils but he should not have striking ideas which would make unity hard to achieve. He should be modest and, no matter how old and wise he was, wait to speak until he was asked. He should never quarrel or speak evil. His ambition

13*

should be to achieve the status of responsible patriarch, able to support and protect others. In addition, if he had had a vision which gave him power, it was desirable, for thus he could better help his family. But individual power was an idea extraneous to the main Papago scheme and never logically incorporated with it.

The good woman had much the same virtues as the good man for, in her household sphere, she also took council and responsibility. With her, there was little question of a vision and industry headed all the virtues. Her conduct in sex matters was not, by any means the distinguishing mark of her behavior for both she and the man had a fair amount of latitude. But she had a ceremonial duty never to injure men by her presence while menstruating. If she was careful in this respect and was industrious, she was always a good citizen.

The achievement of this ideal was perfectly possible for any average group member and the society was correspondingly contented. The unadjusted person was the ambitious individual, with startling ideas. He would always be listened to, — at least if he waited until he was old enough to speak in council — for the society suppressed no one. But he would suffer the stigma of being uncooperative, talking too much and being "big headed." Only the most urgent conviction could nerve a man to put himself thus outside the pale, or only the most robust ambition. One imagines that shamans must have had such an ambition for they alone took the risks and received the rewards of the business adventurer. In psychology, they came nearest to the normal individualists of a modern society. But the average group member was not likely to diverge. The emotional drive to unity was great, experience was limited and ideas hard to come by. If a man had one which differed from the ideas of the council and if he could maintain it until he was elderly and entitled to speak, it was valid indeed.

Group unity is now being rapidly broken up by the impact of White ideas, but it is still found among the older men, and one of the greatest misfortunes of the returned student is to find himself debarred from this unity and from the feeling of individual importance which it gave. He must now either convince his whole group. of his new ideas, fighting against the stigma attached to putting himself forward, or he must achieve enough to be important in his own right. The second problem is the burden of White youth also, but the latter are not conditioned to shyness nor to an audience which rejects publicity methods.

When the individual had once submitted himself to the group pattern, he had no oppressive duties, other than the constant one of working hard enough to keep alive. Papago life does not involve the rigid obligations which burden many primitive societies, with their corelative fear of supernatural punishment for omissions. It may have been their very preoccupation with getting food which prevented the Desert People from evolving such a ceremonial framework. Their communal ceremonies are formulae meant to increase the food supply by singing of rain and plenty, but they are enjoyable in themselves and their chief activity is dancing and feasting.

However, they provide an outlet for other emotions than those required by the peaceable life. The Papago had a good deal of sex freedom but at certain feasts the rules were abrogated entirely; the monotony of toil and good behavior was lifted and the orgiastic in human temperament had its expression. Chief among these was the communal drinking feast, when it was the duty of men to saturate themselves like plants in the rain and the resulting madness was celebrated in song. On this occasion, men and women were absolved from marriage bonds and the light and "playful" woman was glorified. Two other occasions, the scalp dance and the girl's puberty dance permitted sexual license as they did through out almost all the West. The Papago culture contained strains not completely assimilable to peace and unity.

Other ceremonies supplied satisfaction to the restless individual. If he could be content to have his major expression in dreaming, there was the vision. Not the vision of the Plains, which could mean violent individualism, torture and keen ambition! The Papago, absorbing the wide-spread conception of the animal guardian and the song, had dimmed its outlines to as great a conformity as possible with their fundamental ideal. They fasted with the partly utilitarian object of growing used to hunger which was their frequent lot and, with the power achieved, to earn meals for the family. Such power, with many peoples who have a similar custom, expresses itself in a song, but with the Papago, the song was the important thing. The temperament to be cultivated was not so much that of the fighter and leader as of the singer and dreamer. All acts of prowess culminated only when the hero, fasting afterward, had dreamed a song and thus the achievements of the executive were made subordinate to those of the artist and creator. But a very moderate achievement in creation was sufficient and failure no detriment.

The points of stress for the average individual were few. As a child, whether or not he had parents, he had plenty of affection, no punishment and a gradual inculcation into responsibility as early as he could stand it. The daily discourses of his grandfather conditioned him, even before he could understand the words, to the same virtues required of adults: industry, peaceableness, modesly.

As an adult, he found little difficulty in coming up to the requirements of his society. Acquisitiveness and ambition need not burden him since all had about the same amount of property and prestige was discouraged. He could avoid the demands of war by becoming a shaman or a berdache. The feelings to be suppressed were: extreme ambition, desire for dominance, cruelty, curiosity. He might give a free rein to sex, (though there were a few restrictions for women) to play and to poetic imagination (phrased as the dreaming of songs.) Executives were not needed in a society which ran in such regular grooves, and it was the non-executives and artists who were at a premium.

Granted the form of understatement proper for Papago speech, he might indulge freely in various kinds of expression forbidden by modern society. He could say that he was afraid in battle and most warriors did say so. He could openly express grief and could weep in public. He could admit without shame that others were more intelligent than he. What he could not do was to show anger or stinginess, or jealousy, worst of all to admit that he did not love his relatives.

Almost everyone could live up to these conditions and few acknowledged failure by being driven to suicide or insanity. Two ancient cases of suicide were reported, both for typically Papago reasons: one, inability to bear opprobrium and one the fear of being a burden in old age.

No insanity is reported from former times except that of a shaman who "got too much power, ran around like a horse and died under a cactus." One case known now is being treated by the shaman with a crucifix. Several feeble minded and deformed children are to be seen at present though "we never had them before," and one wonders if the reason was that they were exposed in infancy.

The peaceable ideal was expressed in outward behavior by a constant, smiling calm. Much talking and loud laughter are, even now discouraged and a group of kin, reunited at a feast, take their pleasure by sitting together in smiling silence. When they do speak, it is in a low tone of voice made almost inaudible by the many whispered syllables of the language. Ceremonial speakers use the same tone and a shout is an anomaly even between cowboys in the open.

Facial expression varies between a good humored calm and a

smile. When one is angry, his face simply becomes expressionless. The writer has heard of Papagos who attacked one another in anger but in a fairly long experience has seen no demonstration of the emotion except for people to walk away muttering, or sit, head down in silence. Laughter is constant, but it expresses good nature rather than amusement. Humor being so tied to time and place as it is, the writer found difficulty in grasping Papago jokes, but she noted a large number which turned on tricks of pronunciation. Endless amusement was derived by ridiculing the dialect of another group and many of the Coyote stories would have been pointless were it not for the speech of Coyote himself who always talks tongue-tied. There were the usual number of obscene tales, told in any group and before any relative. And there was always huge enjoyment in applying a name to anyone, even such simple names as Broken Basket or He Fell in the River.

Public behavior is very restrained. People do not touch one another or show affection except to children. There are no small words of courtesy. Instead of greeting, one stands smiling at the door of a house, waiting to be invited in. As a farewell, one says: "I am going" and receives the permission: "Go then." "Thank you" and "forgive me," are considered futile substitutes for deeds which should show the speaker's attitude. In the rare cases when blame is voiced by a father or some qualified person, there is no positive word which can be used. He must say, "it is not good," or, "not like people," *i. e.*, not polite.

Praise also is rarely used. The individual, feeling himself a necessary part of the group, does not need the constant flattery which comforts the lonely fighter in a different form of society. Papagos are so unused to this version of politeness that the lightly spoken compliments of Whites disconcert them. They consider the speaker to be either grovelling or making an important communication.

But while avoiding the extremes of blame or praise, communication proceeds with great etiquette so as not to hurt any one's feelings. The writer, having asked the interpreter to make the proper approach to a new subject, was always impressed by the almost courtly care with which polite openings were sought and cautiously followed up. One may ascribe some of the courtliness to Spanish influence but a wholesale adoption of Spanish manners would involve flattery also.

Motions and thinking are in slow tempo. Much of this can be credited to the heat, but it is to be remembered that the Papago, like many Indians, have a slower heartbeat than Whites. Their calm rhythm, achieved, perhaps, over centuries, is one of the factors in their contentment and good nature and one to be considered in any educational system which would involve their speeding up. The writer, having long admired the lack of nervous irritability in the Papago found herself, on two or three occasions, in situations where she had to urge her Papago friends to extreme haste. They went to pieces under it much more quickly than Whites who are prepared for such a strain. It would be futile to expect them to bring their admirable nervous control into the atmosphere of speed and strain which often accompanies White activity.

Papago culture is still an integrated one. The two hundred years and more of leisurely and voluntary contacts with the Whites have not disturbed the balance of organization between the individual and the community and have left the life such that the average individual can still live it with contentment and satisfaction. But this culture is breaking up and Whites who oversee the process have the interesting problem of inculcating a set of virtues and inhibitions almost directly opposite to the former ones, without too destructive a period of transition.

## ACCULTURATION

The picture of the Papago given here is that of a people forced by their environment to a low subsistence level. Due to old habits and old alliances, they did not move out of that environment or even make raids on the agricultural kinsmen about them. Their solution was hard labor, peaceableness and the cultivation of friendships that would protect them. Their informal social system was held together by ties of family and of community duty which could not be broken without danger to livelihood. But as livelihood changed, organization changed with it. These pages follow the change in social customs consequent on a raised standard of living.

The Papago were fortunate in being able to take their Spanish acculturation slowly. Kino's visits were long enough for benefit and stimulus, not for tyranny, and when they ceased his charges were left, for two centuries to adapt themselves to the new tools and ideas, without many more to distract them. The result was a thorough assimilation of wheat and horses into their scheme of life without much disturbance, either economic or social. Wheat had to be raised in small quantities, due to water conditions and did not lead to commercial production. Cattle, until recently, were also owned in small quantities, just enough, in fact, to substitute for the man's occupation of hunting, which was interfered with by the gradual population of the surrounding area.

The Papago became acquainted, in the Spanish period, with the Mexican house of wattle and daub and with the full clothing recommended by the Fathers. But these things were of no use to a wandering people in a hot country. It was not until much later, when their frequent contacts with Whites made houses and clothes a matter of prestige, that the Papago built and dressed in the Mexican style.

They took from Mexico two social institutions, the whipping post and the governor. There is some room for doubt as to whether the governor's office was new but his powers certainly were. We must lay their effectiveness to the priests rather than to the distant Spanish officials, for the priests were empowered by law to supervise the governor's election and his activities. It was the priests who gave the Papago their wheat and cattle and thus gained respect for the powerful charms recited in church to bring blessing. The Papago were used to ceremonial leaders and easily accepted dictation from these who had a more wonder-working ritual than their own.

But once appointed, the governors had little supervision and they and the whipping posts lapsed into a Papago pattern. Whipping was done in an informal and neighborly manner and as much for Papago ceremonial offenses as for those against Spanish law. The governor's function became so like that of the old ceremonial leader that tradition confuses the two. The organization of the extended family and the village remained untouched.

The Papago have their Apache enemies to thank for this isolation. Had the Spaniards been able to populate Pimeria as they did Sonora there would have been the same mixture of races and the same complete adoption of Spanish forms as there was to the south. The Papago, in their sterile desert, might have been neglected, but the Pima would have been overwhelmed and the influence would have spread from there. As it was, the conditions summarized above held on until Mexican independence in 1821.

The thirty years of turmoil comprised in Mexico's war of independence and the internal fighting which preceded and followed it, involved as much change for the Papago as the century preceding. There was skirmishing in Papago country; Papagos were given guns, horses and food for their help against counter revolutionists and against the Apache; Papago villages were broken up and there was racial intermixture. This affected only the south of the area, part of which is now in Mexico. But where it occurred, it was a potent factor in breaking up residence, causing the loss of clan affiliations and even of clan names and the abandonment of ceremonies because there were no longer villages to conduct them. It seems to have been at this period that the southerners began to build Mexican houses of wattle and daub. Such a house could not be burned or moved after a death and it was too valuable to abandon; so the ancient custom of moving to avoid the ghosts was allowed to lapse.

The north seems hardly to have felt the disruption whose greatest effect was to provide a yeast of people acquainted with new ways and amenable to further acculturation. Indeed, for some forty years after Mexico's independence, there was very little change. The Gadsden Purchase passed almost unnoticed by the average Papago, and an old man was recently found who still supposed he was under Mexican rule. The Americans, at first, were too occupied with subduing the Apache and organizing Arizona to pay much attention to the Desert People. They gave them some supplies and tools; a school finally became available at Phoenix though few of them went there, and there was, eventually, a small reservation at San Xavier with a farmer in charge.

But during this period the Papago themselves worked out an important change. Since 1750, more or less, one of the chief preoccupations of their lives had been fear of the Apache. It had caused their concentration in large villages and the infrequent communication of these villages with one another. It had raised to extreme importance the duties of a warrior and his consequent dreaming and song making. In fact, no man in his prime thought much of any other duties, which may have been one of the reasons for the small change in agriculture, housing and furnishing.

As the Americans took over the Apache problem, the Papago began to move out of their concentrated villages and the formation of daughter villages began. This gave larger fields and more opportunity for cattle. It did not loosen the family tie, in fact, it strengthened, it, since each village was founded by relatives. But it did loosen the village organization and the power of public opinion. It tended toward the loss of ceremonies, since the new village had no fetish and found it hard to get a ceremonial orator. I conjecture that it was this moving rather than conscious White influence which brought the first important shift in Papago culture.

But conscious White influence followed. Miners and ranchers were appropriating Papago land and, in order to protect the Indians' rights, it was necessary to establish a reservation. When the Papago came under governmental guidance in 1917, they had, perhaps, a more integrated culture than any other Indians under similar conditions. Groups in the east and northwest met the experience when they were already disintegrated by war, and removal. The Pueblos who had not suffered these disadvantages, had kept their culture by a conscious effort which, in itself colored their organization. But the Papago had suffered neither dispossession nor threats to their integrity. Theirs was what might be called an aboriginal self sufficiency.

There was no plan to interfere with such a sufficiency. Where Spain had installed the governor and the whipping post, America left Papago social organization untouched. Schools, hospitals and extension service were put into operation, missions were encouraged. Their aim was, while leaving the Papago "unspoiled and independent" to bring their standard of living up to that of the neighboring Whites. Said the Board of Indian Commissioners:[1]

> "If the tribe is helpfully aided in education, water health and livestock improvement, and subjected to the minimum of

[1] 50th Report, Board of Indian Commissioners, 1919.

governmental jurisdiction, and that only of the most helpful kind, there is little question that, within a generation, the Papago Indians will be self supporting citizens of the United States and Arizona, respected by their white neighbors and a most valuable national asset."

More than a generation has passed and it is now obvious that the aid provided has involved complex changes. Raising the standard of living must mean an economy of scarcity instead of one of abundance. It must mean the substitution of investment by saving for investment by giving. It must, therefore, without wise and inventive supervision, loosen the ties of obligation which held Papago society together.

Such a process has begun and it raises the interesting question of whether a system of group responsibility evolved, like that of the Papago, over centuries of conditioning, can be carried over into a new order. Cooperation and group responsibility are ideals much talked of by Whites and hard to achieve in a society with European history. They exist among the Papago ready made but tied to an economic system that is hard to continue. The devices and adjustments by which this attitude, valuable to society could be preserved during the coming periods of disruption form a problem of the first importance to the practical sociologist.

In 1917 the difficulty was not obvious. School, hospital and extension service were started on the reservation. Missions were encouraged. Indians were helped to get horses, wagons and tools on a loan basis and were employed on the improvements at a money wage. The first problem of all seemed to be the sterility of the land and several deep wells were dug at the larger villages so that people need no longer move in the dry season.

The south, already accustomed to change and with its village organization disrupted, welcomed the improvements and the first missions were established there. Ever since, the south has provided the yeast which spread progressivism through the country. But the north was reluctant and still is. Old people, with an obscure sense of the maladjustments to come, resisted the changes and the well at one village was dug against opposition. But once the improvements were there, all made use of them.

They did so with an attitude unknown before among the Papago. Heretofore, their village had been their own creation and no improvements had been made without their efforts. Now an unknown power had placed a machine there without their consent and they felt no bonds of obligation. They do not feel them yet, and though the well serves the village as well as the school, it is sometimes in danger of stopping because few villagers will give their time to run it. Nor will they buy gasoline. Communal responsibility had broken down at one point and never has been built up.

It is easy to see, after the event, that there might have been an agreement with the community before the pump was put in, establishing corporate responsibility and placing the government in the familiar role of patriarch caring for his family. But the arrival at such an agreement would have been a slow and disheartening process while the necessary improvements, which the public could understand, would seem to be sacrificed.

The improvements went forward and schools, hospital and stock supervision were instituted. In each case there was opposition, sometimes bitter and threatening, from a section of the people. There was such opposition on most reservations but with the Papago, who had never fought the Whites, it was benefits, not cruelty which aroused the first hostility and produced the resistant group now called montezumas. They are not organized, for open political opposition is foreign to Papago custom. They remain at home, spreading through their patriarchal families the emotional conviction that things should remain as they were.

They were once in the majority and it is possible they are so still. But in the south, where old ties were already slackened, there were Papago who gladly accepted the new order. In all the changes which follow, we must assume the presence of two parties, conservatives and progressives. The dividing line does not pass between old and young, as it does on so many reservations for the schools have not been operating long enough to produce a rift. It is rather between north and south, with exceptions on both sides. Neither party has knowledge enough to form any plan by which modern improvements could be fitted to ancient institutions. The conservatives reject completely; the progressives accept completely. Both inevitably take advantage of the improvements offered, both evince a lessening of the old obligations though in different degrees.

Communal duties to the village, which once took the place of a tax, have very nearly lapsed, since the government is responsible for the principle communal interests of pump, school and stock supervision. The Papago, who have never had a national organization, have still to develope their relationship to such a centralized authority. The fact that the stockman cannot get help on roundups and that parents must be organized from the beginning for school cooperation is not a proof that the Papago cannot cooperate. Rather, they are unprepared for cooperation of the sort proposed.

Family ties have not suffered so much, for as we shall mention later, the patriarchal family has amazing vitality. But the tie has loosened at a point where maintenance of unity often meant an economic strain: the responsibility for distant relatives. It had been the custom for every extended family to take care of its own dependents though the drain sometimes reduced the whole family to a low subsistence level. According to the new standard such families needed help and they could have it by giving up responsibility for old uncles and cousins, even grandparents. Many did so. When the writer first visited the reservation, applications for government charity were almost unknown but within four years they reached a point where a social worker was needed to take care of them.

The first move of a social worker, faced with a case of dependency, is generally to place some of the responsibility on the family. But the Papago honestly feel themselves poor according to the new standard. Their economy of abundance has been abandoned and with it the system of gifts. With teachers and extension workers earnestly laboring to establish the new standard, it is inevitable that the government take some of the financial burden. Here is one of the institutions of White social life seen in its very incipience. Can dependency be controlled among the Papago so that it shall not reach the proportions found among Whites ?

We have considered the situation as it is affected by outright giving. But earning had its part and, in so far as they earned, the Papago themselves contributed to the demolishing of the old order. Papagos have always been workers and they eagerly accepted the paid work offered by the government and by neighboring Whites. The city of Tucson grew up at the east of the reservation and families migrated there to live on its outskirts, their women working steadily as household servants, their men intermittently as day laborers. The copper mine of Ajo developed at the west and several hundred Papago sometimes lived in its slums, supported entirely by money wages.

A temporary migration to work for pay had been an old expedient of the Papago to eke out their subsistence. Families had gone for a few weeks, individuals for a whole winter, their pay being their food while working and some knives, cloth or wheat to take home to the family. But money pay was different. It was more than enough for subsistence and the surplus could be concealed so that any one so tempted might fail to contribute at all to the family support, without detection. Individuals who got steady work detached themselves from the kin group for long periods, perhaps permanently. Young men ventured to marry as they liked, knowing that they could support a wife without their fathers' aid. The family still raised food for its own support but now the store was available for bartering the surplus and investment in gifts could be given up. It was given up by some and since the others could not rely on the return which was once unquestioned, they too became slack or capricious. The gift system, built up by economic conditions, was being broken down by the same means.

Through all the stress, the institution which showed the greatest vitality was that of the patriarchal family. Though its distant dependents were lopped off, though its young people were educated to new desires at school, though some of them even seceded to wage work, a core of the family kept to the old customs. The writer has talked with many an educated young man who would make no plans without the permission of his conservative father. She has found men unable to take paying work because the family head had requested their services. The sense of security and importance derived from membership in such a group still bulks large in Papago life.

One of the reasons for the survival of patriarchal organization was that the family, in the majority of cases, kept its old lands and worked them jointly as before. Where the means of support was chiefly agriculture, change had to be slow, even with the entrance of money into the situation. Farms were not big enough to produce much money by sale of produce and there were relatives expecting to share the harvest unless actual concealment was practised. A Papago living and working in Tucson like any White, told the writer that on the farm on the reservation in which he shares the whole extended family is still invited to come and help themselves at harvest. Many of them make no return and so the farm barely supports itself.

But, with cattle raising, there was opportunity for further development. The Papago have had cattle since 1700 but it was only recently that they realized the possibility of raising them as a business. Beef cattle were allowed to roam wild and only hunted and killed when the family needed meat. As the country was settled and the deer and antelope frightened off, cattle raising moved gradually into the place once occupied by hunting. A patriarchal family had formerly had, in all its component households, no more than one or two hunters, bringing in ten or fifteen deer a year. Now such a family might kill the same number of cows, distributing the meat just as they once distributed venison. One or more of their young men was designated as cowboy while the others did his share of the farmwork and bought his clothes. The cattle ran on the vaguely designated range which had once been the old hunting range and the unpaid local stockman who worked under the government stockman was, in one case, the hereditary hunt chief.

It was at the south, were village organization had been broken up and where Mexican cattle ranches served as patterns, that families first began raising and keeping cattle. It was a business in the Papago manner, the patriarch at the head and the cattle of all his family herded together, his relatives acting as cowboys. Now there are six establishments, mostly in the south, which merit the term of cattle ranches and their patriarchal heads are powerful persons, whose neighbors give them a feudal obedience.

How did two or three Papago accumulate a herd and build large ranch houses with wells and gardens, while the majority were barely self supporting ? The answer given the writer was: "They took care of their cows, sold them and bought more." In other words, they made the change from investment by gift exchange to investment by saving. Land is open to all. Any one may build a large house, fence off a garden and dig a reservoir. But the adjustment needed is too great to appeal to the majority who watch mistrustfully while the minority become capitalists. It is the very beginning of the process among a people who once discouraged all individual prominence.

During these changes affecting individual attitudes, the forms of village government remained ostensibly the same. The nightly meeting of the council, the only source of news and companionship while the Apache kept the Papago beleaguered, has long been a thing of the past. But the council still meets for business purposes, it still comes to a unanimous decision and the young men still feel that until the opinion of the old men has been announced no action can be taken. But there is not time, now, for the long deliberations which once produced unanimity. The White government makes proposals which require quick decision, the governors are called to the agency to hear them and, on returning, they dictate to their constituents rather than consult them. As a result, the governor's power has developed tremendously.

The authority which he holds was obvious when the Papago were asked to elect delegates to decide on a constitution under the Indian Reorganization act. The Pima, much longer under White influence than the Papago, elected, under such circumstances, their young English speaking men, discarding the older ones unacquainted with the situation. But trusting the young men is contrary to all tradition and the Papago have not reached such a point of·change. They elected the elderly governors and, as a consequence, the whole tone of their constitution and of their government is likely to have a different tinge.

But a new economic change is likely to affect the village profoundly. In 1933 Emergency Conservation funds were alotted for the crying economic problem of the reservation — the development of a water supply. In the next two years wells, pumps, and reservoirs were installed wherever it was possible. This means that the yearly migration to the hills which has been such a determining factor in Papago life, is no longer necessary. People who live the year round in one village will build better houses and have more furniture. It will be more worth while for the government to build them a good school and for them to help with it. Many who used to camp for the winter with another group, will now have an undivided allegiance. The village should gain in membership and in importance.

Before these pages go to press, further developments will already have taken place. The new constitution will be in operation and the establishment of the Papago as commercial cattle raisers will be in process. Organization in local family groups whose frugal subsistence was dependent on the unity of all the members must gradually give way to institutions contingent on the new economy. Investment in goodwill must yield to investment in goods and, therefore, must produce the financial superiority of some over others.

Those men least in accord with the old order, that is, those with unfulfilled personal ambitions, will be the first to drop the code of humility and generosity and to start on the road to success open for the aggressive individual.

Such men have appeared already and the attitude shown toward them is an interesting variant of that shown toward those who had animal guardians by those who had none. The favor of an animal guardian was, under the old order, the one road to individual success but it came by chance, not by planned industry. Of several youths who were industrious and good runners, the Hawk would appear only to one "because he liked his ways". We may assume this phrasing in terms of the supernatural to have been the outlet provided for the ambitious and active man not content to be a member of the working group. But it applied only to a few. The majority looked up to the favored individual and accepted his gifts, without hope of emulation.

This attitude often carries over toward individuals who achieve economic success. The majority, without the pattern of rivalry current in a White society, tend to regard them, with resignation, as people successful by supernatural means. If kinsmen, they expect

14

gifts from them: if strangers, they tend to accuse them of mysterious luck much in the nature of sorcery. It will be long before the idea of success open to all and, in fact, obligatory on all, has full acceptance.

In the meantime, those most easily freed from the old economic obligations will have made long strides ahead. But they will not go alone: indications are that each will take at least the core of his patriarchal family with him. We have mentioned what vitality the family shows, even when customs associated with it drop away. We have also mentioned the ingrained habit of the Papago of relying on the local patriarch for advice and guidance. As prestige shifts from a ceremonial to an economic basis, the signs are that this reliance on the powerful man will increase rather than diminish. Such men are now surrounded by small groups of relatives who accept gifts and obey orders almost like feudal retainers. Since the new customs do not require the powerful man to be modest and self denying, we might perhaps expect a development like that of the old political ward boss, himself a reproduction of an Irish local chieftain.

The further shifting of elements which will form new patterns for Papago behavior can hardly be conjectured at this point in time. But there are at least grounds for rejecting the premises of a worker on another reservation who planned: "We want them to stay Indians but, in business matters, to act like White men."

# APPENDIX I

1. Group at Kuitatk (Mesquite Root) about 1850—1860, informant 26

Mesquite Root was an ancient town in which people had gathered for many generations for fear of the Apache. Containing 300 people, it was too large to be composed only of relatives but related groups clustered together. All the land around Mesquite Root was inherited in different families and those who needed more land had to move.

The group under consideration were the five children of a widow who had married in *Kuiwo*, Sloping Ground, but returned to her native village after her husband's death. Since she had few brothers, she had always retained a share in the family land there, and her eldest son had come back in the summers to cultivate it. When her husband died, she left his land at Sloping Ground to his brother and returned to use her own family land. She lived in a house with her oldest son and his family, while the other sons and one daughter clustered about them in a half circle.

In the dry season, instead of using the Well of Mesquite Root, the family went back to that of their father's family, Badger Well. Here they met paternal relatives, two great uncles and a distant female cousin, with whom they had the same gift relations as they did at Mesquite Root with the mother's relatives.

## House A

1. The Gambler, governor of Mesquite Root
2. wife of A 1
3. mother of A 1
4. daughter
5. son
6. son

Living arrangements: A 1, the oldest son built his house in a central position, the houses of his three brothers and one sister grouped around it. Each house had its own kitchen and storehouse, but the women took turns cooking for the whole group. Each woman cooked for one day (two meals) choosing what she would use from her own storehouse. Children were sent to the neighboring houses to collect empty bowls and return full, one bowl for each married couple, one bowl for their children.

Land: The four sons divided their father's land, giving a strip also to their sister (see below) and to a father's older brother's son, called older uncle.

14*

Work sharing: They worked the land together but each stored his
     share of the harvest separately. They needed no outside help.
Gifts: When A 1 killed a deer, he gave enough for two meals to each
     of the sibling families. Any left over went to more distant
     relatives in rotation. They made return in kind. When he
     killed a steer, which was larger, he sent to all relatives in
     Mesquite Root. A 2, after picking cactus fruit, took gifts to:
     the siblings in the home group: to a female 1st cousin and L,
     a distant uncle. Food gifts were sent twice a week to a "distant
     paternal cousin" at Whirling Water (1, 2 Gl).

### House B

1 Rat Ears y b of A 1
2 wife of B 1
     small children, not remembered
Living arrangements, land and gifts as with A 1

### House C

1 Big Vulva y b of A 1
2 wife of C 1
     small children not remembered
Living arrangements, land and gifts as with A 1

### House D

1 head
2 Maria Ignacia, y si of A 1
     small children not remembered
Living arrangements, work and gifts as with A 1

Land: D 2 had married a man from Whirling Water, but he was an
     orphan with no relatives there; so he came to work with his
     wifes' family who allowed him a strip of land.

### House E

1 Corncob y b of A 1
2 wife
Living arrangements, land, work and gifts as with A 1
Other relatives living in Mesquite Root but not in the above group

### House F

1 Head
2 Running Clouds, wife of F 1, m o si d of A 1
Children
This house was much nearer than those of all the other relatives
and almost one of the family group.

Living arrangements: The family had separate living arrangements. Although brothers of F 2 were in the village, they were too far away for cooperative housekeeping.

Land: The land belonged in the family of F 2, whose mother had been the sister of A 3, but these two women, having no brothers, had remained on the land. The husband of F 2 also lived in Mesquite Root and cultivated his own land there as well as his wife's.

Work sharing: The brothers both of F 1 and F 2 gave assistance at harvest and exchanged harvest gifts.

Gifts: The household sent almost as many food gifts to houses A B C D E as to the nearer relatives, G and H. The reason seems to have been geographic nearness which brought intimacy.

### More Distant Houses at Mesquite Root

All these sent occasional food gifts to houses A B C D E F, invited them into their fields at harvest time and sent them venison now and then, all of which was reciprocated in equal quantity.

### House G

1 Head, b of F 2

Living arrangements: Cooperative housekeeping with House H
Land: Shared land with H 1
Work: Called in House H
Gifts: Food gifts at almost every meal to House H. Occasionally, in turn to all others.

### House H

1 Head, b of F 2 and G 1
arrangements as with house G

### House I

1 Head, m o half si s s of A 1

### House J

1 Head, b of L 1
Houses I and J had cooperative housekeeping and shared their fields. Sent regular food gifts to houses G and H, their half cousins.

### House K

1 Head, m o s s of A 1

### House L

1 Head, yb of A 2

### House M

1 Head
wife "distant older sister" of A 1

## House N

1 Pointed Shoes head, distant nephew to A 1
    (House O same as I, 2, House G)
1 Little Eyes ffss to A 1
This family lived five miles away in the valley, whence water
was fetched when the pond at Mesquite Root began to dry.
The daughter of A 1 was sent there almost once a week with
food gifts.

## House P
### at Sloping Ground, father's old home

1 Head fb of A 1
2 wife
3 son
4 son
5 son
6 son

Land: P 1 used the land belonging to the father of A 1, B 1, C 1,
D 2, E 1. This land had been deserted when its owner, his
brother, died and the widow A 3 moved back to her own
family land at Mesquite Root.

Gifts: This family was invited at harvest and given produce which
they reciprocated.

    About thirty relatives of A 2 lived at Kaka, in a different
valley. At harvest, they sent for House A to come and help
themselves and the guests once stayed a year. At their own
harvest they gave a similar invitation.

## 2. Households at Sikorhimat (Whirling Water) about 1860—1870
### informant 26

Whirling Water was an old settlement with inherited lands. The
well was Covered Wells, used also by Santa Rosa. However, the
two groups did not mix but kept, the one to the wash, the other to
the high land. There was no gift exchange between them even though
some of their members were distantly related.

## House A

1 household head, (a shaman) f o b s of B 1
2 wife of A 1 m si to B 1
3 Shady Bow, son of A 1 and A 2 f o b s of H 2
4 Maria Chona, wife of A 3 f f b d to C 1
5 Winged, son of A 1 and A 2
2 Feather Tips wife of A 5
7 Skirt String, son of A 1 and A 2
8 wife of Skirt String, d of C 1
9 Basket Unravelled, son of A 1 and A 2
Shining Evening, son of A 1 and A 2, transvestite

Living arrangements: All lived in one large house with shade for cooking, common storehouse, women all worked together at cooking, men in fields. Even before the father's, death A 5 and A 7 built separate sleeping houses for themselves and their wives. After the father's death, all built separate houses, the mother living with the transvestite. All still cooked together and used a common storehouse.

Land: The land was hereditary in the father's family and the sons all worked it together. When they needed more land "they simply moved the boundary line."

Work sharing: For help in the field, the family called on the father and mother of A 4 who lived in Mesquite Root. They were the only parents-in-law who found it convenient to come. They would be given two large winnowing baskets of beans or a pile of unhusked corn some four feet in diameter. Others asked were E 2, paternal aunt of A 1 and G 1 and his wives who were second cousins to A 4.

Gifts: The men of this family were good hunters and famous for their gifts of meat. When A 1 killed a deer, he sent his daughter-in-law A 4 with a full carrying basket of the meat to her parents some 15 miles away. They re-filled the basket with corn, beans, and cactus syrup. The son, A 3, killed a deer three or four times a month and always sent a piece to his parents-in-law. "They liked meat. That was why they married their daughter into a hunting family." Meat was also given at every killing to House E and House H, where lived the brothers of A 2 and House C, a classificatory brother of A 2. The other households received their turn in rotation. The household sent produce to the wife's relatives at Mesquite Root, these being m y b and a second cousin of A 2. She had no nearer relatives.

### House B

1 Yellowlegs, household head, first cousin of A 1
2 co-wife no. 1, si of A 1
3 s of B 2
4 s of B 2
5 co-wife no. 2, si of A 1 and B 2
6 s of A 5
7 d of A 5
8 d of A 5

Living: All lived in one house until the parents' death, then moved to Pima country.

Land: The women, sisters of A 1, should have moved to their husband's land, but it was not good. On the other hand A 1, the only man in the family, had plenty of land; so B 1 moved to Whirling Water and cultivated part of it for his wives. When he and the wives died, it should have gone to the sons, but one son and a daughter died at almost the same time; so the others did not care to stay. They moved to the Pima country.

### House C

1 Tattooed Old Man, household head, ffbs to A 2
2 kuiwonyi wife
3 Riboso, son of A 1 and A 2
4 wife of C 3
5 Singing Instrument son of A 1 and A 2
6 Wife of C 5
  (a daughter married to A 7 in same village)

Living arrangements: The two sons built separate sleeping huts as they married, but the family had a common storehouse and kitchen.

Land: The brothers kept the land in common and pooled the produce.

### House D

1 Woman-Lover, household head, f m m  d s of A 2 Distant relative A 1
2 wife
3 vilantatc, son of C 1 and C 2
4 wife of C 3
  (two sons dead, a daughter married at the Hollow)

Living arrangements: One large house with common kitchen and storehouse.
Father and son worked the field together.

### House E

1 Iron Eyes (name bestowed in joke by a transvestite)
2 Flower Dew, co-wife no. 1 f ss to A 1
3 Running Ahead, son of E 1 and E 2
4 Chona (Encarnacion) co-wife no 2, sis of D 2 ffs to A 1
5 Pitakito, son of E 1 and E 6
6 Haviala, d of E 1 and E 6

Living: All in one house with common storehouse and kitchen. On the head's death both wives were too old to remarry. One went back to her brother, the other to her married daughter.

Land: The land was hereditary in husband's family. Two of his sons used their wives' land in the same village. E 5 continued to work his father's land but he had no sons and on his death the land was deserted.

### House F

1 Salty Forehead, household head, b of D 1
2 wife si of A 2

3 son of D 1 and D 2, (died)
>(sons all married and lived on their wives' land, there being no one to take care of it. Wives of first 2 were sisters and orphans. Wife of third had no brothers.)

When F 1 and F 2 grew old, there was no one to care for their land. They went to Topawa where lived a brother of F 1.

Gifts: Sons, living at a distance, would send for F 1 at harvest time 85 miles away and would load his saddle bags and pack horse. He made the trip three or four times every harvest.

### House G

1 Little Eyes, head f f f s s of A 4
2 Salomena, co-wife no. 1, f f b s d of A 4
3 Tcucuuwuk, co-wife no. 2, y si of G 2
4 Rustling Leaves, co-wife no. 3, y si of G 2 and G 3
5 Gold, yb of G 1
6 Wife of G 5, si of G 2, 3 and 4
7 Flower Shoes, y si of G 1

Living arrangements: cooperative housekeeping
Land: G 1 and G 2 had land at Santa Rosa but all their relatives had died; so they had come to use the land of their wives.
Gifts: Occasional food gifts to other households at Whirling Water but also sent back to Santa Rosa. One connection from there now lived at Mesquite Root (House A) and with this family gifts were exchanged once a week.

### House H

1 Feeling Happy, household head, yb of A 2, ceremonial leader
2 Pilito, co-wife no. 1
3 Dolores, d of G 1 and G 2
4 Having Spanish Beans, son of G 1 and G 2
5 Wife of G 4
6 Water Scum, co-wife no. 2
7 Woman Magician d of G 1 and G 6
8 Malia, d of G 1 and G 8

Living arrangements: The whole family lived in one house. The two daughters of G 6 married one man and went with him to Mesquite Root. Wives of G 6 died and the son and his wife continued to live with the father. When he died, son tore down the house, then rebuilt it and lived there, using the land. Son's wife died and he took another, unrelated.
Land: Hereditary in the family

A second group, distantly related to the first and exchanging gifts with them only rarely. (informant 43)

### House H

1 Letting-Go, head
2 Wife
3 Widowed daughter of H 1 and H 2 who had returned home after her husband's death
4 d of H 3

### House I

1 head
2 wife, si of H 1
3 Margarita, d, died young
4 Tilisa (Theresa), d, died young
5 Lilian
6 d, died in infancy
7 d, died in infancy

Living arrangements: H and I were organized as one, with two brush huts and a common kitchen. H 2 managed them both, and directed the other women. She decided what food was to be used and went to the storehouse for it; the others did not go without permission.

Land: The land was hereditary in the family of H 1. He shared it with his sister's husband, I 1, because he needed a man to help him. The two men worked the land as a unit and formed a common household. H 3, the widowed daughter of H 1 came home from Archie and was given no land but simply formed a part of the household.

Work sharing: H 1 and I 1 pooled labor and results.

Gifts: Food gifts were given only when there was plenty for a meal. A basket of food containing about a quart was sent every two or three days to House J which contained the only near relatives. Much more rarely a small gift of cactus syrup or other delicacy was sent to House A. H 1 was a hunter and always took part of his kill to House J. An equivalent amount of corn and beans was returned the same day. He did not give meat to his more distant relatives but dried and kept it.

### House J

1 widow of younger brother of A 2
2 d of J 1
3 d of J 2
4 d of J 2
5 d of J 2
6 s of J 2
7 s of J 2
8 b of J 1
9 si of J 1

Living arrangements: All the family lived in one house, the younger
women working under the direction of J 1 who was almost senile
but domineering.
Land: The land had been in the family of J 1 who had returned
there after her husband's death.
Work sharing: All the men worked the land together and pooled the
products.
Gifts: A quart basket of cooked food was sent every two or three
days to Houses H and I. When H 1 sent meat, this family
reciprocated the same day with corn and beans.

### 3. Households at wahw kihk (Standing Rock) 1870—1890
### informant 26

This was a new settlement founded by a group of relatives from
Mesquite Root because the latter town was crowded and had insufficient water. The discoverer who made Standing Rock habitable
was Dried Seeds, mother's younger brother to A 1 and B 2, both of
whom followed him to the new place. Other relatives and connections followed, the women bringing their husbands so that in this
case patrilineal residence broke down for economic reasons. The
special group described is that of informant's second husband with
his sisters and half sisters, all of whom lived close together. They
lived at Standing Rock all the year without needing to move because
of the abundance of water.

### House A

1 Household head, Pisali
He had had two wives simultaneously but both had died.
His sons by them married and were living in separate
houses.
2 Current wife, Maria Chona, had left a husband at Whirling
Water.
3 Son of A 1 and A 2, Two Bits
(Wife's daughter by the former husband was with her
maternal uncle, in the home village.)

Land: New, taken up on emigration from Mesquite Root
Work sharing: Before the son of the family was old enough, help in
the fields was given by sister's sons of A 1, B 5, B 9 and B 12.
They planted their own fields first and then, without being
asked, came over to work for their uncle. They were given
their food and were asked to help themselves from the harvest.
No criticism was made as to the quantity they took, but they
returned an equal amount from their own harvest. Sisters of
A 1: B 2, 3, 4, C 2, and D 2 always came to help cook during
harvest, and were given a basket of beans each or its equivalent.

Gifts: A 1 was "rich" and kept cattle. When he killed a cow, he
summoned all his sisters and their families, Houses B, C, D,
to cook and eat at his house and on their departure gave each
a three or four pound piece of meat. If any was left, he distributed
it to unrelated villagers. They all returned equal amounts of
meat or produce if possible. From the poor ones less was
expected.

On ordinary occasions, when the family were eating porridge
or vegetables, the wife cooked a five gallon pot. A large portion
was sent first to husband's own sister, B 2; the family ate and,
if any was left, it was sent to the half sisters, C 2 and D 2, who
reciprocated in equal amounts. Five or six times a year the
husband and wife got on a horse with saddlebags loaded with
produce and visited the wife's family, bringing back equal
amounts. The husband, A 1, who kept cattle, usually gave
beef, while the wife's brothers, who were hunters, returned
venison.

### House B

1 Thundering Wind, household head.
2 Maria Juana, co-wife no. 1, y si of A 1 above by the same
mother
3 Water Drops, younger half si of A 1 and B 2, her mother
being their father's co-wife no. 2
4 Sprinkling Flowers co-wife no. 3, half si of A 1 and B 2, own
si of B 3
(There was a fourth co-wife, married in old age because she
was the widow of a classificatory younger brother. She
remained living at her home village.)
5 From Nowhere, son of B 1 and B 2, village governor
6 Tree-Leaves-Circling, co-wife no. 1 of B 5
7 Milky-Way co-wife no. 2 of B 5 and si of B 6
8 Brilliant Leaves co-wife no. 3 of B 5 and si of B 6 and B 7
9 Apache Ears, son of B 1 and B 2
10 Scattered Songs, co-wife no. 1 of B 9
11 Luisa, co-wife no. 2 of B 9 and si of B 8
12 Nolinzo (Lorenzo) son of B 1 and B 2
13 Wife of B 12
14 Pilanzo (Esperanza) d of B 1 and B 2, died young
15 Around the Corner, son of B 1 and B 3 (other children died)
16 Tinella, wife of B 15
17 Maria, d of B 1 and B 4
18 Paula, d of B 1 and B 2 (lived in separate hut)
19 kolowinyi, husband of B 18

Living arrangements: All this family lived in one house, the various
wives of the men each having a separate mat. In a separate

house adjacent, lived B 18, daughter of B 1 and B 2, who had brought her husband to share the land because it was better than his own. She and her husband cooked and ate with the main family. On the father's death, the sons tore down the main house and each built himself a separate one. The three sons of B 1 and B 2, with their own sister, B 18, continued to have a common storehouse and common cooking arrangements, and their mother lived with the oldest brother, B 5. B 15 had a separate house in which he lived with his mother.

Land: B 1 had hereditary land at Mesquite Root but had emigrated with his wives when their family found better fields at Standing Rock. He retained his old field at Mesquite Root and his sons from all three wives took turns in living there in the summer and working it. When B 1 died, his two parcels of land were divided among all the sons. Sons B 5, 9, 12, kept their land in common. B 15, their half brother had a separate strip, as had their sister B 18. When B 15 died, his widow's second husband took the land.

Work sharing: Until B 1's death, all the sons worked under him, the daughters-in-law sharing the work of the one house. After his death, the three sons by co-wife no. 1 worked their land as a unit with a common storehouse. If they needed more help, they called on B 15, the half brother, and B 19, the brother-in-law, giving each a sack of produce as pay. These latter two sometimes called for help and paid in the same way. All the brothers, but particularly the oldest, B 5, worked for their uncle, A 1, and later for his widow.

Gifts: The mother of the three wives lived with a fourth married sister, C 2, who had more room but was made free of the storehouse of this family. A sister of the wives was married at San Luis, and her husband occasionally brought some of his harvest which was reciprocated. He did not bring much to the above sisters because they were married to a rich man, but gave more to C 2 who was not so rich and who had arranged his marriage.

Jesus, the fourth wife, lived thirty miles away at the village of her paternal family, where she had retired after her first husband's death. B 1 visited her once a week with saddlebags full of meat, vegetables, cheese (he kept cows), or cloth. She filled his saddlebags on the return with vegetables. Once a year she came to visit him and her co-wives, stayed two or three days and was loaded with gifts.

## House C

1 Household head, Echoing Songs
2 Second wife, Susannah (first wife, no relative of Susannah, dead)

3 Son of 1 and 2, Pedro Leon

4 Daughter of C 2 by a former husband; she called her stepfather, who had not been related, by the term for father's
younger brother.

5 Mother of C 2, A 1, B 2, 3, 4

Living arrangements: The family lived in one house, taking care
of the mother of C 2. C 2 was this woman's second daughter, the
oldest one being one of the wives of B 1 whose house was
crowded. The mother had lived with her third daughter, D 2,
at Whirling Water; when the latter followed the rest of her
family to Standing Rock, the mother came too, and C 2, then
a widow joined them. C 2 finally met C 1 at a liquor festival
and married him. Then she set up a separate house and her
mother came to her. Her household always kept up extremely
intimate relations with House D, where she had lived.

Land: C 2, when she joined her married sister at Standing Rock,
was given a field by her nephew, B 5, the village chief, and he
and his brothers worked it for her. When she married C 1 the
work was turned over to him. C 1 had land of his own at Whirling Water, but that of his wife being better, he abandoned
his own field.

Gifts: House C and House D, poorer than the other siblings, were
especially intimate. They used the same storage hut, though
they kept their property separate. They had different kitchens
but exchanged food gifts at every meal. Two other daughters
of C 5 were married to B 1, who threw his storage hut open to
the mother at all times. Another daughter was married at
San Luis, and her husband came twice a year to bring gifts which
he presented to C 2 for distribution among all the sisters. This
was because she had been instrumental in getting him her
younger sister to wife. He always summoned her to help with
his harvest and gave her a share of the returns. C 2, known
to be the poorest of the sisters, frequently received gifts from
the house of her brother, A 1, which she was not expected to
return.

### House D

1 Hot, household head, ob of C 1

2 Katari (Caterina) wife, own si of a A, B 2, half si of B 3, B 4,
C 2

3 Juan, s,of D 1 and D 2

4 Evening Waving, wife of D 3

5 Martina, d of D 1 and D 2

6 kolowinyi, husband of D 4

7 ïhna, d of D 5 and D 6

Land: D 1 was from Whirling Water. He married his wife while she
was still with her family at Mesquite Root, and took her to

Whirling Water. When the wife's family emigrated to Standing Rock, the couple joined them there, abandoning their field at Whirling Water. Their son D 3 brought his wife home in the regular way. The daughter married a man from Mesquite Root but all his family were dead so he left his land and joined his wife's family. His wife's mother was at that time with them but on arriving at Standing Rock she went to her older daughter Susannah.

Gifts: This family and that of Susannah, House C lived close together and used the same storehouse. They did not eat together but exchanged food gifts at every meal.

4. Group of relatives at San Pedro (Tobacco Mountain) from about 1900 to the present (informant 2)

This group had moved from Coyote Village, a settlement in the hills. A mountain spring was near enough to the village so that the people did not need to move in winter but they did so, going to Mesquite Root, a larger place, for fear of the Apache. In summer they had to go into the valley, some times three or four miles away, to plant. The informant, A 1, discovered that water was obtainable near Tobacco Mountain and dug a well there. Two of his "distant" paternal uncles followed him and the three started a new permanent settlement. of which A 1 was made governor. Relatives from Coyote Village joined them for planting but returned to the old village in the winter.

### House A

1 Donkey Shoulder, head
2 Wife
3 Ramon, son of A 1 and A 2
4 son of A 1 and A 2

(A daughter married in Coyote Village 17 miles away)

Living arrangements: All lived in one house until the two sons married and built separate shelters but the family used the common kitchen.

Land: A 1, on coming to Tobacco Mountain fenced off a field for himself which he works with his sons.

Work sharing: When the help of his sons is not sufficient, A 1 calls on the two senior "uncles" who joined his pioneer venture. He continues to call on their families though nearer relatives have now joined him. For large operations, such as plowing, which is done with White man's tools, the whole village works together, taking the fields in rotation.

Gifts: The women of the family sent out food gifts two or three times a week. "Not much because there was not much food." Only one or two families received gifts on one day; they were taken in turn, the senior uncles' turn coming oftenest. The gifts were reciprocated the same day. When A 1 kills a beef, he invites the whole village (all connected) to partake. This may happen two or three times a year. He always fills his saddlebags and takes a large portion to the married daughter in Coyote Village.

Heads of families living at Tobacco Mountain who exchange food gifts with A 1 and who are given beef when he slaughters:

B Teviso Luis, ffobs s called "older uncle" one of the pioneers
C Wilamin ffobs s called "older uncle" one of the pioneers
D Sipela (Cypriano) ffybss called "younger uncle"
E Nestoro fob to C
F Nicola fbs to C
G Filomeno fsi s to E and F
H Nasio fsi s to E and F
I Francisco brother of F
J Avilano (his wife is mbd to F)
K Manuel Chappo m b s to wife of D
L Narisco Lopez obs to A
M Tomaso obs to A
N Domingo son of H

5. Group at tciaur (Devil[1]-Sitting) about 1890, informant 21

Devil-Sitting was a summer planting ground settled by a group of paternal kin. Some moved in winter to the well at Comobabi (Mulberry Well) where they met a group from the other side of the family. The camp of these other relatives was about three-quarters of a mile away and, though it contained some who were closely related, the group from Devil-Sitting had no gift relations with them (21).

### House A

1 Ego's f, a widower
2 Ego,
3 d

### House B

1 m of A 1

### House C

1 yb of A 1, unmarried
2 yb of A 1,
3 yb of A 1

Living arrangements: The three houses above were small huts whose function was that of rooms in a single dwelling. The

---

[1] "Devil" names omitted since informant objected to giving those of the dead.

place had been the home of the father of A 1 who was dead. A hut had been built for his widow near by and another for her three unmarried sons. The married son, now a widower, lived in another hut with his two children and the grandmother cooked for all.

Land: All the sons together worked the dead father's land, undivided.

Work sharing: Work was done by five brothers, four in one household, one separate. A 1 and C 1, 2, 3, kept their share together, D 1 separate. At harvest time, the first four sent for the relatives of the dead wife of A 1, to help work. A man and wife would receive one sack of produce (harvest sometimes ten sacks.) Only one couple was asked each year, since there would not be enough to pay more. The Akchin relatives reciprocated. A 2 was frequently sent by A 1, his father, to help his senior uncle in his field, since the latter had not many sons. He fed the boy and gave him moral advice.

Gifts: Cooked food was sent every day to D 1, father's older brother. It was sent about three times a week to E 1 and when F 1 arrived, also to him. "We would have given to more relatives but there were no others there." Gifts were sent by turns to three brothers of B 1 at a distance. Some four gallons of corn mush were cooked each night, the gifts were sent out and the family ate the remainder. Gifts came in each evening. When A 1 killed a deer, he took portions to Houses D, E, and F. About six times a year he carried meat to the relatives of his dead wife, at Akchin (25 miles). A senior first cousin of A 1 used to visit him at the Well, bringing corn and cooked mescal. A 1 went to Coyote Sitting in return, taking produce.

### House D

1 head, ob of A 1
2 wife
3 son
4 son
5 son

Living arrangements: D 1 had moved from the family group of huts even before the father died and set up separate housekeeping.

Land and Work: He used a separate portion of the father's land. Though he and his brothers tilled all together, he took the harvest from one strip. His nephew, A 2, was often sent in to help him.

Gifts: When D 1 killed a deer, he distributed meat as A 1 did. Occasionally he sent gifts to his wife's people, and at harvest time called the neighboring relatives in to help themselves.

15

## House E

1 wife's m b to A 1, with wife and children

Land: Had moved to Devil when his niece, now dead, had married, because there was more land.

Work Sharing: Cultivated his own field with sons, called the others in at harvest time to help themselves.

Gifts: Sent food gifts frequently to House F, his relative, less often to A, B, C, D, affinals.

## House F

1 ob s of dead wife of A 1, with wife and children

Land: F 1 had land in Achin where the wife of A 1 had lived. Being crowded there, and finding more at Devil, he moved without asking permission. He kept with the Devil people even in summer, when they moved back among his own relatives.

Work sharing: He worked his field with his sons, but when he needed help he called on his nearest relative, E 1.

Gifts: At harvest time affinal relatives at Devil were asked to help themselves and paternal kin from Akchin were sent for.

In winter, when water failed at Devil, Households A, B, C, and F moved to Mulberry Well, the winter camp used by the people of Akchin, the home of the dead wife of A 1. Here they met a group of this woman's relatives, but camped three quarters of a mile away from them and exchanged gifts only rarely. Their customary gift giving went on in their own circle. It may be mentioned that E 1 and F 1 were both Akchin people but, having moved to Devil, they now made their winter camp with its residents and formed part of their gift giving circle, not that of their nearer kin.

## Group at Comobabi (Mulberry) Well

Houses A, B, C, E, F, as at Devil

## House G

1 f of dead wife of A 1
2 wife of G 1
3 f of G 2

## House H

Brothers of dead wife of A 1 with wives and children

## House I

Mother's brothers of dead wife of A 1

A few relatives of A 1 himself also came to Mulberry Well, but stayed near the relatives of A 1's dead wife and exchanged gifts with them because they had fields near them at home and had "got used to it." These were:

House J

f si of A 1

House K

f f o s s to A 1

House L

m brothers of A 1

## 6. Households at Anegam (The Willows) about 1880
### (informant 5)

The family had headquarters at the Willows, where they built brush houses. When the water gave out there, they went to the foothills to hunt, living in roofless circular enclosures. During planting time they moved to and fro between The Willows and their fields, some of which were five miles away at the base of the hills, where flood water collected.

### House A

1 Never-Says-Anything, head, o b of B 1, C 2, m o b of D 2
2 wife of 1 (elderly, no children)
Living arrangements: A 1 was the head of a group of relatives, inclouding a younger brother and a sister and a niece. All had separate houses for sleeping, but cooked and ate together in a common kitchen, the younger women dividing the work and taking food from a common storehouse.
Land: The four relatives used their inherited land in common. They had two fields, one near the mountain for melons and one at home for other crops.
Work sharing: Work was done by the men of the four households without outside help. They took turns living in a windbreak near the mountain to tend the melon field.
Gifts: Gifts of dried meat, salt and cactus syrup were sent to distant cousins at Santa Rosa (5 miles away) three or four times a year.

### House B

1 head, yb of A 1, o b of C 2, m ob of D 2
2 wife of 1
3 Coyote-Skin-Quiver s of B 1 and B 2
4 Pitala d of B 1 and B 2
5 Chawa s of B 1 and B 2

Living arrangements: Separate house but shared meals as with A1.
Land: Father's field shared with ob, ysi and y si d as with A 1
Work sharing: Shared by men of four families
Gifts: as with A 1.

15*

### House C

1 head
2 Having a Belt, wife of C 1
3 Licenza (Crescenza) d of c 1 and C 2, other daughters died

Living arrangements: Separate house but shared meals as with A 1
Land: The husband was from another village but came to his wife's
family because they had more land.
Work sharing: The men of the four families worked the fields in
common.
Gifts: As with A 1.

### House D

1 Hugging-an-Owl, head
2 Flowering Wind, wife of D 1, si d to A 1, B 1, C 2
3 Dionisio, s of D 1 and D 2
4 s of A 1 by a former wife
5 s of D 1 by a former wife
(A daughter of D 1 and D 2 had married a Pima and was
living at Sacaton. Another lived at Akchin six miles away.)

Living arrangements: Separate house and shared meals as with A 1
Land: D 1 came from Santa Rosa (5 miles away) where he had land
but he had left it to live with his wife's uncles who had more.
But he still pented his field at Santa Rosa and visited it
occasionally. His younger sister's daughter, had married at
Santa Rosa and her husband had made a new field where D 1
sometimes planted. When D 1 died, his sons left the Willows
to the other families and went to their sister at Sacaton, then
a widow. They used her land until her sons grew up, then
returned to The Willows, broke new land and planted.
Work Sharing: D 1 worked the Willows land with the men of the
other families keeping the produce in common.
Gifts: D 1, the youngest of the group, was a hunter. When he
killed a deer, he sent word to his daughter in Santa Rosa and
younger sister's daughter in Akchin, who came to help butcher
and cook. They feasted with the rest of the family and each
took home a large piece. This family sent out everything they
had cooked for a meal and ate the return gifts. At harvest they
sent for the daughters at Akchin and Sacaton, and the niece
of D 1 at Santa Rosa bidding them help themselves.

### 7. Group at Imikah, [(Field of) the Relatives,] about 1870 (informant 41)

This group contained only three families, two brothers and a
sister. Their father had moved from Hikiwanyi a few miles away
and broken new land. The two brothers had always used it and the
sister, when she lost her husband, returned there. In the dry

season, they went to Red Well, where they met other paternal kin but the three families camped close and kept their gift exchange circle as before. The informant, in this case, would not use the names of the dead.

## House A

1 head
2 wife of A 1
3 s
4 s
5 d
6 d

(One son had married a woman at White Clay and lived with his father-in-law who had no man in the family)

## House B

1 head
2 widow of B 1, si of A 1
3 d
4
5

Living arrangements: The two houses were the equivalents of rooms in a large dwelling; the families cooking and eating together under a large shade. As between the two older women "there was no particular head."

Land: The fields were new, having been first broken by the father of A 1. They were divided between A 1 and his brother and the produce kept separate. No separate land was given to B 2. She was part of the family of A 1.

Work sharing: A 1 and his brother, C 1, sometimes worked the fields as a unit, sometimes each worked his own, the one who finished soonest helping the other.

Gifts: Dishes of food were sent between this family and House C at their meals, twice a day. The married son, living with his wife's people, was invited to come at harvest and help himself. A brother of A 2 living at a distance was invited in the same way to stay through harvest and took home a large storage basket (three feet high) full. The guests asked for the particular kind of produce which they lacked. They reciprocated at their own harvest with equal amounts but different produce if possible.

## House C

1 head yb of A 1
2 wife of C 1
3 d with husband and children part time
4 d with husband and children part time
5 d with husband and children part time

Living arrangements: The daughters were not at home all the time
but, the father having no sons, one of them was generally there
with her husband.

Land: The land, having been first broken by the father of A 1, was
shared between him and his brother. His sons-in-law had land
of their own at Kaka, across the mountains, which they cultivated.

Work sharing: C 1, when there were no sons-in-law to help him,
called on his brother's family who had two sons, but more
people to feed. All worked in both fields until the work was
done, but kept the produce separate.

Gifts: Cooked food was exchanged with Houses A and B at the main
meal every day. At harvest the sons-in-law, whether they had
helped or not, were asked to come and help themselves. They
brought gifts with them from their own fields.

### 8. Households at Tecalote (Owl's Hoot) about 1890—1900
### (informant 32)

This group of relatives had been migrating for several generations,
about the southern part of the reservation and over the Mexican
border. They had settled at Tecalote, then they went to Poso Verde
(Mexico) Baboquivari, San Miguel, Vamori, leaving a few of their
members at each place. One family finally returned to Tecalote
and there dug a reservoir in a low spot. Their fields they planted in
a wash some three miles away. Every summer, at cactus time,
they joined the relatives from the above mentioned places and went
into the foothills of Mexico to pick organ cactus. In the winters they
worked in Mexico.

When the father of the single Tecalote family died, four of the
children, two sons and two daughters used his field until the oldest
son made himself a new one. The other three divided up the old
field, though they worked it all together. Of the remaining two, a
daughter married a man with a field at Wamori and a son acted as
cowboy for the family cattle.

### House A

1 Acting-Like-a-Girl, family head
2 "The Head Woman", osi of B 1, C 1, D 2, E 1, F 1
3 Manuel, son of A 1 and A 2
4 Salvador, son
5 Cecilia, d
6 Jose, s
7 Anton, s
8 Candelario

Land: A 2 should properly have gone to her husband's land but
he was from a Mexican village where the men were day laborers

without land; so she brought him to the land her father had cleared. This she shared with her younger brother C 1 and her sister F 2, the land being divided into three plots.

Work sharing: The men of Houses A, C, and F, cultivated the land together though each kept his produce in his own storehouse. When they needed help, they called on E 1 who cared for the family cattle herd, paying him in produce. Before E 1 was married, he lived with A 1 and worked as a member of her family without extra pay. She objected to E 1's marriage because it deprived her of a farm hand.

Gifts: Houses A and B, belonging to the oldest brother and sister of the family maintained special intimacy, sending small food gifts, enough for one person, every day. They gave produce to sister D 2, deserted by her husband, whenever she was at home.

### House B

1 Jose Juan, nickname kuksali (cucharo) spoon, head. He was ob of C 1, D 2, E 1, F 2, yb of A 2
2 Listiana (Christiana) Mexican
3 Marcanton son of B 1 and B 2
4 Jose Maria son
5 Juan Jose son
6 Josepha, d of B 1 and B 2
7 Lucia d
8 Maria d
9 d of B 2 by former husband
10 d of B 2 by former husband

Land: B 1, the oldest son in the family, broke a new field, leaving the inherited land to his siblings. He considered the new land entirely his property and never made gifts from it.

Work sharing: B 1 worked his land with the aid of his sons, rarely called on his brothers. He, like them, shared in the herd of cattle which was in charge of E 1 and all paid E 1 in produce.

Gifts: The intimate relations of B 1 were with A 2, the oldest of the family. These two oldest lived close together and sent food gifts almost daily. The gifts were only a gesture, perhaps a portion for one person. They went occasionally to visit F 2 who lived three miles away, took a gift and received and equal amount. They gave produce to D 2, deserted by her husband, whenever she was at home.

### House C

1 Pedro, head yb of A 2, B 1, F 2, o b of D 2, E 1
2 Lipinza
3 Silapo, son of C 1 and C 2
4 Ramon, son
5 (Daughter Isilia married and went to Vamori)

Land: C 1 who was the second son, shared the father's land with his sisters A 2, and F 2, the land being divided into three portions.

Work sharing: C 1 shared the work on the land with A 1 and F 1, the husbands of his sisters. When they needed more help, they called on E 1 who had no land but cared for the family herd. They paid him in produce.

Gifts: Houses C, E, and D were close together, C 1, E 1, and D 2 being the three youngest of the family felt a solidarity, and exchanged small food gifts daily. They never sent to B, the older brother whose house was farther off and who had made a new field, and they rarely sent to A 2, the oldest sister who was disagreeably domineering. When D 2 was deserted by her husband, the brothers C 1 and E 1 supplied her food.

### House D

1 Dolores, head
2 Jesus, wife of D 1, o si of E 1, y si of A 2, B 1, C 1, F 2
3 Margarita, d of D 1 and D 2
4 Jose, son
5 Joaquina, d
6 Luis, s
7 s

Land: This sister married a man with land at Vamori, the next village but continued living at Tecalote because of the reservoir. Her husband went to school at Hampton and afterward deserted her. She went periodically to Tucson to work for the Whites, and in the intervals brothers C and E supported her.

Gifts: House D was within 200 yards of E which was the same distance from C. All three exchanged food gifts daily. D 2, E 1 and C 1 were the three youngest of the family and felt a solidarity.

### House E

1 Juan Diego yb of A 2, B 1, F 2, C 1, D 2
2 1st wife, Mexican, left
3 2nd wife, left
4 3rd wife
5 son
6 son
7 Carmen, d

Living arrangements: E 1 was the youngest of the family and after the death of his parents lived with oldest sister, A 2. When he took a wife, he brought her home there, but the sister, A 2, scared her out so that her father took her away. E 1 then took another wife and built a separate house but his sister, who wished his services for herself made life miserable for this wife also until she left. E 1 then took a third who was the mother of his children.

Land: E 1 never had any land. The land left by his father was divided between brothers B 1 and C 1 and sister F 2. E 1 the youngest, helped them work it. When he was old and his children grown, he broke some new land at Tecalote and began to plant.

Work sharing: The father of all the siblings had been a shaman and had accumulated some cattle as payment. These were kept in a common herd, though marked with the brands of the individual siblings. E 1, as youngest, was told off to ride herd on them and did so until he was too old to ride. He was paid in goods and some of the cattle. Says A 2, the oldest sister never let him have his share.

Gifts: Houses C, D, and E were 200 yards apart. The two brothers, C 1 and E 1 and the sister D 2, were the three youngest of the family and felt specially intimate. They exchanged food gifts every day, sending a very small amount, such as a bowl holding two cupfuls of cooked beans and three tortillas. Once or twice a year they sent such delicacies as chile or meat. They sent much more rarely to A 2, the domineering older sister. When she made her return gifts to E, they were never food but soap, thread needles. She would admonish the child who brought the food gift to go home and tell her mother to do some sewing for her. With the older brother, B 1, there was no gift exchange, his field being in Vamori, the old family home. The sister, F 2, was three miles away; she gave when any of the E family visited, but there was no regular exchange. Family E went in winters to Mexico and always stopped with F on the way back, bringing her a sack of figs, chile, and pomgranates. Relatives of E 4 lived in the neighborehood and were sent occasional food gifts. When E 1 butchered a deer, he was accustomed to give to relative and neighbors alike, all reciprocating with farm produce.

## House F

1 head
2 Maria Juana, o si of C 1, D 2, E 1, y si of A 2, B 1
3 Luisa d of F 1 and F 2
4 Ramon, s
5 Jose, s
6 Serafina, d
7 Charlita, d
8 Rosita

Land: This sister lived near the planting field three miles from the other houses. She kept her cattle near the house instead of with the family herd and made a business of making cheese which she traded in Mexico for fruit and dried meat.

Work sharing: F 1 worked the field with A 1 and C 1. When they needed more help, they called on E 1 and paid him in produce.

Gifts: F 2 was too far away to exchange gifts with any of the family, but she gave them a cheese if she came to visit. They reciprocated with produce.

DISTRIBUTION OF PAPAGO TRAITS MENTIONED

| | Shoshoneans, Basin and Plateau | Shoshoneans, Calif. | Western Pueblos | Eastern Pueblos | Mexico | River Yumans | Upland Yumans |
|---|---|---|---|---|---|---|---|
| No distinction parallel and cross cousins | × | | | / | × | | |
| Age distinctions between siblings ... | × | × | × | / | × | × | × |
| Age, sex, lineage in uncle class ..... | | × | | | / | × | × |
| 4 grandparental terms ............. | × | | | / | × | × | × |
| Affinals singled out as a class, not merged ...................... | / | × | / | / | | / | |
| Moieties ......................... | | × | | × | | | |
| Sibs ............................. | | × | × | × | | × | / |
| Sib names for individuals .......... | | / | / | | | × | |
| Localized lineage.................. | | / | × | / | × | / | / |
| Set of hereditary village officers .... | | × | × | / | | | |
| Star names....................... | | × | | | × | × | × |
| Organized warfare ................ | | | | | × | × | |
| Scalps rather than prisoners ........ | | | × | × | | / | |
| Warrior purification .............. | | | × | / | × | × | |
| Intervillage games ................ | | | / | | × | | |
| Birth segregation ................. | × | × | / | | | / | / |
| Presentation to sun ............... | | | × | × | × | | |
| Postnatal purification ............. | | | × | × | × | | |
| Girl's segregation at puberty........ | × | / | / | | | / | / |
| Menstruation dangerous ........... | / | / | | | | | / |
| Animal guardian ................. | × | | | | | × | × |
| Power in dream .................. | × | | | | | × | × |
| Exogamy rules extend equally both sides family .................... | × | / | / | / | | / | / |
| Temporary matrilocal residence ..... | × | | | | / | / | |
| Light woman ..................... | | | | | × | × | |
| Sororate and levirate.............. | × | | | | / | / | |
| Bury and cremate ................ | × | | | | × | | |
| Destroy property at death ......... | × | × | | | × | × | × |
| Exorcism at death ................ | | × | × | × | × | | |
| Name of dead taboo .............. | × | × | × | | × | ✗ | × |

# APPENDIX II

## COMPARATIVE DATA

The elements from which the Papago built their social system were shared with a large area. We cannot ignore the fact that not only the practices of the Papago but some of their emotional attitudes have somewhat continuous distributions in the neighborhood. These distributions are by no means all in the same direction. A map would show the areas of the different traits, extending now north, now southeast or west, with overlapping, intensifying, weakening or adaptation always at different points. We have attempted to follow some of these permutations and combinations, showing how the combination of two traits has sometimes produced a highly specialized one — as the sacredness of the enemy trophy and the fear of ceremonial uncleanness brought about the paramount importance of Papago warrior's purification. Also, to a slight degree, we have attempted to show what circumstances among the Papago or their neighbors, invited the spread of a trait or prevented its adoption. The areas studied are those mentioned in the first chapter as being accessible to the Papago. Spier and Gifford[1] have already discussed the relations of some of them to the Pimans but neither used material from the northern Shoshoneans or from Mexico. The reason is lack of information, particularly from Mexico, but the striking likenesses which appear, even in scattered and incomplete data, make it seem worth while here to plot what there is. A trait found only among Yumans, as are some in the data mentioned, may well be of Yuman origin, with the Pimans as recipients, but when it appears again in Mexico, though only in one group and without data for the intervening area, it opens up a possibility of spread from the south. The areas studied are, therefore, the following:

## I. Gila Pima

Unless otherwise stated, it is to be assumed that the practices of Pima and Papago were the same. We have already stated that the division of Upper Pimeria into a Pima and a Papago section is an artificial one, sponsored mostly by white Americans. The native division would be along a north and south line, leaving the

---

[1] AA 1936, no. 4, pp. 679–82.

more advanced people, with traces of pueblo influence, at the east and the more primitive ones at the west. This division, however, appears chiefly in dialect and ceremonies. Social organization seems much the same for the whole area[1] except in tribal organization and warfare where there are traces, at the north, of Maricopa influence. These have been noted below but otherwise we shall speak here of Gila Pima and American Papago as the Pimans. Mexican Papago and Lower Pima are not included for lack of data.

## II. Mexico

This region which contains the home of the Opata and the Pimas Bajos, often treated in Spanish accounts as one with the Pimans, is the one on which we possess least information. Through it the Uto-Aztecans, Pima congeners, stretch in an unbroken line down to the Cora. All of them are agriculturalists, some prosperous village dwellers, some hidden in remote gorges, and, though their culture is essentially one, it can be broken up into sub-areas. A classification by Beals[2] with revision by Bennett[3] results as follows:

1 Pimans (Pima, Papago, Nevome or Pima Bajo)
2 Sonora-Sinaloa (Opata, Yaqui, Mayo)
3 North Sierra (Tarahumare, Varohio and others)
4 South Sierra (Tepehuane, Cora, Huichol, Acaxee, Zacateco, etc.)
5 Tepic-Culiacan

If our data were full enough, we should confine our discussion to two groups, that of Sonora- Sinaloa, which is nearest geographically, and that of the South Sierra which includes the Tepehuane, of Piman dialect. But information relates now to one sub-area, now to another, and some of the fullest concerns the Aztecs. It has seemed worth while to gather all these scattered fragments because, though they may cast little light on the Papago place in Mexican culture, they change our perspective for the area farther north. Therefore all available data for the Mexico Uto-Aztecans have been included, much of it coming from the excellent compilations of Beals and Bennett. For convenience in using the data, a number indicating the sub-area has been placed after every group cited, the Nahua being added as group 6.

---

[1] cf. Russell, 1926.
[2] Beals, 1932.
[3] Bennett, 1935.

## III. Yumans

These neighbors of entirely different speech live in the same sort of country as the Papago, have the same house and the same pottery, yet their customs coincide with Papago customs at only a few points. It is with the River Yumans that likeness to the Pimans is found, while the Upland Yumans, as already noted by Spier[1] have much in common with the Basin Shoshoneans. Therefore, in this study, the two groups have been treated separately.

## IV. Shoshoneans.

West and north of the Yumans is the great group of Shoshoneans, stretching from southern California up into Nevada. As the sub-groups were listed, those of southern California fell constantly into one category which included Cahuilla, Cupeño, Luiseño and Serrano, now and then Gabrieliño and Juaneño. The more northern Shoshoneans, beginning with the Chemehuevi, showed sufficient similarity to be placed under a second heading which has been called Basin. This northwesterly affiliation of the Papago is a very important one. In view of the constantly recurring similarities noted, we might well carry our study further north on the Plateau and even follow it west through California, finding some of these areas no more out of focus from the Papago point of view than are the Eastern Pueblos, in spite of the latter's geographical nearness. The selection of the Basin peoples quoted is a matter of convenience and the availability of data, and we look to forthcoming studies on that region to fill the very obvious gaps.

## V. Pueblos

To the north and the northeast of the Papago are their Uto-Aztecan congeners, the Hopi, westernmost of a pueblo group which often shows very different affiliations. Looking at the whole area from the point of view of organization, it seems obvious that a simple division can be made on geographic lines. Hopi and Zuni, on the west, fall into one category, and, on the eást, the Tanoans, no matter how they differ among themselves, fall into another. The Keres, between the two, show likenesses to both, with eastern influences predominating. Acoma is marginal, aligning now with the western pueblos which are its geographic neighbors, now with its linguistic relatives to the east.

---

[1] Spier, 1928.

## VI. Athapascans

It is hard to see how there could have been much borrowing from these deadly enemies to the east who were so feared that all their property was taboo and from whom no prisoners were taken except young children. Yet likenesses do appear. Very often they can be traced to a borrowing from the Pueblos by both Athapascans and Pimans and at other times to a common likeness with Mexico. Occasionally, as with the guardian spirit usages, the Pimans seem nearer to these aliens than to any of their more friendly neighbors. We may even look further eastward, to the southern Sioux and find scattered but striking resemblances such as sib names for individuals, fear of the menstruant and individual guardian spirits.

Throughout this area, we find Papago affiliations peculiarly complicated and intertwined. Our data concern only social organization and therefore present a slightly different picture from that which would result if we studied material culture. The accompanying chart gives some indications of its nature though it must be accepted merely as a summary of facts presented in the text not as a complete analysis. The traits taken up are those described in the preceding chapters, in the order of their appearance.

### MOIETY

The Piman patrilineal moieties, with their animal names and distinguishing paints and colors and their occasional ceremonial functions[1] most resemble those of the southern California Shoshoneans.[2] Even their names, Coyote and Buzzard, suggest the Shoshonean names, Coyote and Wildcat. North of the Shoshonean area stretch the Californian Yokuts and Miwok with similar moieties originating, according to Strong, from the same source and the Papago thus find themselves close to a wide stretch of moiety organization. However, their relation to it is distinctly marginal for their moieties have not, now, the exogamy nor the various ceremonial functions which characterize those of California. These functions, among the Pimans, are associated with the village, while the moiety retains only a name and a few atrophied functions.

Moiety is absent in the wedge of Yuman peoples which separates California Shoshoneans from the Pimans. Only the vaguest

---

[1] Pima, Russell, p. 97. Herzog reports a former function in games. AA vol. 38, no. 3, p. 520.

[2] Serrano, Desert Cahuilla, Mountain Cahuilla, Pass Cahuilla, Cupeño, Luiseño. All have paternal descent, exogamy, ceremonial functions, distinguishing paints, and also divisions according to natural phenomena. Strong, 1927, p. 46.

suggestions of it can be found in Mexico[1] and even less in the western pueblos.[2] It appears again in the eastern pueblos but shorn of many of its western characteristics for here it has neither the animal name, the color nor the paint.[3] From this statement we must except Acoma which here aligns with the west in having no moiety at all. Exogamy is not always observed[4] and, when we reach the Tewa, the tendency is even toward endogamy.[5] Functional importance is, however, even stronger than in the west where moieties are active only on certain occasions. Among the Keres, most ceremonies are conducted by moieties,[6] while, with the Tewa, moieties are the outstanding feature of organization, not only ceremonial but social[7] and the same seems to hold, though to less degree, with the Tigua.[8] We might follow this importance of moiety in government far to the east again, where we find it among southern Sioux and Iroquois. But such a use of dichotomy is entirely foreign to the Pimans who in this respect align themselves decidedly with California.

## SIB

Sibs are to be found throughout our area, the distinction being that in part of it they are patrilineal, in part matrilineal. Patrilineal sibs appear at the south and west, among Pimans, southern Californian Shoshoneans[9] and their neighbors the Diegueño;[10] and River Yumans[11] and some Mexicans.[12] As with the moities, we are at once struck by the similarity of Shoshonean sib names to those

---

[1] Beals, AA vol. 43, pp. 467–475.
[2] Parsons, 1933b, p. 55, detects faint traces of ceremonial dichotomy at Hopi.
[3] Keres, Parsons, 1924a, p. 337.
[4] Santo Domingo: White, 1935, p. 72. Santa Ana: Parsons, 1920a, p. 64, Cochiti: Kroeber 1919b, p. 97. Laguna is marginal, its moieties being not only non-exogamous but changeable at will: Parsons 1924a, p. 337.
[5] Parsons, 1924a, p. 337, 1936a, p. 116.
[6] Parsons, op. cit.
[7] Parsons, 1924a, p. 337, 1936a, p. 116.
[8] Taos has double chieftaincy according to season: Parsons 1924a, p. 337. Isleta ceremonial dichotomy and double chieftaincy: Parsons, 1930, p. 261.
[9] Strong, 1927, 1929.
[10] Kroeber, 1925, p. 719.
[11] Mohave: Kroeber, 1925, p. 741; Yuma: Forde, 1931, pp. 142–3; Cocopa: Gifford, 1933, p. 387; Gila Yumans: Spier, 1933, pp. 186–196.
[12] Cahita: localized patrilineal sibs, Beals, AA vol. 34, p. 468, 1932; Acaxee; Ibid, p. 469; Tepecano (4): Bennett, 1935, p. 395. Aztecs (4): localized patrilineal sibs, each owning land and house; Bandelier, pp. 402, 406.

of the Pimans. In both cases the names are untranslatable but several close resemblances suggest a common origin.[1]

The Shoshonean sibs of southern California are important organizations. They are exogamous and localized, one sib sometimes constituting a village, and they are units of government, each having, or having had, a sacred house, fetish and ceremonial leader. In Mexico, the same sort of organization is indicated among the Aztecs though there is no data for tracing it among northern Mexican tribes. The River Yumans, though having patrilineal sibs, lack all this further organization. The Pimans seem very like the Shoshoneans in having the sacred house, fetish and ceremonial leader but, as with the moiety, these functions have been transferred to the village, while the sib is little more than a name.

To the north and east is the area of the matrilineal sib, among the Pueblos[2] and the western Apache, who have many Pueblo characteristics.[3]

Hopi forms the link between east and west for, as pointed out by Strong, its sibs, though matrilineal, have the leader, house and fetish of the southern Californian Shoshoneans. To the east, the importance of the matrilineal sib dwindles, under the influence of the patrilineal moiety, which takes over ceremonial functions, leader and sacred house, either sharing them with societies as among some Keres, or operating in its own name as among the Tewa.

---

[1] i. e. Papago *aapap*, Mountain Cahuilla *apapatcem (itcem* means people) (Strong, 1929, p. 148), Cupeño *apapas* (Ibid p. 215); Papago *maam*, Serrano *mamaitum*; Papago *apki*, Serrano *apihavetum* (Ibid p. 11); Papago *waahw*, Desert Cahuilla *wa'atcem* or *wawitcem* (Ibid p. 41).

[2] WESTERN PUEBLOS. Sibs matrilineal, exogamous, non-localized but with ceremonial functions, house, property and leader: Strong 1927, p. 55; Lowie 1929, pp. 330, 338. Acoma resembles the western pueblos in having matrilineal exogamous sibs with definite functions: White, 1930, pp. 34–35. Laguna may be put in the same class though sib functions are fewer: Parsons, 1923b, pp. 206, 212, 219, 225, 226; White, 1936, pp. 70–71.

EASTERN PUEBLOS. Keres: all have matrilineal sibs but with few or no functions. Sibs exogamous at Domingo: White, 1933, pp. 70–73, and Cochiti: Goldfrank, p. 12. At Sia exogamous only in theory because of depopulation: Stevenson, 1890, p. 19; at Santa Ana no exogamy mentioned.

Tanoan: 1) Towa: Jemez sibs feeble: Parsons, 1925, p. 25. 2) Tewa: three or four matrilineal sibs exist in each village but as names without function: Parsons, 1924, p. 333; 1929, pp. 82–85. Sib membership can be changed Ibid, p. 84. 3) Tiwa: Isleta sibs are related to those of their western neighbors in being exogamous with a few ceremonial functions: Parsons, 1920a, pp. 57, 61. Taos, no sibs: Parsons, 1936a, p. 38.

[3] Goodwin, 1935, p. 58.

## SIB NAMES FOR INDIVIDUALS

Scattered sparsely through our area there appears a custom of bestowing on sib members a name or title indicating the sib. It is unknown in the Basin; but suggested here and there among southern California Shoshoneans where the men of one sib may all be called pine trees.[1] The custom is fully developed among the River Yumans where all women of å sib bear its generic name, sometimes with an additional name describing the totem.[2] The Pimans have a less elaborate system by which all children call their father not by a kinship term but by the name of the sib. Different but related is the Hopi custom by which sibs have a stock of personal names which may be given by women to their clansmen's offspring.[3] No such usage can be traced among the other pueblos but a stock of clan-owned personal names is, of course, found in other tribes of North America as among the southern Sioux[4] and the Iroquois, where names were clan property doled out by officials to young sib members.

Summing up the affiliations of the Piman moiety and sib, we find them decidedly to the west. In name and in specific characteristics such as associated paint and color, these Piman divisions are very like those of the southern California Shoshoneans but the more important functions of sib and moiety found among these Shoshoneans have, with the Pimans, been transferred to the village. Since the southern California sib is localized and may even constitute a village, this makes the resemblance between the Papago and these Shoshoneans very close. The difference is mainly one of emphasis: on kinship with the Shoshoneans, on locality with the Papago. Only in the matter of sib names for individuals is there a peculiar distribution which brings the Pimans closest to the River Yumans.

## EXOGAMY

Related to sib and moiety organization are rules of exogamy which limit the incest group to sib or moiety while allowing marriage with relatives outside it. This is not the case in our area. Throughout its extent, except among some Yumans,[5] there is prohibition

---

[1] Strong, 1929, p. 19.
[2] Mohave: Kroeber, 1925, p. 741; Yuma: Forde, 1931, pp. 142—3; Cocopa: Gifford, 1933, p. 287; Gila Yumans: women's names have totemic sib reference; Spier, 1933, p. 187.
[3] Parsons, 1933b, p. 38.
[4] Fletcher, p. 137.
[5] Mohave: Kroeber, 1925, p. 795; Gila Yumans: Spier, 1933.

of marriage of any blood kin, and where sib or moiety rules exist they are added to the taboo on the marriage of blood relatives instead of replacing it. In the center of the area is a north and south extension of bilateral family organization, from the Basin and Plateau through the Pimans into Mexico. In its northern portion the only rule is that against marriage of blood kin[1] and this area includes the Pimans whose sibs and moieties have not influenced their bilateral kin system nor their marriage rules. Beals suggests patrilineal exogamous units for northern Mexico[2] but one wonders, from his data, whether the situation here was not like that of the Papago, exogamy of village or *barrio*.

At either side of this region of the bilateral family are groups organized in sibs and moieties and with a unilateral system. But in addition to other rules, they place a taboo on all blood kin. This is the case with southern California Shoshoneans[3] and with all the Pueblos, some of whom even omit the sib or moiety taboo and invoke only that of blood kin.[4]   Only some of the River Yumans, whose difference from their neighbors is so frequently emphasized, practice sib exogamy with no reference to blood kin.[5]

---

[1] Shivwits: Lowie, 1924, p. 275; Paviotso: Ibid p. 276; Wind River: Ibid p. 278; Surprise Valley: Kelly, 1932, pp. 164—5; Owens Valley: Steward, 1933, p. 294, apparently village exogamy; W. Mono: Kroeber, 1925, p. 588.

[2] Unilateral Organizations in Mexico, AA vol. 34.

[3] Desert Cahuilla: no marriage within sib or moiety or to any blood kin; Strong, 1929, pp. 73–4; Pass Cahuilla: moiety exogamy, Ibid pp. 112—4; Mountain Cahuilla: moiety exogamy plus taboo on blood kin, Ibid pp. 171—2; Cupeño: no moiety control, only taboo was on blood kin, Ibid pp. 239—44; Luiseño: sib exogamy, Kroeber, 1925, p. 719, plus taboo on blood kin, Ibid p. 617.

[4] Hopi: Exogamy of linked matrilineages, plus taboo on father's sib Beaglehole, 1935, p. 47; Lowie, 1929b, p. 387. Zuni: No Marriage in mother's sib nor to actual kin in father's sib, Kroeber, 1917, p· 98. Acoma: No marriage in the matrilineal sib, White, 1930, p. 34. Laguna: No marriage in the matrilineal sib, nor in the father's sib, Parsons, 1923b, p. 206. Cochiti: No marriage in matrilineal sib, Goldfrank, p. 12. Santo Domingo: No marriage in matrilineal sib, disapproval of marriage into father's sib, White, 1935, p. 70.   Sia: No marriage in matrilineal sib nor into father's sib, Stevenson, 1890, p. 19. Tewa: Sibs matrilineal, unimportant; marriage forbidden between blood kin, Parsons, 1924a, p. 333. Jemez: No marriage to blood kin, Parsons, 1929, p. 32. Isleta: No marriage to blood kin, Parsons, 1930, p. 235. Taos: No marriage to blood kin to fourth degree, Parsons, 1936a, p. 47.

[5] Mohave: Sib exogamy, Kroeber, 1925, q. 795. Yuma: Sib exogamy, Forde, 1931, p. 142. Cocopa: No data. Maricopa: Sib exogamy plus taboo on blood kin, Spier, 1933, pp. 186, 219.

## LOCALIZED MALE LINEAGE

Though with the Pimans sibs are of very little importance there is another group which forms the essential unit for economic and social activities. This is the localized male lineage. In small hamlets this unit is often coincident with the village which is theoretically the settlement of a group of patrilineal kin joined from time to time by other relatives. Such a localized male lineage is found not only among the southern California Shoshoneans[1] but throughout California[2] and apparently in Mexico.[3] Even with the River Yumans it seems the most usual arrangement.[4] But it ceases abruptly as we turn to the pueblo and eastern area. In the matrilineal western pueblos, there are some indications that the female lineage is an important ceremonial unit, though not localized[5] and the Navajo and Apache, pueblo imitators in many respects, even show localization.[6] Otherwise, the importance of a localized lineage of any sort is not reported. Again, the affiliations of the Pimans are decidedly with the west.

## VILLAGE ORGANIZATION

Looking at the northern part of our area we find, in the Basin, an almost complete lack of organization and leadership though there are suggestions[7] of a hereditary band leader who might function when families gathered for a hunt or ceremony. Coming south to the southern California Shoshoneans, we find the well organized system already referred to: a localized sib with hereditary

---

[1] Serrano, Cahuilla, Gabrieliño, Cupeño, Luiseño had, as their unit, the localized male lineage, Strong, 1929, p. 321.

[2] Gifford, 1926.

[3] Localized male lineage among Acaxee (4), Beals, 1933, p. 19, and Cahita (2). Beals lists also "barrios" *i. e.* local divisions of a town all the way from Sinaloa to Mexico City, Beals, 1932, pp. 202—203; Beals, AA 34: 467—475; these may or may not have been inhabited by related groups but Bandelier has marshalled evidence to show that the Mexican *calpulli*, clan group, did have local residence, Bandelier, 1879, p. 398; Thompson, 1933, p. 105. Says Parsons, 1933a, p. 630: "As yet there is no evidence anywhere in Mexico either pre-Conquest or modern, for any organization other than the compound family group with bilateral descent and some emphasis upon inheritance, through the father, of property, position and functions."

[4] Mohave, field work by the writer indicates patrilineal residence; Yuma, residence optional, Forde, 1931, p. 156; Maricopa, residence first with man's parents, then optional, Spier, 1933, p. 222.

[5] Hopi: Lowie, 1929a, p. 329; Parsons, 1933b, p. 25. Zuni: Kroeber, 1919, pp. 91—134; Parsons, 1923b, pp. 226—8.

[6] Western Apache, Goodwin, 1935, p. 57. Eastern Apache, Opler, 1936, p. 620. Navajo, Reichard, 1928.

[7] Surprise Valley, Steward, 1933, p. 83, and Owens Valley, Ibid, p. 304.

ceremonial leader, in charge of a sacred house and fetish. This leader had, as assistants, a crier and a singer, sometimes an executive officer, concerned with the distribution of food and money at ceremonies.[1] Temporary war leaders were chosen when needed[2] and for the Luiseño, a hereditary hunt leader is suggested.[3]

We cannot trace this organization to Mexico. where data is insufficient but we find it among the Pimans, where the village had hereditary ceremonial leader, house and fetish, often a crier and a singer. There is always a hereditary hunt leader, and, the Pimans having more need of war than the southern California Shoshoneans, a hereditary war leader also. But this leader had almost the functions of a priest and the Pimans followed the custom of their Shoshonean kinsmen in choosing a temporary war leader when needed.

In the western Pueblos we find traces of this organization, already noted for Hopi. The hereditary leader, house and fetish are certainly to be found but, with the Hopi, they belong to the sib, and there being many sibs in one village, their importance is obscured. In the organization of the village as a whole, one sib leader is given the position of head and there is a crier but no war chief or hunt chief. The actual guidance of affairs is much more the concern of a council of chiefs than of individuals. At Zuni this tendency is carried even further and, instead of individuals we find priesthoods and societies carrying on all the functions of government and ceremony.

With the eastern Pueblos, the list of officials again shows resemblance to those of the Shoshoneans for we find a ceremonial leader (with the Tewa one for each half of the year) and a very important war chief or two, perhaps with assistants. There is no hunt leader, for hunting is still the concern of a society. But the difference here is that the leaders are not hereditary but appointed by their groups (societies, priesthoods or moieties) in which membership is voluntary. From the southern California Shoshoneans, through the Pueblos, there is a change from hereditary officers, through group government to appointive officers. The Pimans, with their hereditary officers, align again with the southern California Shoshoneans, though the actual officers, particularly the hunt chief, suggest the Keres.

The River Yumans fall into an entirely different category for they were tribally organized, with officers not usually hereditary

---

[1] Strong, 1929, pp. 15, 108, 163, 249, 292.
[2] Ibid, p. 57.
[3] Sparkman, 1908, p. 215.

but gaining their authority through dreams.[1] These officers were:
a tribal leader, a temporary war leader and a very important
scalp keeper. There was no sacred house nor fetish. Here there
seems an intrusion of an entirely different governmental system
from that of the other groups considered. The tribal leader reported
for the Pima[2] may well have been borrowed from the Yuman
Maricopa, for the Papago have no hint of such an official.

Again with village organization, as with that of sib and moiety,
we find the closest resemblance of the Pimans is to southern California Shoshoneans.

### KIN GROUPINGS

Spier[3] has classified the Papago kin terminology as of the Yuman
type, on the basis of one of its outstanding features, the seniority
distinctions. This is, however, to extract one element of the terminology and give it the key position, while others, perhaps equally
significant, have quite different distributions. As these are followed
out, Papago and Pima show themselves affiliated now with the
Basin, now with Mexico, or in sporadic but intimate ways, with
their kinsmen, the Shoshoneans of southern California. We shall
trace four of the more obvious features through some of their
permutations and combinations.

1. The equating of cross and parallel cousins with siblings is
a characteristic of the Basin, where the bilateral family prevails.[4]
It is found also in Mexico[5] where Parsons assumes the same form
of organization.[6] Even in the pueblos there are examples among
the Keres[7] and again among the easternmost of the Apache, who
differ from Western Apache and Navajo in having no sib system.[8]

---

[1] One chief for whole tribe, shepherd and advisor, hereditary with Mohave:
Kroeber, 1925, p. 745; and Maricopa: Spier, 1933, p. 157. Yuma and
Cocopa got power by dreams: Forde, p. 135; Gifford, 1933, p. 298; other
leaders, the scalp keeper and the temporary war leader, also got power
through dreams. An informal council mentioned for Yuma: Forde, p. 139,
and Maricopa: Spier, 1933, p. 158.
[2] Russell, p. 195.
[3] Spier, 1925, p. 75.
[4] Tübatulabal, Kawaïsu: Gifford, 1917, pp. 222, 230; Wind River Shoshoni,
Uintah Ute, Southern Ute: Spier, 1925, p. 75; Paviotso, Moapa: Lowie,
1924, pp. 289—90; Owens Valley Paiute: Steward, 1933, p. 299; Kaibab
Paiute: Gifford, 1917, p. 245.
[5] Yaqui: Kroeber, 1931, p. 24; Tarahumare: Bennett, 1935, p. 221; Cora:
Radin, 1931, p. 6.
[6] Parsons, 1933a, p. 630.
[7] Acoma, San Felipe, Cochiti: Parsons, 1932, chart.
[8] Mescalero and Chiracahua; Opler 1936b, p. 626.

In the area of sib importance, the cousin-sibling category has been replaced by the usual arrangement for a unilateral society, that of placing parallel cousins with siblings while cross cousins are in an entirely different category. This is the practice of southern California Shoshoneans[1] and Yumans.[2] It is found, of course, in many of the pueblos[3] even the Tewa whose sibs are of the weakest, and spreads to the east among those pueblo imitators, the western Apache, Navajo and Jicarilla.[4]

2. Four Grandparental Terms.

Another Piman practice which should belong, logically, to peoples with a bilateral terminology, is the use of four terms for grandparents, thus giving equal weight to the father's and the mother's line. This terminology does, to some extent, follow the distribution of the sibling-cousin classification just mentioned. We can trace it through the Basin,[5] part of Mexico[6] and the eastern Apache[7] and it appears also among the River Yumans.[8] Occasionally there are only two terms for grandparents but they represent the two lineages and therefore constitute a simplification of the same idea.[9] In the rest of the area, sib organizations predominate and, as we should expect, the four grandparental terms are missing. However, the variations which take their place have no logical relation to a unilateral system but focus attention on sex of the grandparent[10] or of the grandparent and the speaker.[11] We can find in a few of the pueblos, and those not the most likely ones, a differentiation of grandmothers, as though a matrilineally

---

[1] Serrano, Desert Cahuilla, Cupeño; Gifford, 1922a, pp. 49—50, 54—55. Luiseño: Kroeber, 1917b, p. 348.

[2] Yuma: Gifford, 1922a, p. 62; Cocopa and Southern Diegueño: Ibid, p. 67; Kamia: Ibid, p. 65; Walapai: Kroeber, 1925, pp. 127—128. There are variations in that with some of the above, cross cousins can be siblings under certain circumstances. The Yavapai are of a group not classified here, which makes three categories for siblings, parallel cousins and cross cousins.

[3] Hopi, Zuni, Jemez, Laguna, Tewa; Parsons, 1932, chart.

[4] Opler, 1936b, pp. 627, 629, 630.

[5] Kawaïsu, Eastern Mono, Northern Paiute: Gifford, 1922a, p. 128. Wind River Shoshoni, Uintah, Southern Ute: Spier, 1925, p. 75. Kaibab Paiute have two terms which nevertheless distinguish lineage.

[6] Northern Tepehuane: Spier, 1925, p. 76; Tepecano: Kroeber, 1934, p. 25.

[7] Chiracahua, Mescalero: Opler, 1936b, pp. 625, 626.

[8] Yuma, Mohave: Spier, 1925, p. 75; Cocopa: Gifford, 1922a, p. 67; Maricopa: Spier, 1933, p. 216.

[9] Kaibab Paiute: Gifford, 1917, p. 245. Yaqui and Opata: Kroeber, 1934, p. 25.

[10] Hopi, Zuni, Tewa, Taos: Parsons, 1932, chart. Jicarilla Apache: Opler, 1936b, p. 627.

[11] Keres; Parsons, 1932, chart.

organized people, confronted with grandparent terms which recognized sex only, had felt obliged to differentiate between the grandmother who was clan ancestress and the one who was not.[1] Outside the pueblo region, there is more emphasis on lineage but still not in the direction which would seem most natural. The patrilineal southern California Shoshoneans differentiate the mother's parents and class those of the father together[2] while the matrilineal Western Apache distinguish those of the father, not the mother.[3] However we explain the variety of practice, it is evident that this part of our area has been the meeting place of several different principles in the matter of grandparent terms, with much resulting confusion.

3. Age, sex and lineage in the uncle class.

The Pimans, in common with many groups in the area, practice the junior sororate and levirate, which would demand that the father distinguish his older and younger brothers and the mother her older and younger sisters. With siblings of opposite sex, no age distinction would be needed. In the uncle class of the area, we should expect at least six terms and these six do occur. They coincide, however, neither with the bilateral family nor with the practice of junior sororate and levirate. The Shoshoneans of Basin and Plateau, who have the junior sororate and levirate, do not have the terms[4] though part of northern Mexico does.[5] There are hints as to sororate and levirate in this region but no adequate data. On the other hand, the six terms are found at the west, among both River Yumans[6] and southern California Shoshoneans[7]

---

[1] Isleta, Hano, Jemez: Parsons, op. cit.

[2] Gifford, 1922a, pp. 128—9.

[3] Opler, 1936b, p. 629.

[4] Mono, Northeast and Southeast, no age distinctions: Gifford, 1922a, p. 49. Uintah Ute: father distinguishes ages of his sisters, mother of her brothers: Spier, 1925, p. 76. Kawaïsu same: Gifford, 1917, p. 245. Northern Paiute sex and lineage only: Kroeber, 1917b, p. 359. Kaibab Paiute age and sex: Gifford, 1917, p. 245. Owens Valley sex distinctions, not age: mother's siblings equated with spouses of father's siblings: Steward, 1933, pp. 299—300.

[5] Age, sex, lineage noted for Tarahumare: Bennett, 1933, p. 220 and Opata: Radin, 1931, p. 3. Tepehuane note all three items for uncles, sex and age only for aunts; Radin, p. 4. Spier, 1925 says that Northern Tepehuane distinguish the age of father's sisters and mother's brothers, a practice opposite to the requirements of levirate and sororate.

[6] Mohave six terms, one uncle merged with sibling: Kroeber, 1917b, p. 341, Yuma, Cocopa, Northern and Southern Diegueño six terms: Gifford, 1922a, pp. 63, 67, 69, 70, Maricopa six terms: Spier, 1933, p. 216, Walapai six terms: Kroeber, 1935, p. 127, Southeast Yavapai six terms: Gifford, 1932, p. 193.

[7] Serrano, Desert Cahuilla, Cupeño six terms: Gifford, 1922a, pp. 54, 57, 59; Luiseño six: Kroeber, 1917b, p. 348.

although the practice of junior sororate and levirate is denied by all the Yumans and by one group of Shoshoneans, the Cupeño. The Pimans, having sororate and levirate, should have six terms but here there is an efflorescence of eight terms for no other reason, apparently, than that of carrying the process to its final conclusion. Beside the Pimans, only the Tarahumare[1] indulge in this fullness of nomenclature.

The Pueblos, where sororate and levirate are absent, follow the logical custom for a unilateral family, classing the mother's sister with the mother and the father's brother with the father.[2] Zuni adds a distinction in the age of the mother's sisters.

4. We turn now to that trait of the Piman system to which Spier[3] has given most importance and which caused him to classify it with those of Yumans and southern California Shoshoneans. This is the age distinction among siblings. Spier does not make the category such a simple one, for he includes in it elements of the three other usages just discussed. However, it seems obvious that the distribution of these three is fairly different and only overlaps at certain points, so it seems better to follow the age distinctions separately. They are extremely wide-spread to north and west of our area, in the Mackenzie Basin, the Plateau[4] and California.[5] We can in fact follow them around the circle, through northern Mexico,[6] the pueblos[7] and back to the Jicarilla Apache and Navajo.[8] But they have a very different aspect, according as the area of age distinctions among siblings overlaps with one where all cousins have the sibling title thus making age the paramount consideration among Ego's contemporaries or with one where only parallel cousins are siblings, and age distinctions become a perogative of the unilateral group. Also they change their scope in areas where the sex of the sibling is noted and where age distinctions may apply to both sexes alike. At times too, the man's brothers and woman's sisters may be singled out as though for purposes of sororate and. levirate[9] or serving a similar purpose, sex is noted only among

---

[1] Bennett, 1935, p. 220.
[2] Parsons, 1932, chart.
[3] Spier, 1925, p. 75.
[4] Spier, 1925, pp. 76—77.
[5] Gifford, 1922a, p. 139.
[6] Yaqui, Opata, Cora: Kroeber, 1934, p. 23. Tarahumare: Bennett, 1935, pp. 220—221. Tepehuane: Spier, 1925, p. 75.
[7] Parsons, 1932.
[8] Opler, 1936b, p. 627, 629—30.
[9] Northern and western California.

seniors or only among juniors.[1] The Pimans have combined these possibilities in an unusual way. With them, all cousins are siblings and therefore age distinctions apply to everyone in Ego's generation. They are however the only ones which apply, for sex is not noted. This extreme simplification of traits in Ego's class is recorded only for the Tepehuane[2] and tends to emphasize the difference between the Pimans and the Yumans with whom they have been classed.

At another point, however, Pimans and Yumans are one; the calculation of sibling seniority, not by the ages of siblings themselves but by those of their parents. Since the parents may themselves have been cousins, called senior and junior according to the status of *their* parents, this leads to a highly artificial system of age terms. Its distribution is in southern California, reaching up to the Basin[3] and down to northern Mexico.[4]

The Pimans seem to have combined elements of a northern system, (that of equating all cousins with siblings) with a detail from a more southern one (reckoning seniority through that of the connecting relative) and, since they omit the factor of sex, have produced an almost unique result.

Another point which might have been followed out is the treatment of affinals but here the usage is so complex that it is hard to draw significant conclusions. In some minor details, however, the Pimans show resemblances to their neighbors so close that they should be noted in a distribution study. Such is the altering or severing of the affinal relationship under certain circumstances, i. e. the birth of a child or the death of the connecting relative. This is a feature of Piman terminology, where the affinal is called "that woman" or "that man" and addressed as "friend" until the birth of a child gives biological connection with the family. Conversely the death of all children severs the connection. Here there is likeness with the southern California Shoshoneans, who give the affinal a title, but alter it when the marriage has issue[5] or, again when the connecting relative dies.[6] Some neighboring Basin Shoshoneans the Kawaïsu, follow the same custom[7] and so do some southern Yumans.[8]

---

[1] River Yumans: Gifford, 1922a, p. 139. Jicarilla and Lipan Apache: Opler, 1936b.
[2] Radin, p. 4.
[3] Spier, 1925, p. 75.
[4] Tarahumare: Bennett, 1935, p. 221.
[5] Serrano, Desert Cahuilla, Cupeño: Gifford, 1922a, pp. 50, 51, 55, 57, 60.
[6] Serrano, Luiseño: Gifford, 1922a, p. 257.
[7] Gifford, 1917, p. 231.
[8] Diegueño, Mohave, Yuma, Cocopa, Kamia: Kroeber, 1917b, p. 393.

The Pimans share with the Luiseño and Northern Paiute the custom of describing an affinal not by a special word but by a descriptive phrase, such as "father of my grandchild".[1] With Papago and Luiseño, there is the further peculiarity that such phrases become "frozen" and used as reciprocals by people for whom they are not appropriate. Such likenesses would seem to argue a connection holding its own with surprising persistence.

Other traits of the Piman system which might have been followed out are the use of separate terms for child by man and woman thus carrying out the idea of reciprocity; the use of a term for mother's younger sister which duplicates or resembles the mother term and similar practice with father's older brother. There is not space for carrying comparisons to this extent but the examples given at least illustrate the varied distribution of even related elements in the Piman terminology. Through the various overlappings and adaptations presented there appears a basic similarity with the Shoshoneans which, at times, is carried into surprising detail. In all but age distinctions, the Pimans appear nearer to the Shoshoneans, particularly those of the Basin, than to the Yumans with whom they have been classed.

KNOWLEDGE

In the matter of star names there is little data for comparison. We may note the recognition of Orion under the name of Mountain Sheep as common to Pimans, Yumans[2] and under a different name among Tarahumara,[3] and Hopi.[4] Pimans and southern California Shoshoneans show one of their scattered but close resemblances in that both recognize a constellation called the Hand[5] while other groups either do not recognize it or call it by a different name.[6]

In the naming of months, the Pimans differ sharply from the River Yumans, whom they resemble in so many practical matters. Yumans generelly employ a series of six names, repeated[7] and, among the Maricopa at least, with totemic connotation. The Papago[8] name all twelve months with standardized names.

---

[1] Kroeber, 1917b, pp. 348, 351, 387.
[2] Spier, 1928, p. 171.
[3] Bennett, 1935, p. 348.
[4] Parsons, 1936b, vol. 1, pp. 9—10.
[5] Spier, 1928, p. 170.
[6] Havasupai: Spier, 1928.
[7] Summary in Spier, 1928, p. 170; additions, Spier, 1933, p. 143.
[8] Russell gives no mention of the Pima custom.

Piman recording of history has been fully discussed in another place,[1] with the conclusion that there may well be a single distribution area for Plains skin records and Piman stick records, both possibly originating under white influence.

## WAR

The northern part of our area was occupied by peaceful peoples who fought, according to tradition, only in self defense. In the Basin, before the coming of the Whites they hardly fought at all. Such war parties as did take place in this northern area were of the guerilla type involving few men, a surprise attack and a scalp or two. This holds for Basin, Upland Yumans, southern California Shoshoneans and Pueblos. With the River Yumans[2] we reach an area of organized warfare with large armies and a formal challenge. The Pima, who have the same customs[3] might be thought to have learned them from their Yuman neighbors, the Maricopa, except that they are reported for the ancient Pima and quite widely in Mexico.[4] Even the Jicarilla Apache when they fought the Plains tribes, prefaced the battle with a challenge and a duel by the chiefs.[5] The Papago, however, have no trace of such formalities, but align, in the matter of war organization, with the peaceful Plateau and Basin peoples. These last reduced operations to the bare essentials, rarely even taking scalps,[6] nor is there record of scalping by any of the southern California Shoshoneans except the Luiseño.[7]

South and east of the Luiseño begins an area characterized by scalping or some other form of trophy taking. It may once have been a matter of convenience as to whether the trophy should be a live prisoner, his head alone, the hair of his head or a small portion of that hair. The taking of prisoners is still dependent largely on practical considerations but scalp or head taking, despite Kroeber's opinion to the contrary,[8] seems to have something of an areal distribution.

[1] Underhill, 1938.

[2] Mohave: Kroeber, 1925, pp. 751—3; Yuma: Forde, pp. 162—3; Cocopa: Gifford, 1933, pp. 299—300; Maricopa: Spier, 1933, pp. 16—26.

[3] Russell, p. 120.

[4] Pima Bajo, Rio Fuerto, Ocoroni, Sinaloa, Chiametla, Tepic: Beals, 1932, p. 190; Aztecs (with neighbors) pitched battles with challenge and insults: Thompson, p. 120.

[5] Opler, 1936a, p. 211.

[6] Scalps taken by Uintah Ute, Lemhi, Paviotso: Spier, 1928, p. 259, but there is a question if this was done by the nearby Pyramid Lake Paiute: Kelly, 1923, p. 188, or by those of Owens Valley: Steward, 1933, p. 306.

[7] Kroeber, 1925, p. 721.                              [8] Kroeber, 1925, p. 844.

The greatest amount of trophy taking of all sorts is found among the Aztecs, who took prisoners and, after sacrifice, kept their scalps or skulls.[1] With their treatment of prisoners was associated a ceremonial cannibalism repeated among some of their neighbors.[2] Going north, we find that the usual trophy was heads[3] with an occasional substitution of the scalp[4] until, with the Opata, just south of the Pimans, there is mention of scalps only.[5] It is unfortunate that we do not know the size of the scalps taken in Mexico for, from this point, the records show a differentiation in size between east and west. The River Yumans took the whole scalp with ears,[6] a custom which extends northward through most of California.[7] The Papago, on the contrary, took the smallest possible trophy, sometimes only four hairs. The symbolism by which the whole enemy was thought to have been brought into camp and made a slave could hardly have gone much further.[8] From the Papago, the area of the small scalp extends eastward through the pueblos[9] and is characteristic of all eastern North America. Here is another of those instance where Papago affiliations, are, unexpectedly, to the east rather than the west.[10]

A smaller area, not coincident with either of those just mentioned, but combining portions of both, considers the scalp to be not a mere sign of conquest but a source of supernatural power, requiring magical treatment. The Aztecs identified prisoners with gods and

[1] Prisoners sacrificed, captor kept hair and bones, Thompson, p. 124. Skull rack in front of temples, Beals, 1932, p. 191.

[2] Acaxee (4) Yaqui (3) Tepehuane (4): Beals, 1932, p. 16.

[3] Tarahumare, Acaxee, Yaqui, Tepehuane: Ibid.

[4] Tepahue, Sinaloa; Beals, 1932, p. 191.

[5] Ibid.

[6] Mohave: Kroeber, 1925, pp. 751—52; Yuma: Forde, p. 165; Cocopa: Gifford, 1933, pp. 299—303; Maricopa: Spier, 1933, p. 177. The custom does not continue through the Upland Yumans except Southeast Yavapai: Gifford, 1932, pp. 184—86; and instead we find the torturing of prisoners and cannibalism. Yavapai: Ibid. Walapai: Kroeber, 1935, pp. 175—76.

[7] Kroeber, 1925, p. 844.

[8] The size of Pima scalps is not recorded. The Pima, like the Papago, took child captives whom they sold as slaves in Mexico. These, too, were regarded as dangerous. Russell, p. 197.

[9] Hopi: Beaglehole, 1935, pp. 22—3. There is mention, however, of occasional women captives, Ibid, and of whole heads: Parsons, 1936b. Zuni, scalps of all slain: Bunzel, 1930, pp. 674—75, but no mention of prisoners. Scalps but not prisoners mentioned for Acoma: White, 1930, p. 96; Cochitti: Dumarest, p. 198—200; Sia: Stevenson, 1890, p. 121; Tewa: Parsons, 1929, p 137; Isleta: Parsons, 1930, pp. 326—7; Taos: Parsons, 1936b, p. 21; also captives.

[10] The writer has no information on Athapascans except that the Navajo took small or large scalps as they preferred. Hill, 1936, p. 15.

sacrificed them to keep the sun on its rounds. Though, as mentioned above, scalps were not the most usual trophy, the ceremonial dancing in the skins of sacrificial victims and the skull racks in front of temples are sufficient indication that all trophies had a ceremonial significance. North of the Aztecs, though trophies were kept there is no information as to how they were regarded. When we reach the Colorado Desert, however, we find scalps endowed with a decided magical significance and handled only by qualified ceremonialists. Among the Papago, who have so little group organization, the scalp handlers are purified Enemy Slayers, each one owning his trophies as personal property.[1] Among River Yumans and some of the Uplanders, there is a special scalp keeper, qualified by ceremonial fasting[2] and the lightly organized Jicarilla Apache, on the other side of the pueblos, have a similar arrangement.[3] The western pueblos, after their usual organized style, confide the scalps to a priesthood or a society and beyond that, show such fear of them that they keep them outside the village.[4] We might pause here to inquire how much dread is associated with the scalp, beyond that normally accorded to the supernatural. It is true that all sacredness connotes danger among River Yumans, Pimans and pueblos, but the exile of the scalp from the village and other rites to be mentioned seem to single out this trophy for special dread. The explanation might be that an area revering the enemy trophy has here overlapped an area noted for its fear of the dead[5] producing a particular horror of the trophy. This horror is

---

[1] There is no record of scalp magic from the Pima but the Slayer's purification seems to indicate it. Russell, 1926, p. 204.

[2] River Yumans: scalps kept by a special official, in his house. Mohave: same, Kroeber, 1925, p. 752. Yuma: Forde, p. 166. Cocopa: Gifford, 1933, p. 301. Maricopa: Spier, 1933, p. 177. Upland Yumans: South-eastern Yavapai: gave scalps to the chief of camp who kept them at a distance for fear of ghosts, Gifford 1932, p. 184.

[3] Scalps kept away from war party at night. On return, put in charge of old men with requisite ceremonial knowledge. These purified the scalp by washing and singing over it, also going through a fast themselves. Opler, 1936a, pp. 211—212.

[4] Hopi: Scalps thrown into fissure on mesa edge and guarded by war chief. Fed once a year by kwan society. Beaglehole, 1935, pp. 23, 24. Zuni: after exorcism, scalps are kept in a shrine outside the village, in charge of a scalp chief who performs occasional ceremonies, Bunzel, 1930, pp. 674—5. Laguna: in this case aligns with the western pueblos and keeps scalps in a cave in the hills as dangerous. They are in care of the Warriors' Society: Parsons, 1920b, p. 122.

[5] See below, under death. The area, stretching west into California includes River Yumans, Pimans, southern Athapascans and Hopi. There is no mention of fear of the dead at Zuni, but note that the scalper, there, is treated exactly like the widower. Bunzel, 1930, p. 503.

not to be found in the eastern pueblos, who allow the scalp in the village though under ceremonial guardianship.[1] It appears however among the Jicarilla Apache[2] and the Navajo[3] who reflect the customs of the western pueblos much more than those of the eastern. But as we go further out in the Plains both reverence and fear drop away.

We have, then, followed the disposal of the scalp from Mexico, where it shares with other trophies a sacredness entirely unconnected with fear, through the area of Pimans, River Yumans, and a group of Athapascans where its sacredness involves fear of the dead, then through the eastern pueblos where sacredness is formal and fear very little indicated, to the Plains where both fear and sacredness disappear.

At the point in the area where scalp fear is greatest, we find also a ritual of cleansing for the scalp taker. The conception of ceremonial uncleanness here involved is often associated with the fear of death but not necessarily so. All the way north to the Eskimo, there are requirements of purification for people in situations which the culture considers supernaturally dangerous. The treatment — generally fasting and segregation — may be applied to the women at times of crisis[4], to the priest,[5] to those who handle the dead[6] or, as in our present area, to the scalp taker. The fast and segregation required of the Papago warrior applies also to the Pima[7] and, even more strenuously, to the Hopi and Zuni.[8] The difference is that noted previously: Hopi and Zuni integrate the whole procedure with their group organization and make the ordeal an initiation into priesthood or society. Pimans, with no group

---

[1] Keres: Acoma keeps scalps at headquarters of head war chief, under his care; White, 1930, p. 99. Sia: Scalps kept by Knife Society, Stevenson, 1890, p. 121. San Felipe: Scalps in house of cacique in his care; White, 1932, p. 13. Tewa: Scalps kept in village, sometimes in charge of a scalp keeper, sometimes of winter chief or of old women with some kind of ceremonial war duties; Parsons, 1929, pp. 136—38. Tigua Isleta: Scalps kept in kivas, cared for by Warriors' Society; Parsons, 1930, p. 327. Taos: Scalps kept in Water Kiva, in charge of war chief; Parsons, 1936a, p. 21. Picuris: Still has official scalp house, not a kiva. R. U.
[2] Opler, op. cit.
[3] Scalps are sung over, outside the hogan of the scalper, then put away in a rock crevice. Later used in war dance to cure those suffering from contact with strangers. Hill, 1936, p. 17.
[4] Morice, pp. 162—64.
[5] Bunzel, 1930, pp. 503—506.
[6] Reichard, 1928, p. 143.
[7] Russell, 1926, p. 204.
[8] Beaglehole, 1935, p. 23; Bunzel, 1930, pp. 674—5; Parsons, 1924b, p. 36.

organization, make the end of the process simply individual power. Jicarilla and Navajo[1] and River Yumans,[2] also without organized ceremonial groups, follow the same principle though all three who share an extreme fear of the dead, give more prominence to the neophyte's escape from danger than to his acquisition of power. With the eastern pueblos, group membership is the whole point and the rigors of initiation are reduced or absent.[3] In Mexico, where there are any signs of the custom at all, it seems to be an initiation, unaccompanied by lustration or fear.[4] The unwarlike Shoshoneans of southern California, have no sign of the custom at all, nor do those of the Basin.

The Piman area, then, has been the scene of a overlapping of three different concepts: sacredness of the trophy, fear of the dead, and ceremonial uncleanness, all tending to magnify the importance of the scalp. We might go even further in this disen-

---

[1] Jicarilla: "ceremony over warriors to drive away danger from the enemy", Opler, 1936a, pp. 211—212. Navajo warrior "purified himself" by taking sweatbaths and singing songs. If these were not efficacious, a war dance must be performed. Hill, 1936, p. 17.

[2] Mohave: both killers and scalpers have four day vigil, fast, continence, bathing (field work by the writer). Yuma: same; Forde, p. 166. Cocopa: killers 4 day continence, fast, bathing; Gifford, 1933, p. 301. Maricopa: killer-scalper a 16 day vigil, fasting, bathing, vomiting; Spier, 1933, p. 181. Southeastern Yavapai: all warriors and leader washed in creek, and fasted 2 days; Gifford, 1932, p. 184. Walapai: killer induced vomiting and hid his clothes in a cave; Kroeber, 1935, p. 147.

[3] Keres: Acoma has no purification, warrior throws scalp on an anthill, then goes through short ceremony; White, 1930, p. 96. But the elaborate initiation of war captains who are continent for one year, Ibid, pp. 45 seq., seems to concentrate killer taboos upon them. Laguna: Scalper must be continent for 12 days and then is taken into war society; Parsons, 1920b, p. 122. Santo Domingo once had a warriors' society, but there is no mention of initiation; White, 1935, p. 40. Cochiti: War priest is head of scalpers. No mention of initiation; Dumarest, pp. 198—200. San Felipe: War society extinct, no details; White, 1932, p. 19. Sia: Scalper dances with War and Knife Societies, then four days continence; Stevenson, 1890, p. 121. Tewa: Scalp takers constitute a society, no details; Parsons, 1929, p. 136. Tigua Isleta: During scalp ceremonial scalpers live at home four days, continent, take emetic; Parsons, 1930, p. 327. Taos: No society, no purification. Honors to scalp taker and scalp touchers have slight resemblance to Plains coup counting; Parsons, 1936a, p. 21.

[4] Tlaxcala: For initiation into high warrior rank, a ceremony, then 4 days fasting in house of priest with blackened body. Instruction from the priest, little sleep, food four small balls of maize, then one year less severe penance, finally a feast and presentation of rank, Torquemada, quoted in Thompson, p. 114. Aztec ruler, at temple of the war god, was painted black by the priest and given a mantle with scull designs, then fasted alone in a room four days, Thompson, p. 105.

tangling of psychological threads by following the distribution of the fast and dream. This, however, must receive its full treatment under ceremonies,[1] as must the subject of purification, paramount in Papago ceremonial life.

However there is one aspect of Papago purification which has bearing on the comparative study of organization. This is the singling out of at least three classes of men for ceremonial purification leading to supernatural power. The scalp taker, the eagle killer and the salt gatherer all go through long ordeals, after which they are re-admitted into the community with the status of "ripe" men. True, the ripe men are not organized and each man's power is his individual possession. Nevertheless it might be possible to regard these purifications as a desert version of initiation into a society. In that case, instead of being surprised that the Papago regard three different classes of men as needing discharming, we should consider that the large number of societies to be found in the pueblos has here been reduced to three which have special interest for Papago life. The exact relation between Papago ordeal and pueblo initiation is too intricate to be traced at present but the forms of the two are so alike that we must assume some connection of ideas.

GAMES

No attempt is here made to trace the distribution of the Papago games which are common in the Southwest and whose occurrence is noted by Culin[2] and by Spier.[3] Culin has also noted the fact that all games commonly have ceremonial significance and it may be assumed that this will vary according to the interests of the group. Thus, for the Papago the purpose, when stated, is rain as it is for the Tewa[4] but there is some magical affiliation of the course of the kickball with that of the sun as in Isleta.[5]

Interesting in any study of social organization is the selection of the groups taking sides in games — or at least in the important ones. Piman games are held between villages:[6] a habit shared with Mexico[7] where we have mentioned that the Acaxee game

---

[1] See Underhill, Papago Ceremonies. In preparation.
[2] Culin, 1902.
[3] Spier, 1928, pp. 345—55.
[4] Parsons, 1929, pp. 230—4.
[5] Parsons, 1930, p. 83.
[6] Pima played against Papago. Probably villages were matched, not whole tribes, Russell, p. 172. Such matches reported from early times, Velarde, p. 133.
[7] Opata (2); Bandelier, 1892, p. 240. Tarahumara (3): Bennett-, 1935, p. 335. Acaxee (4): Beals, 1933, p. 11. Sinaloa (5): Beals, 1932, p. 190. Mayo Yaqui (2): Bennett, 1935, p. 395.

preliminaries almost duplicated those of the Papago. Although there are not data enough for listing, we might find some connection between the permanent racetrack maintained by every Papago village and the permanent ball courts of Mexico. Such courts are now being found in archaeological sites in the Pima valley and even further north. They represent a permanent provision for games not found in the modern pueblos except at Taos and Picuris[1] which also have permanent racetracks. This is one of the rare likenesses between the Papago and the Eastern Pueblos as contrasted with Western ones.

In other respects, Pueblo game organization differed from the Piman, even though the two peoples played the same games. In the Pueblos, both western and eastern, competition was not between villages but between groups within a village such as moieties[2] sibs[3] ceremonial groups[4] even streets or sexes. Data is insufficient for following game organization through the rest of our area.

The Piman custom of payment to the visiting village, which dances for its hosts, has not been listed since all the peoples considered make gifts, in greater or less degree, on cermonial occasions and gift giving becomes too complicated to chart. We may observe that the Papago raise games to a high importance and make them an occasion for gift giving, which therefore takes place between villages. The Southern California Shoshoneans make death observances their greatest ceremony and giving occurs at that time, between sibs or moieties. With the Pueblos, the gifts are between smaller ceremonial groups: certain clan members, certain society members, or individuals, and the occasions for giving are numberless. Here again, the Piman village has taken over activities which elsewhere belong to sib or moiety. This absorption of functions by the village is one of the outstanding facts of Piman social organization.

### LIFE OF THE INDIVIDUAL

## Ceremonial Uncleanness of Women

Piman birth customs, which involve segregation of the mother, can hardly be studied apart from the Piman conception of woman's uncleanness in any female function, such as childbirth, puberty and subsequent menstruation. Over a wide area in the west of the

---

[1] Parsons, 1936a, p. 96.

[2] Tewa; Parsons, 1929, p. 41; Taos; Ibid 1936a, p. 96; Isleta; Ibid 1930, pp. 239—240.

[3] Zuni, information from Dr. Parsons.

[4] Hopi: Parsons, 1936a, p. 59; Isleta, op. cit.

United States and another in the east, there is a feeling that the woman at one or more of these times, is in contact with supernatural power and therefore to be classed with the shaman, the scalp taker or other functionary singled out by the culture. In such a condition she is subject to several kinds of restrictions, designed to protect both herself and others. For the benefit of others, she is segregated. Cultures which stress her dangerousness keep her outside the house: others merely keep her away from any one or anything specially susceptible, such as men, their weapons, the deer (men's especial concern), or the sick.

For her own benefit, she is subject to restrictions which have to do with diet, with touching her head or her lips and with bathing. The result is a fast, more or less severe, the use of scratching stick, drinking tube or both, and one or more purification baths. The whole treatment is similar to that of the warrior just described, though woman and warrior are seldom both singled out for it by the same culture, as they are with the Papago.[1]

A third requirement relates usually to the first menstruation and is based on the belief that the girl, at this time, is in a magically crucial condition where any act of hers will set a pattern for her whole future life. For this reason she must be a model of cleanliness, good behavior and sometimes beauty. Above all, she must exhibit the height of industry, often symbolized by running.

These three components of an attitude toward woman exemplify the interpretation of the supernatural so common in our area; it can be dangerous or beneficial, according to the way it is handled. The woman, therefore, must be treated like a sacred object, not safely approached by the average person; she must counteract her sacredness by purifying herself as the priest and neophyte do and she must take advantage of its power to get a blessing. The man, in a similar situation often receives his blessing in the form of a dream but the woman, less connected with ceremonial life, aims for such practical boons as industry and beauty.

The negative emphasis on woman's malign power is more widespread than positive emphasis on her power to bless. Doubtless there was an unbroken area of menstrual fear all the way from the old world for we could find examples from Yukaghir of Siberia[2]

---

[1] We may note that in Aztec belief the childbearing woman was equal in honor to the warrior who captured a prisoner and the two had the same destiny after death. But since the Aztecs seem not to have emphasized the dangers of contact with the supernatural there were no purification rites.

[2] Jochelson, Vladimir, The Yukaghir, p. 194.

through the Eskimo[1] the Northwest Coast, the Mackenzie Basin and Plateau.[2]

Coming south to the Shoshoneans, we find among the northern ones a fear strong enough to demand the segregation hut[3] while the southern ones observe the milder quarantine of keeping the menstruant away from men.[4] The Pimans have the hut and a profound fear of the menstruant, expressed in special ceremonies to discharm the tools or weapons of men which might have been exposed to her. The writer has found no record of menstrual fear in Mexico, and among the Huichol its absence is definitely recorded.[5] Among the pueblos there are vestiges of taboo in that Zuni menstruants do not to go kachina dances, nor Isleta menstruants to the Catholic church[6] while the Hopi girl, at least at puberty, uses the scratcher and is secluded from the sun.[7]

In the myths of all the pueblos we can find suggestions of a belief that the menstruant is dangerous to the weapons of warriors and hunters and at Taos such fear is definitely expressed.[8] The Jicarilla Apache, too, consider menstrual blood dangerous to men[9] though the Navajo do not and the attitude of other Athapascans is not recorded. Again among the southern Sioux we find hut, restrictions and a vivid sense of dread.[10]

In the whole area, side by side with fear *of* the woman there exists fear *for* the woman which demands that she purify herself by a varying number of restrictions. We shall not follow in detail the changing requirements for diet, bath and implements which are found in all combinations while the drinking tube, at least, has a distribution of its own[11] with other connections. We simply note that wherever, in the area mentioned, there is any form of quarantine for the menstruant, there are also requirements, more or less

---

[1] Boas, The Eskimo of Baffin Land and Hudson's Bay AMNH-B, vol. 15, p. 120. Nelson, E. W., The Eskimo about Bering Strait, BAE-R, pt. 1. p. 291.

[2] Thompson, Teit, J., Thompson Indians, AMNH-M, no. 11, p. 326. Carrier, Morice, pp. 162—4.

[3] Lemhi, Paviotso, Wind River, Ute: Lowie, 1923, p. 93: Surprise Valley Paiute: Kelly, 1932, p. 162.

[4] Lowie, 1923, p. 145; Steward, 1933, p. 293.

[5] Klineberg, Otto. Notes on the Huichol. AA vol. 36, 1934, p. 454.

[6] Information from Dr. Parsons.

[7] Parsons, 1936b, pp. 139—42.

[8] Parsons, 1936a, p. 20.

[9] Opler, 1936a, p. 221.

[10] Omaha: Mead, Changing Culture of an Indian Tribe, p. 189; Fortune, Reo, Omaha Secret Societies, p. 31; Oto: Whitman, The Oto, p. 83.

[11] Birket Smith, quoted by Loeb, 1931, p. 532.

stringent, for her self purification. Turning to California, we find, in the northern part, an extension of Plateau usages, with segregation hut and restrictions.[1] But as we go south there seems, at least from the written material, to be a difference of emphasis. True, in southern California the touch of the menstruant was avoided;[2] she was secluded, either in her own house[3] or outside it[4] and she observed restrictions, for years or perhaps for life.[5] The reason given, however is "her health and her husband's",[6] the emphasis being on the positive side of supernatural power, not the negative. The Luiseño girl might fast voluntarily for two or three years after puberty,[7] but her purpose was apparently to secure additional blessing. The suggestion of positive emphasis seems slight at this point but as we follow out the puberty and childbirth observances, we shall find it constantly reiterated.

Puberty restrictions are much more widespread than those for the subsequent periods. Often the requirements for self-purification are confined to an initial effort at this time when the girl apparently immunizes herself and must guard, in the future, only against her effect on others. Data on this subject are not exact but, at least where there is no hut, the restrictions seem to be confined to the first menses. Combined with them are what we might call the *crisis requirements* designed to set the pattern for the girl's future. Such are silence or taciturnity, to prevent gossiping; industry, such as corn grinding, fetching firewood or running; health and beauty, induced by shielding the eyes; moulding the figure or baking the body in hot sand.

Industry, represented by genuine hard work, is found at the north among Shoshoneans[8] and Californians.[9] The Papago have it also and the Hopi, who later impose no restrictions, exploit this opportunity for having the women grind corn. Taos, where we have already met the taboo, demands industry, and a glimpse at the eastern area shows fast and seclusion among the southern Sioux though without any positive emphasis on crisis requirements.

[1] Yurok; Kroeber, 1925, p. 299; Pomo, Ibid, p. 254. The likeness of this part of California to the Plateau has already been noted by Lowie, 1924, p. 147.
[2] Desert Cahuilla, Strong, 1929, p. 82; Luiseño, Waterman, pp. 281—88, DuBois, pp. 91—96.
[3] Cahuilla.
[4] Luiseño.
[5] Cahuilla and Luiseño as above. Also Cupeño, Strong, op. cit., p. 257.
[6] Strong, op. cit., p. 82.
[7] Du Bois, p. 96.
[8] Paviotoso: Lowie, 1924, p. 147; Steward, 1933, p. 293.
[9] Karok, Hupa, Shasta, Achomawi, Maidu: Lowie, 1924, p. 147.

Sometimes the industry demanded does not mean actual hard work but is symbolized by running in a more or less ritual manner[1] the idea being, perhaps, that running is a necessary activity of the food gatherer. It is the practice of the Yumans, River and Upland;[2] running is not mentioned for the Mohave but their girls, as a symbol of industry, pick leaves from greasewood bushes.[3] It appears among Eastern Apache[4] and reaches its height among the Luiseño who terminate a public treatment of the first menstruant with a formal run, face painting, admonition, and pictograph.[5] There is no mention of running for the other Shoshonean groups, an admonition to good behavior and industry taking its place.

But the crisis requirements for industry, in this area, are entirely dwarfed by those for health and beauty. Both the southern California Shoshoneans and the Yumans follow the custom of "baking" their adolescent girls in a bed of hot sand, an adaptation of the well known baking pit to the purpose of keeping a human body warm. The Mohave, who used "baking" for various illnesses, have explained it to the writer as a therapeutic expedient for invalids unsupplied with blankets. Certainly the reason given for it by those who "bake" their girls is not exorcism of evil but the insuring of a straight spine and a healthy body. The "baking" is often done in public, in the presence of important personages and to the accompaniment of speeches and singing.[6]

The southern Athapascans have a similar positive attitude, specially remarkable in view of the negative one taken by their congeners in the north.[7] The accounts show no suggestion of fear and, at least with the Apache, the girl is in a position of high honor. In all cases she practices restrictions, ending with ritual running. Health and beauty are again of paramount interest but they are insured, in this case, not by baking but by moulding and kneading

---

[1] Southern Ute, Maidu, Achomawi, Hupa: Lowie, 1924, p. 147.

[2] Cocopa: Gifford, 1933, p. 290; Maricopa; Spier, 1933, pp. 324—26; Diegueño; Kroeber, 1925, p. 716; Havasupai; Spier, 1928, pp. 325—26.

[3] Kroeber, 1925, p. 748.

[4] Opler, 1936a, p. 215, information Dr. Benedict, Reichard, 1928, pp. 135—9.

[5] Strong, 1929, p. 30—31.

[6] Baking is reported from the Plateau and Basin for southern Ute, Lowie 1924, p. 148; and Owens Valley Paiute, Steward 1933; p. 293, but it is in southern California that we find it featured. Note that Zuni women at puberty kneel over heated sand on the floor, Stevenson, 1902, p. 303, a pit in the house being impossible.

[7] Jicarilla: Opler, 1938, p. 48; Mescalero and Chiracahua, personal information, Dr. Benedict; White Mountain: Goddard, Indians of the Southwest, p. 173; Navajo, Reichard, 1928, pp. 135—9.

of the girl's body. We might note, however, that the Navajo do pitbake a ceremonial cake.

It would be interesting to study, over the area discussed, the various channels for fear of the supernatural, such as the sorcerer, the dead, the scalp taker and to note how far their use has augmented or displaced the fear of the woman. This study makes no pretense to such exhaustive analysis but it is suggested that we might by this means get a ray of light on the presence of what we have called the positive attidude at one point or the negative at another.

CHILDBIRTH

We have left restrictions concerning childbrith until the last because they are far less widely distributed than those for the woman at puberty or at subsequent menstruation. In general it may be said that, wherever there is a segregation hut, the parturient retires to it as well as the menstruant. Where fear has been reduced merely to that of contact by men with menstrual blood, the same fear is generally felt for the blood of childbirth and men (except shamans) are not present at delivery. There is less emphasis on self purification by the mother although we have not full data on this subject. Such is the situation for Basin, Plateau and northern California, all in the fear area.[1] In this area there is some use of the hot sand bed, surely a highly practical expedient at such a time. But its use would seem to be ceremonial rather than practical. Only a few of the Paiute employ it[2] and further north, where parturients suffer severely in cold weather, there is no mention of it. Neither do the Pimans allow the woman this sort of comfort and the suggestion seems to be that, despite its usefulness, it is little employed in the area of segregation and fear. Pimans segregate the mother but with little emphasis on restrictions, their attention in that regard being all focussed on the warrior.

The pueblos differ from the rest of the area in placing more ceremonial emphasis on childbirth than on menstruation. The mother is segregated, not from men but from the sun;[3] takes only gruel but does not fast. Often, too she bathes and goes through

---

[1] Basin and Plateau, the mother is confined to the house with food restrictions and sometimes a scratching stick. Southern Ute, Wind River Shoshoni: Lowie, 1924, p. 148; Owens Valley Paiute: Steward, 1933, p. 290; Surprise Valley: Kelly, 1932, pp. 158—9.

[2] Owens Valley: Steward, 1933, p. 290.

[3] Hopi: Beaglehole, 1935, p. 30; Isleta: Parsons, 1930, p. 215; Taos: Parsons, 1936a, p. 40. Presentation of the baby to the sun in other pueblos may be the obverse of a previous seclusion of the mother from the sun.

various ceremonials not of the usual restrictive sort but connected with pueblo patterns.[1]

Restrictions for the mother are found throughout almost all of California[2] but here they overlap with the couvade, which is concerned with the father, not the mother. The result is diet restrictions for both but, both being under the same supernatural influence, there is no point in separating the woman from her husband and the menstrual lodge is often not used.[3] In northern Mexico where no couvade is reported, restrictions for the mother are even lighter,[4] while with the Aztecs the woman after childbirth was praised and honored. Mother's segregation is a northern custom practiced only in the upper part of our area and reaching the Papago in an attenuated form.

A purification ceremony for the mother like that practised by the Pimans would seem a natural termination to the mother's seclusion and we should expect to find it among the people using the menstrual lodge. On the contrary, it is a southern ceremony, occurring among the Aztecs[5] and Tarahumara,[6] and again in the pueblos.[7] A part of this area[8] is included in that just discussed, where purification for the scalp assumes such importance. We are led to think that the treatment of the parturient has been assimilated to the same pattern, though in mild degree.

Mother's purification has about the same distribution as that of the third birth ceremony described for the Papago: presentation

---

[1] However, Zuni women have the hot sand bed. Parsons, 1919, p. 169. Sia women deliver their bebies on a bed of *unwarmed* sand "symbolic of the lap of mother earth" Stevenson, 1890, pp. 134, 145.

[2] Kroeber, 1925, p. 840.

[3] Mohave: No segregation mentioned, ritual fast for a month, Kroeber, 1925, p. 747. Yuma: No segregation but scratching taboo for four days, Forde, p. 158. Cocopa: No segregation, but ritual fast and scratching taboo, eight days, Gifford, 1933, p. 289. Maricopa: Segregation of mother eight days in special shelter, ritual fast, "hot bed", Spier, 1933, p. 312. Diegueño: After childbirth no avoidable work or exposure, diet restrictions one month, Kroeber, 1925, pp. 720—1. Southeastern Yavapai: Seclusion in the woods, "hot bed" four days, Gifford, 1932, p. 199. Walapai: No segragation but diet, and scratcher, "hot bed", Spier, 1928, p. 301.

[4] Tarahumara (3): Woman goes to a hidden spot but husband may go too. No restrictions for mother, Bennett 1935, p. 234; Opata (2) Tepecano (4): Post birth restrictions for woman, Bennett, 1935, p. 395.

[5] Sahagun, Jourdanet, pp. 456—7.

[6] Bennett, 1935, pp. 234—5.

[7] Hopi: Beaglehole, 1935, pp. 30—37; Zuni: Stevenson, 1902, p. 303; Acoma: White, 1930, p. 134; Sia: Stevenson, 1890, p. 140.

[8] Western pueblos and possibly Aztecs.

of the baby to the sun.[1] We might easily connect this custom with the importance of the sun in all Aztec ceremonies but, in negative fashion it also recalls the north where the segregation lodge keeps the woman away from human beings *and from the sun*. Papago male neophytes and their wives also keep out of the sun. The presentation of the baby might signalize an end of this taboo.

### THE "LIGHT WOMAN" A RECOGNIZED INSTITUTION

The "light woman" of the Papago is mentioned for the Pima at least in songs[2] and field work by the writer revealed the existence of such a woman among the ancient Mohave. The Aztecs also had a "daughter of joy", of whom Sahagun says: "her heart is restless (the expression is used in songs by the Papago): she laughs with everyone, she wants to be well paid".[3] The kindly aura thrown about her by the Pimans is not reflected by Sahagun who quotes a rebuke to her: "You are a whore... You beckon men, whistle to them... allow unnatural practices, you paint yourself with cochineal, you run about on the roads everywhere, you never go home, you are always restless, you tell jokes to make everyone laugh".[4]

### DREAM POWER AND CHOICE OF CAREER

In the Papago version of the acquisition of power, we distinguish four elements. Power came from an animal. It came in a dream in natural sleep. It was open to anyone. Its acquisition was solitary, not a group experience. There has been discussed in the text the fact that power, although open to anyone, did not fit him for all functions but stopped short at the barrier of hereditary office. Also the fact that the dream, although it appeared involuntary, was definitely motivated.

According to the foregoing references, it appears that the Papago were in an area where animals were the usual givers of power[5]

---

[1] Aztecs, Sahagun: Jourdanet, pp. 456—7; Hopi: Beaglehole, 1935, p. 37; Zuni: Parsons, 1917, p. 257; Acoma: White, 1935, p. 80; Santo Domingo: White, 1935, p. 80; Cochiti: Goldfrank, p. 48; San Felipe: White, 1932, p. 60; Sia: Stevenson, 1890, p. 141; San Juan: Parsons, 1929, p. 63; Laguna: Parsons, 1920, p. 127; Isleta: Parsons, 1930, p. 214; Tewa: Patsons, 1929, pp. 13, 16.

[2] Russell, p. 283. Unpublished songs collected by Dr. Benedict speak of her as a source of blessing.

[3] Sahagun: Jourdanet, Book X, chap. XV.

[4] Sahagun: Seler, pp. 366—7.

[5] The Shoshoneans of Basin and Plateau: Benedict 1923, p. 147; Kelly, 1932, p. 110; Steward, 1933, p. 308; Kroeber, 1925, p. 600; The Apache: Opler, 1936a, pp. 65—70; Goodwin, White Mountain Apache Religion,

except for the foreign Yumans, whose visions showed mountains or a complete supernatural experience.[1] The method of conferring power was the dream, found from the northern Shoshoneans down through the Yumans (who raised it to heights of importance) and again on the eastern edge of our area among the Apache. In this area, power dreams were usually open to every individual though here and there they were limited to shamans, a practice which finds its fullest development in northern California.

But toward the south of the area the power experience undergoes a decided change. Among the southern California Shoshoneans, it was induced by the taking of a drug, toloache, and the drug theme is repeated among the Tarahumare[2] and Huichol[3] whose visions came from another drug, peyote. Here, too, instead of occurring to individuals, power acquisition was a social experience, either at a boys' adolescence ceremony or after the peyote pilgrimage. There could hardly be a greater change from the dream idea as it occurs among the Paiute.

The Pueblos align themselves rather with the south than with the north. We admit the few examples of the individual vision, induced by fasting and admit also that fieldworkers are now and then bringing in more. But these are still exceptions and the typical power experience, both in Western and Eastern Pueblos, is the ritual of the medicine society whose members are shamans who achieve not a dream but merely heightened powers through a socialized performance. The society members are, moreover, mature men and women, not boys at adolescence as are all the others mentioned.

The power experience, in this case, has gone far from the Papago version, which resembles in almost every detail that of the Paiute and, somewhat surprisingly, of the Apache. But the Papago allow the vision not only to the boy who falls asleep but to the man who is purified after a heroic act. These acts, it has been

AA vol. 40, p. 28; Pueblos, animals give songs to societies, Hopi, Stephen xxix, are patrons of curing; Zuni: Bunzel, 1930, p. 528; Acoma: White 1930, pp. 116—121; Sia: Stevenson, 1890, pp. 93, 100, 102, 103. Santo Domingo: White, 1925, p. 121; Tewa: Parsons, 1929, p. 274; Isleta: Parsons, 1930, pp. 307—314; southern California Shoshoneans: Boscana, p. 17; in Mexico, Zapatecans: Parsons, 1936b, pp. 133, 225.

[1] Mohave: Kroeber, 1925, p. 26; Yuma: Forde, p. 202; Cocopa: Gifford, 1933, p. 308; Southeastern Yavapai: Gifford, 1933, p. 242; Walapai: Kroeber, 1935, p. 188.

Note: These notes were published before the publication of Dr. Park's summary of the subject.

[2] Bennett, 1935, p. 292.

[3] Lumholtz, 1900, p. 96.

pointed out elsewhere, are very similar to the initiation into a society. In their scattered desert life the Papago have no societies, and the vigil of the initiates has been amalgamated with the idea of the dream. The result is a somewhat incoherent one. To the boy, a dream comes in sleep, without fast or vigil. To the would-be "ripe" man it comes during fast and vigil which have, as their first purpose, purification. Established ritual has here prevented the spread of the democratic dream experience to all walks of life. Does this mean a reflection of ritual from the pueblos on cultures otherwise committed to the idea of individual dream power?

## THE DEAD

Pimans buried their dead in a sitting position, in rock crevices often enlarged to the semblance of a small house by additional walls and a roof. The body was accompanied by some of its principal possessions.

Crevice burial, a natural expedient for people in rough country, with no tools but digging sticks, is the usual practice in Basin and Plateau,[1] and is continued into Mexico.[2] It was the custom of the ancient Basket Makers and Pueblo dwellers though modern pueblos have discontinued it, all but Hopi.[3] It still is followed by Apache[4] and Navajo.[5] Other groups in the pueblos and Mexico bury their dead in graves, extended in the Christianized manner but, in general, the Basin, pueblos, Pimans and north Mexico, form a continuous area of burial. Westward into California, there is an extension of this area plotted by Spier,[6] but to north and south of it are areas of cremation. One, including Yumans and southern California Shoshoneans, extends from the Colorado Basin west to the Pacific and south through the peninsula. The other includes central and northeast California. Between the two is the burial area just mentioned, an extension, geographically, of the burial area in Basin and Plateau.

The division between regions which burn and regions which bury seems definite but, throughout the Basin and Plateau we find exceptions to the burial practice, not unlike that made by the Pimans. Pima and Papago cremate people of any sort killed by the

---

[1] Moapa and Shivwits; Lowie, 1924, p. 149; Paviotso: Ibid, p. 281; Uintah Ute: Ibid, p. 280; Wind River: Ibid, p. 282; Southern Ute: Ibid p. 279; Lemhi: Lowie, 1909, p. 214; Surprise Valley: Kelly, 1932. p. 168.

[2] Opata, Yaqui, Tarahumare, Tepehuane, Huichol: Bennett, 1936, p. 395.

[3] Voth, 1912, p. 101; Beaglehole, 1935, p. 12.

[4] Jicarilla: Opler, 1936a, p. 223.

[5] Reichard, 1928, p. 143.

[6] Spier, 1928, pp. 293—96.

enemy; Surprise Valley Paiute cremate quarrelsome people;[1] Owens Valley cremates shamans executed for witchcraft and people dying of snakebite;[2] Western Mono once cremated those dying in an epidemic[3] while elsewhere cremation is occasionally mentioned, though without details.[4]

It is possible that these scattered instances represent merely a shift from one form of mortuary practice to another under influence from nearby peoples. We notice, however, that the persons cremated represent a group of individuals sometimes classed together in ceremonies and who might be roughly defined as those suffering supernatural violence. From that point of view, they are not dissimilar to the Papago exceptions made for people killed by the enemy, for such warriors are thought to be victims of dangerous magic which must be exorcised by fire. We might compare all these scattered instances with the practice of the Aztecs, which also included burning and burying. With them, however, those cremated were warriors and women dying in childbirth, held equivalent to warriors,[5] while a special group of people dying of causes connected with water (drunkenness, drowning, etc.) were buried and went to the rain gods.[6] It is true that, in the Aztec case, cremation was the rule also for the rank and file[7] while the small class of buried people formed the exception. Nevertheless, it is interesting to note a certain thread of logic in the dual mortuary practices found scattered among the Uto-Aztecans. Such duality is not unknown elsewhere in the world for the hill tribes of India, whose normal practice is cremation, habitually bury those dead of violence. Is it possible that the Uto-Aztecan case represents, not a symptom of change from one form of disposal to another, but a relic of very old custom ?

A trait harder to explain is the scattered and discontinous custom of preservation of the bones in a special receptacle. This occurs in such scattered instances as the Shoshonean Luiseño,[8] Yuman Diegueño,[9] Aztecs,[10] and, possibly Owens Valley Paiute.[11] It was

---

[1] Kelly, 1932, p. 167.

[2] Steward, 1933, p. 297.

[3] Spier, 1928, p. 295. Papago consider an epidemic a supernatural visitation, to be dealt with by special ceremony.

[4] Shivwits and Moapá: Lowie, 1924, p. 279.

[5] Sahagun: Seler, pp. 301—2.

[6] Ibid, pp. 300—301. Note that duality extends to the Maya, with whom common people were buried and nobles (warriors ?) cremated. Thompson, p. 74.

[7] Sahagun: Seler, pp. 298—9.

[8] Waterman, pp. 305—6.

[9] Strong, 1929, p. 299.

[10] Sahagun: Seler, pp. 298—9.

[11] Steward, 1933, p. 297.

the method used by the Hohokam and, not only in their area but south of it in the trincheras of Sonora, there are to be found hundreds of such funerary jars.[1]

The other elements mentioned in Piman mortuary custom are related ones. Fear of the evil influence of the dead is found, to some extent, over the whole area, where the dying are often avoided and the dead adjured at the funeral to go away and not return. It is this fear which motivates the destruction of property immediately after death practiced throughout our area, except in the pueblos.[2] and the taboo on the use of the name, which can be found even at Hopi,[3] and Zuni.[4] At Hopi, though the houses do not lend themselves to burning, the expressed fear of the dead equals any in the area.[5]

Allied with property destruction and name taboo is the ceremony of exorcism held, as a rule, when the dead is supposed to have completed his four days' journey to the other world. The northern Shoshoneans seem to have nothing of this sort but every pueblo practises a cleansing rite in more or less Christianized form.[6] The Papago custom of taking food to the grave on the fourth day is probably a means of speeding the dead on his journey and so, at bottom, are the elaborate "death fiestas" of northern Mexico.[7] The southern Athapascans, however keep to the idea of exorcism with all its stringent force.[8] To the west, in the ceremony of

---

[1] Personal Information, Dr. Brand.

[2] Basin: Eastern Mono, Kroeber, 1925, p. 589; Surprise Valley: Kelly, 1932, p. 167; Shosshoni: Lowie, 1908, p. 214; Chemehuevi: Kroeber, 1925, p. 599; Owens Valley: Steward, 1933, p. 297; Southern California Shoshoneans: Strong, 1929, pp. 84, 120, 180, 264, 299; Mexico: Tarahumare, Opata, Huichol: Bennett, 1935, pp. 236, 594; Aztecs, Sahagun: Seler, p. 297; Yumans: Mohave: Kroeber, 1925, p. 751; Yuma: Forde, p. 211; Cocopa: Gifford, 1933, p. 294; Diegueño: Waterman, pp. 305—6; Maricopa: Spier, 1933, p. 303; Northwest and Western Yavapai: Gifford, 1936, pp. 302—3; Southeastern Yavapai: Gifford, 1932, p. 232. Apache: Opler, 1936a, p. 223. Navajo: Reichard, 1928, p. 143.

[3] Beaglehole, 1935, p. 14.

[4] Parsons, 1916, p. 254.

[5] Beaglehole, 1935, p. 11.

[6] Zuni: Stevenson, 1902, p. 310; but note the much more elaborate ceremonial for the widowed, pp. 503—4. Hopi: Beaglehole, 1935, pp. 11—13; Acoma: White, 1930, p. 137; Cochiti: Goldfrank, p. 65; Laguna: Parsons, 1920b, p. 129; Sia: Stevenson, 1890, p. 145; San Felipe: White, 1932 p. 61; Santo Domingo: White, 1935, pp. 86—87; Tewa: Parsons, 1929, pp. 63—66; Isleta: Parsons, 1930, p. 249; Taos: Parsons, 1936a, p. 70.

[7] Tarahumara: Bennett, 1935, p. 240; Tepehuane: Ibid, p. 395; Huichol: Klineberg, AA vol. 36, pt. 3, p. 43. Aztecs (for king and woman dying in childbirth) Sahagun: Seler, pp. 304—5.

[8] Jicarilla: Opler, 1936a, p. 223; Navajo: Reichard, 1928, p.'153.

"covering the tracks of the dead" the California Shoshoneans have combined spectacular burning of property with a use of the occasion for the reciprocal functioning of sibs and for a California ritual which might seem entirely unrelated — the interchange of shell money.[1]

Related to it, is the elaborate and generalized rite which has here been called the mourning ceremony. It would seem to be a final exorcism and presenting of gifts to the dead to ensure against his return and often it is held only for important dead or for those of the whole year. It appears occasionally in the Basin and Plateau[2] and perhaps we might translate the solstice prayersticks for the dead at Hopi[3] in this sense, likewise the "feeding of the dead" on ceremonial occasions at Zuni.[4]  Among the Papago there has been a combination with Christian ritual and the dead are fed on All Souls' Day. Tarahumare ceremonies for the dead are also in Christian guise.[5] A form of exorcism was held by the Aztecs but, as usual, only for important people.[6] The greatest development is in southern California, where the Shoshoneans and the Diegueño burn images of the dead with extreme ceremony[7] while the practice is extended into central California[8] with echoes even further north.[9] River Yumans honor warriors and great men by a slightly different ceremony, which includes a mock war and burning of property.[10]

The mourning ceremony exhibits an extreme variety which we might, perhaps explain by saying that a spectacular occasion for the burning of gifts for the dead and therefore of exorcism, has been enhanced by different ceremonial practices, each important in its own area. The warlike Yumans use the ceremony as an occasion for mimic battle while the Shoshoneans of southern California make it an elaborate display of clan reciprocity and exchange of shell money. The Papago, instead of enhancing the ceremony, have minimized it. They make as much of gift exchange between local groups as do the southern Californians, but not at a death ceremony.

---

[1] Strong, 1929, p.180. The "clothes burning" ceremony not to be confused with the more spectacular image burning held later.

[2] Moapa, Shivwits: Spier, 1928, p. 297; OwensValley: Steward, 1933, p. 297.

[3] Parsons, 1936b.

[4] Parsons, 1916, p. 255.

[5] Bennett, 1936, pp. 239—248.

[6] For king and woman dead in child birth, imageburning at every death anniversary for four years. Sahagun: Seler, pp. 304—5.

[7] Strong, 1929. Waterman, p. 311.

[8] Miwok and Maidu: Kroeber, 1925, p. 860.

[9] Wintun, Pomo, Yuki, Lassik: Ibid.

[10] Mohave: Kroeber, 1925, pp. 750—751; Yuma: Forde, pp. 221—244. Yuma have recently adopted image burning from the Diegueño.

This passes almost without formality while the giving of gifts is connected with a pleasanter occasion, that of intervillage games. The only approach of the Papago to a yearly mourning ceremony is the feeding of the dead, on the eve of All Saints' Day, a practice which is occasionally shared by the pueblos. This aggrandizing of the last mourning rite in California and minimizing among the Papago and the pueblos is in line with Spier's suggestion[1] that the mourning ceremony belongs only to cremating peoples. Our data in the main support this conclusion with some variation in the marginal cases. The Owens Valley Paiute, who are cited as having the ceremony do occasionally cremate and the example for the Aztecs refers to a class of people who were always cremated.

CONCLUSION

The chart (p. 234) lists in concise form the points presented in the text, using a cross to show the presence of a trait, one line to show traces of it. Such procedure gives a result far more clear-cut than the actual facts which, in their present state, are not susceptible of such presentation. The chart is offered only as a convenient summary of what has been said, by no means as a full picture of the area.

The greatest number of resemblances listed is with Mexico. Point after point in war, games, kinship, birth and death practices, is duplicated by one or another of the Mexican Uto-Aztecans — often by many. On some points like star lore and lack of marriage to blood kin, there is no information, but the context argues that, were it obtainable, it might well increase the likeness. We are left, then, with fear and segregation of the menstruant as the chief points where the two cultures do not agree. Fear of the menstruant we must correlate with other examples of an attitude which regards the supernatural as equally potential for good or for evil and therefore to be avoided except by those made magically immune. It is a usual attitude toward the shaman. Applied to the woman, we find it in the plateau and California, with suggestions elsewhere as noted. But it is applied to the scalper by western pueblos, Athapascans and River Yumans and to the priest and those engaged in ceremonial by pueblos and, often, southern Athapascans. The Papago develop all three possibilities by attributing *mana* to the woman, the scalper and also to the salt pilgrim and eagle killer— whom we may regard as ceremonialists. This emphasis on the dangerousness of *mana* is a northern trait which the Papago seem

---

[1] Spier, 1928, pp. 293—96.

to have developed in high degree. No other culture has singled out so many different persons as exposed to it nor focused attention so completely on danger from them, not to them. Fear of the salt pilgrim and the eagle killer, not found elsewhere, are treated in the same way. The Papago constistently emphasize the negative side of supernatural power and consistently regard all vehicles of such power as people to beware of. This fear attitude, though it combines elements from various areas, is uniquely Papago in its emotional aspect.

The second greatest number of resemblances is with the Shoshoneans of Basin and Plateau. The traits having to do with family life: usage at birth, marriage, puberty, death are almost identical in the two cultures. Many of them are to be found in Mexico also, and we might question whether they do not represent a basis belonging to many Uto-Aztecans and still persisting among the simpler members of the stock. As far south as the eastern Tepehuane there are many non-agricultural Uto-Aztecans living in different regions, and, had we data, we might perhaps trace down from the Plateau, through Papago, perhaps Cahita and Tarahumare, a culture of simply organized, food gathering peoples, each influenced at different points by its own advanced neighbors.

The Shoshoneans of southern California are third in order of likeness. With a basic resemblance to the Plateau, these people have moved into an alien area and adopted such traits as shell money exchange and toloache which are completely foreign to the other Uto-Aztecans. Only less foreign are their exaggerated forms of the mourning ceremony and their clans and moieties with reciprocal duties. Still, their basic organization is on the Papago plan, and there are unique resemblances not listed, but which crop up in isolated details. Such is the Luiseño habit of puffing out the breath four times to the sun and of wrapping the village fetish in a mat or basket of special plaited work. Another resemblance is the habit of designating affinals only through their relationship to a child of the blood. The Luiseño have allowed these terms to become "frozen" in the very way found among the Papago. That is, two men will address one another as "father of my grandchild", though one is the father-in-law and the other the son-in-law. (Instance of this practice appears among the northern Shoshoneans also.) The Papago sib names, which are untranslatable, find their nearest likenesses among Cupeño and Serrano. These are the sort of close and detailed resemblances which argue contact.

Fourth place goes to the River Yumans. Spier, in the paper quoted above has argued that these and the Pimans should form a sub-area of the Southwest, while Gifford objected, and our data would uphold Gifford's position. It is true that in pottery, house and other phases of material culture not discussed here, Pimans and Yumans have adopted the same expedients. However, none of their ceremonies correspond. They both have functionless sibs, but they differ completely in tribal organization and all the practices of birth, death and puberty. These are qualitative divergences. Whereas the differences of the Pimans from other Uto-Aztecans to north and south might be explained as successive stages of development along one line, Piman and Yuman differences seem those of alien cultures, meeting only at unrelated points. The two cultures share some phases of the kinship system with the California Shoshoneans and Mexico: organized warfare with Mexico; sibs with the southern California Shoshoneans and the dream power with the Plateau. Their most peculiar likeness is the sib titles for individuals. These are so much alike that they seem definite evidence of borrowing, apparently by the Pimans from the Yumans, whose system is the more complete of the two.

The next resemblances are found among the Western Pueblos, and, if this paper had concerned ceremonial, these would have been much increased. Again, birth and death practices are the same, and, at Hopi, girl's puberty also. Outstanding is the segregation and purification of the scalper, which is not found in the eastern Pueblos nor the Plateau.

Eastern Pueblos and Upland Yumans are last on the list and show about an equal number of resemblances to the Papago. Resemblances in the Eastern Pueblos, like presentation of the baby to the sun and exorcism after death, are usually shared with Mexico. Those of the Upland Yumans are shared with River Yumans, Mexico, and, sometimes, Basin Shoshoneans. In birth and death practices the Yuman group hangs together, while, in general organization, the Uplanders resemble their Shoshonean neighbors, and the River people resemble both Mexico and central California. In view of the break between the two Yuman groups, one is inclined to credit much of the complexity attained by the River people, not to any system of their own, but to influence from the south.

This picture of a north and south diffusion leaves the Yumans aside on the west. We grant that Yumans and Pimans share many points of material culture which bespeak close geographic contact. But the likeness rarely extends to points of organization and ceremony. Where it does, as with the sib titles for individuals, we find it can be traced through a much wider area. Often it is attributable to influence on both Yumans and Pimans from Mexico or the Basin.

In the same way the majority of the Pueblos are left outside our area on the east. Here we must make a sharp distinction between eastern and western Pueblos. The western ones, particularly Hopi, show signs of an old stratum of Basin traits, overlaid with those of a more complex culture. It would be possible to picture the Hopi as once having been semi-nomadic desert people like the Paiute, Papago and Tarahumare and we might attribute to such a stage some of the basic likenesses found among all the group. The striking identities in ceremony which appear now and then between Pimans and Hopi have not such a wide distribution and must date from a later period of contact after the western Pueblos had evolved their complex ceremonial organization.

This picture of diffusion leaves no place for the southern Athapascans who were also neighbors on the east but enemies and intruders. We have stated that most likenesses between them and the Pimans can be traced through the Pueblos with whom both had contact and this is the case with every point but one — that of dream power. This trait Pimans and Athapascans share with a wide area extending both east and west, through the Plains, the Basin and California. The Pueblos are not included. To the east, in the Plains, power comes in a vision, obtained through ordeal. To the west through Basin, Plateau and California, it comes in a dream during natural sleep. As we enter the plateau it becomes more and more the privilege of shamans. Papago and Jicarilla Apache are amazingly alike in their conception of the dream as coming to any one, in natural sleep and in the form of an animal guardian. In noting this likeness of the Papago with the Plains in general and with the Apache in particular, we should not omit to glance even further eastward, and acknowledge the sometimes surprising resemblances of this southwestern group with tribes like the southern Sioux. On such points as the animal guardian spirit, fear of the menstruant, sib names for individuals, Papago affiliations are quite as much with the east as with the west.

Omiting these remote considerations, we might tentatively plot the culture area in which the Papago find their place. Such an area would cut through the Colorado Plateau, leaving Hopi and Zuni within its periphery. It would have a wide northern fringe of Shoshoneans and would include all those of southern California. The Yumans might be admitted as a half assimilated group, highly resistant to some of the traits considered. Beyond the Yumans the outline of our area would sweep down through Sonora, with long projections extending to the south.

18

# BIBLIOGRAPHY

## ABBREVIATIONS

AA           American Anthropologist
AAA-M        American Anthropological Association, Memoirs
AMNH-AP      American Museum of Natural History, Anthropological Papers
   -M        American Museum of Natural History, Memoirs
BAE-B        Bureau of American Ethnology, Bulletin
   -R        Bureau of American Ethnology, Report
CU-CA        Columbia University Contributions to Anthropology
FMNH-PAS     Field Museum of Natural History, Publications, Anthropological Series
MAIHF-INM    Museum of the American Indian, Heye Foundation, Indian Notes and Monographs
M-P          Medallion, Papers, (Gila, Pueblo, Globe, Ariz.)
PM-R         Peabody Museum (Harvard University), Reports
SWM-P        Southwest, Museum, Los Angeles, Papers
UC-PAE       University of California, Publications in Archaeology and Ethnology
   -PG       University of California, Publications in Geography
   -IA       University of California, Ibero Americana
UNM-AS       University of New Mexico, Anthropological Series
   -ESAS     University of New Mexico, Ethnobiological Studies in the American Southwest
UW-P         University of Washington, Publications
YU-PA        Yale University, Publications in Anthropology

Alegre, Francisco Javier.
  1841–42  Historia de la Compania de Jesus en Nueva-Espana, que estaba escribiendo por el P. Francisco Javier Alegre al tiempo de su espulsion. 3 vol. Mexico, Impr. de J. M. Lara.
Apostolicos, Afanes.
  1754  de la Compania de Jesus escritos por un padre de la misma sagrada religion de su provincia de Mexico. Barcelona.
Bancroft, Hubert Howe.
  1884–89  History of the North Mexican States and Texas, 1531—1889. 2 vol. San Francisco, History Co.
           History of the Pacific States of North America. Vol XII. Arizona and New Mexico, 1530—1889. San Francisco, History Co.
Bandelier, A. F.
  1854  Report of an Archaeological Tour in Mexico. Papers of the Archaeological Institute of America, American Series II.
  1879  Social Organization and Mode of Government of the Ancient Mexicans. PM-R no. 12
  1892  Final Report of Investigations among the Indians of Southwestern United States, Parts I and II. Papers of the Archaeological Institute of America, American Series III and IV, Cambridge, Mass.

Beaglehole, Ernest and Pearl.
  1935  Hopi of the Second Mesa. AAA-M 44.
  1936  Hopi Hunting and Hunting Ritual. YU-PA no 4.
Beals, Ralph Leon.
  1932  The Comparative Ethnology of Northern Mexico before 1750.
         UC-IA 2.
  1933  The Acaxee, a Mountain Tribe of Durango and Sinaloa. UC-IA 6.
Benedict, Ruth Fulton.
  1923  The Concept of the Guardian Spirit in North America. AMNH-M
         29:6—97.
  1924  A Brief Sketch of Serrano Culture. AA 26:366—92.
  1934  Patterns of Culture. Houghton Mifflin.
Bennett, Wendel C. and Zingg, Robert M.
  1935  The Tarahumara, an Indian Tribe of Northern Mexico. University
         of Chicago Press.
Bolton, Herbert Eugene.
  1919  Kino's Historical Memoir of Pimeria Alta. Cleveland, The
         Arthur H. Clark Co. 2 vol.
  1930  Anza's California Expedition. U. Cal. Press, Berkeley, 5 vol.
  1936  Rim of Christendom, Macmillan.
Boscana, G.,
         See Harrington.
Bryan, Kirk.
  1925  The Papago Country, Arizona: a geographic, geologic, and
         hydrologic reconnaissance with a guide to desert watering places.
         United States Geological Survey, Water-supply Paper 499.
         Washington, Government Printing Office.
Bunzel, Ruth.
  1930  Introduction to Zuñi Ceremonialism, BAE-R 47.
Castetter, F. and Underhill Ruth M.
  1935  The Ethnobiology of the Papago Indians, UNM-ESAS no. 2.
         With Opler, M. E. The Ethnobiology of the Chiricahua and
         Mescalero Apache, UNM-ESAS no. 3.
Clavijero, Francisco Javier.
  1789  Storia della California. 2 vol. Venezia, M. Fenzo.
Coues, Elliot (Editor)
  1900  On the Trail of a Spanish Pioneer, The Diary and Itinerary of
         Francisco Garces in his Travels through Arizona and California.
         Translation. Frances P. Harper, N. Y.
Culin, Stewart.
  1902–03 Games of the North American Indians. BAE-R 24.
Documentos par a la Historia de Mexico.
  1853–57 Mexico, 3rd series, 7th Series.
Du Bois, Constance Goddard.
  1908  The Religion of the Luiseño Indians of Southern California.
         UC-PAE 8, No. 3:69—186. June 27, 1908.
Dumarest, Father Noel.
  1919  Notes on Cochiti, New Mexico. AAA-M 6: pt 3.
Fewkes, Jesse Walter.
  1897–98 Tusayan Migration Traditions. BAE-R 19, part 2, 573—633.
  1898  Archaeological Expedition to Arizona in 1895. BAE-R 17,
         part 2.

Fletcher, Alice C. and La Flesche, Francis.
    1906   The Omaha Tribe. BAE-R no. 27.
Forde, C. Daryll
    1931   Ethnography of the Yuma Indians. UC-PAE 28, vol. 28, no. 4,
           pp. 83—278.
Gifford, Edward Winslow.
    1916a The Dichotomous Social Organization in South Central Cali-
           fornia. UC-PAE 11:291—296.
    1916b Miwok Moieties UC-PAE 12.
    1917   Tübatulabal and Kawaïsu Kinship Terms. UC-PAE Vol. 12 no. 6.
    1922a California Kinship Terminologies. UC-PAE 18, pp. 1—285,
           Dec. 22, 1922.
    1922b Clans and Moieties in Southern California. UC-PAE 14, no. 4.
    1926   Miwok Lineages and the Politcal Unit in Aboriginal California.
           AA no. 28:389—401.
    1932   The Southeastern Yavapai. UC-PAE 29, no. 3.
    1933   The Cocopa. UC-PAE, 31, no. 5.
    1936   Northeastern and Western Yavapai, UC-PAE 34, no. 4.
Gladwin, Harold S.
    1928   Excavations at Casa Grande, Arizona, Feb. 12—May 1, 1927.
           SWM-P 2.
Gladwin, W. J. and H. S.
    1929a The Red on Buff Culture of the Gila Basin M-P III.
    1929b The Red on Buff Culture of the Papagueria M-P IV.
    1930   The Western Range of the Red on Buff Culture. M-P V.
    1933   The Eastern Range of the Red on Buff Culture. M-P XVI.
Goldfrank, Esther Schiff.
    1927   The Social and Ceremonial Organization of Cochiti. AAA-M 33.
Goodwin, Grenville.
    1935   The Social Divisions and Economic Life of the Western Apache
           AA v 37, no. 1.
    1937   The Characteristics and Function of Clan in a southern Atha-
           pascan Culture. AA v 39, no. 3.
Harrington, John P.
    1912   Tewa Relationship Terms. AA 14:472—498.
    1934   A New and Original Version of Boscana's Historical Account
           of the San Juan Capistrano Indians of Southern California.
           Smithsonian Institution, Miscellaneous Collections 92, no. 4.
Hayden, Carl.
    1924   The Pima Indians and the San Carlos Irrigation Project. In-
           formation presented to the committee on Indian Affairs, House
           ref. 68th Congress, 1st session in connection with S 966 Act.
           Printed for use Commission Indian Affairs.
Halseth, Odd S.
    1936   Prehistoric Irrigation in the Salt River Valley UNM-AS vol.
           1, no. 5.
Haury, Emil.
    1936   The Snaketown Canal UNM-AS vol. 1, no. 5.
Hill, W. W.
    1937   Navajo Warfare. YU-PA no. 5.
Hooper, Lucile.
    1920   The Cahuilla Indians. UC-PAE 16 no. 6:315—380.

Hoover, J. W.
  1935  Generic Descent of the Papago Villages. AA 37, no. 2, part 1, p. 257.
Huntington, Ellsworth.
  1914  The Climatic Factors as Illustrated in Arid America. Carnegie Institution. Washington D. C.
Kelly, Isabel T.
  1932  Ethnography of the Surprise Valley Paiute. UC-PAE 31, 67—210.
  1934  Southern Paiute Bands. AA 36, no. 4.
Kidder, A. V.
  1924  An Introduction to the Study of Southwestern Archaeology. New Haven.
Kino, Eusebio Francisco.
  1919  Kino's historical memoir of Pimeria Alta: a contemporary account of the beginnings of California, Sonora, and Arizona, by Father E. F. Kino, S. J., pioneer, missionary explorer, cartographer, and ranchman, 1683—1711; translated, edited and annotated, by Herbert Eugene Bolton. 2 vol., Cleveland, The Arthur H. Clark Co.
Kissell, Mary Lois
  1916  Basketry of the Papago and Pima. AMNH-P 17:115—264.
Klineberg, Otto.
  1934  Notes on the Huichol. AA 36, no. 3.
Kroeber, A. L.
  1917a  Zuñi Kin and Clan. AAA-M, vol. XVIII, pp. 39—207. AMNH vol. XVIII, part II.
  1917b  California Kinship Systems. UC-PAE 12:339—396.
  1925  Handbook of Indians of California, BAE-B 78:1—995.
  1931  The Seri, S. W. Museum, 44—47.
  1934  Uto-Aztecan Languages of Mexico, UC-IA 8.
Lockwood, Frank C.
  1932  Pioneer Days in Arizona. Macmillan.
  1938  The Apache Indians. Macmillan.
Loeb, Edwin Myer.
  1931  The Religious Organizations of North Central California and Tierra del Fuego. AA v 33, no. 4.
Lowie, Robert H.
  1908  Northern Shoshone. AMNH-P II, part II: 165—306.
  1923  The Cultural Connection of Californian and Plateau Shoshonean Tribes. UC-PAE 20:145—156.
  1924  Notes on Shoshonean Ethnography. AMNH-P XX: 185-314.
  1929a  Notes on Hopi Clans. AA 30, part 4.
  1929b  Hopi Kinship. AA 30, pt. 4.
Lumholtz, Carl Sofus
  1900  Symbolism of the Huichol Indians. AMNH-AP vol. II, pt. 1.
  1902  Unknown Mexico. New York.
  1912  New Trails in Mexico. New York: Scribner's.
Mange, Juan Matheo
  1720  Luz de tierra incognita en la America Septentrienal y diario de las exploraciones en Sonora, por el capitan J. M. Mange. Mexico, Talleras Graficos de la Nacion, 1926.

Morrice, A. G.
  1888–89  The Western Denés. Proceedings of Canadian Institute Toronto. Third Series, no. VII.
Obregon, Balthasar de
  1584  Obregon's History of 16th Century Explorations in Western America Entitled Chronicle, Commentary or Relation of the Ancient and Modern Discoveries in New Spain and New Mexico, Mexico 1594. Translated and edited by George P. Hammond and Agapito Rey. Los Angeles 1928.
Opler, Moris E.
  1935  The Concept of Supernatural Power among the Chiracahua and Mescalero Apache. AA v 37, no. 1.
  1936a  A Summary of Jicarilla Apache Culture· AA v 38, no. 2.
  1936b  The Kinship Systems of the Southern Athabaskan Speaking Tribes. AA v 38, no. 4.
  1937  Apache Data Concerning the Relation of Kinship Terminology to Social Classification. AA v 39, no. 2.
  1938  Myths and Tales of the Jicarilla Apache. AFL-M.
Orozco y Berra, Manuel
  1864  Geografia de las lenguas y Carta Ethnografica de Mexico.
Park, Willard Z.
  1934  Paviotso Shamans. AA 36, no. 1.
Parsons, Elsie Clews
  1916  A Few Zuñi Death Beliefs and Practices. AA XVIII no. 2.
  1917  Notes on Zuñi. AAAM 4, nos. 3—4 (4:151—327).
  1918  Notes on Acoma and Laguna. AA no. 20: 162—186.
  1919  Mothers and Children at Zuñi. Man, XIX.
  1920a  Note on Isleta, Santa Ana and Acoma. AA v 22, no. 1.
  1920b  Notes on Ceremonialism at Laguna. AMNH-AP XIX, part 4.
  1922  Winter and Summer Dance series in Zuñi in 1918. UC-PAE 17, no. 3.
  1923a  Notes on San Felipe and Santo Domingo, AA v 25, no. 4.
  1923b  Laguna Genealogies. AMNH-AP XIX, part 5.
  1924a  Tewa Kin Clan and Moiety. AA 26:333—339.
  1924b  Scalp Ceremonial of Zuñi. AAA-M 31.
  1925  The Pueblo of Jemez. Papers of Southwestern Expedition, no. 3, Department of Archaeology, Phillips Academy, Andover, Mass.
  1928  Notes on the Pima. AA 30, no. 3.
  1929  The Social Organization of the Tewa of New Mexico. AAA-M 36.
  1930  Isleta, New Mexico. BAE-R 47:193—466.
  1932  The Kinship Nomenclature of the Pueblo Indians. AA v 34, no. 3.
  1933a  Some Aztec and Pueblo Parallels. AA 35, no. 4.
  1933b  Hopi and Zuñi Ceremonialism. AAA-M 39.
  1936a  Taos Pueblo General Series in Anthropology no. 2.
  1936b  Editor: Hopi Journal (A. M. Stephen). CU-CA 23.
Perez de Ribas Andres
  1645  Historia de los Triumphos de Nuestra Santa Fe in los Missiones de la Provincia de Nueva España. Madrid.
Radin, Paul
  1931  Mexican Kinship Terms. UC-PAE 31, no. 1.

Recopilacion de leyes de los reynos de las Indias. Madrid, 1756.

Reichard, Gladys A.
1928   Social Life of the Navajo Indians with Some Attention to Minor Ceremonies. CU-CA VII.

Robinson, Will H.
1918   The Story of Arizona. The Berryhill Co. Phoenix, Arizona.
1938   The Apache.

Russell, Frank
1904–05  The Pima Indians. BAE-R 26:3—389.

Sahagun, Fray Bernardino de.
1880   Histoire Generale des Choses de la Nouvelle Espagne par le R. P. Fray Bernardino de Sahagun. Translated and annotated by D. Jourdanet and Remi Simeon. Paris. (abbr. Sahagun, J.)
1927   Einige Kapitel aus dem Geschichtswerk des Fray Bernardino de Sahagun aus dem aztekischen übersetzt von Eduard Seler. Stuttgart, Strecker. (abbr. Sahagun, S).
1932   Translation from the Spanish version. Translated by Fanny Bandelier. Fisk University Press, Nashville Tenn. (abbr. Sahagun, B)

Sauer, Carl and Brand, Donald.
1931   Prehistoric Settlements of Sonora, with special reference to cerros de trincheras. UC-PG vol. 5, no. 3.

Sauer, Carl Ortwin
1932   The road to Cibola. UC-IA 3.
1934   Distribution of Aboriginal Tribes and Languages in Northwestern Mexico. UC-IA 5.

Sparkman, Philip Stedman
1908   The Culture of the Luiseño Indians. UC-PAE 8, no. 4.

Spier, Leslie
1923   Southern Diegueño Customs. UC-PAE 20:297—358.
1925   The Distribution of Kinship Systems in North America. UW-P, vol. 1, no. 2, pp. 69—88.
1928   Havasupai Ethnography. AMNH-AP 29:81—392.
1933   Yuman Tribes of the Gila River. U. Chicago Press.
1936   Cultural Relations of the Gila River and Lower Colorado Tribes. YU-PA 3.

Stevenson, Matilda Coxe
1890   The Sia. BAE-R 11.
1904   The Zuñi Indians: Their Mythology, Esoteric Fraternities and Ceremonies. BAE-R 23.

Steward, Julian H.
1933   Ethnography of the Owens Valley Paiute. UC-PAE 33, no. 3.
1936   Shoshoni Polyandry. AA vol. 38, no. 4.

Strong, William Duncan
1927   An Analysis of Southwestern Society. AA 29, no. 1, pp. 1—61.
1929   Aboriginal Society in Southern California. UC-PAE 26.

Thompson, J. Eric.
1933   Mexico before Cortez. New York: Scribners.

Underhill, Ruth M.
1936   The Autobiography of a Papago Woman. AAA-M. 36.
1938   A Pagago Calendar Record. UNM-B 322. Anthropological Series, 2, no. 5.

U. S. Board of Indian Commissioners.
   1919   Fiftieth annual report of the Board of Indian Commissioners to the secretary of the Interior.
Velarde, Padre Luis (edited by Rufus Kay Wyllys).
   1931   New Mexico Historical Review, vol. 6, no. 2, pp. 111—157 April. Translated from (Relacion de la Pimeria Alta). Translated from Luz de Tierra Incognita, libro II. Documentos para la historia de Mexico IV, tomo 1, pp. 226—402.
Voth, Henry R.
   1905   Traditions of the Hopi. FMNH-PAS VIII.
   1912   Brief Miscellaneous Hopi Papers. FMNH-PAS XI. The Eagle Cult of the Hopi, *ibid.* 107—9. Hopi Proper Names. FMNH-PAS VI.
Waterman, T.
   1910   The Religious Practises of the Diegueño Indians. UC-PAE, no. 6:271—358.
White, Leslie A.
   1930   The Acoma Indians. BAE-R 47.
   1932   The Pueblo of San Felipe. AAA-M 38.
   1935   The Pueblo of Santo Domingo, New Mexico. AAA-M 43.
Winship, George Parker.
   1892–03   The Coronado Expedition, 1540—1542. BAE-R 14, pt. 1:329-613.
Whorf, B. L.
   1935   The Comparative Linguistics of Uto-Aztecan. AA 37, no. 4, Oct—Dec. 1935.